1/17/18

To Ed

Thank you for being such a good friend and generous supporter of our work

David J

The Black Book
of the American Left

The Black Book
of the
American Left

*The Collected Conservative Writings
of David Horowitz*

Volume V
Culture Wars

Second Thoughts Books
Los Angeles

First American edition published in 2013 by Second Thoughts Books.

Manufactured in the United States and printed on acid-free paper. The paper used in this publication meets the minimum requirements of ANSI/NISO Z39.48 1992 (R 1997) *(Permanence of Paper)*.

Book design and production by Catherine Campaigne; copy-edited by David Landau; research provided by Mike Bauer.

FIRST AMERICAN EDITION

LIBRARY OF CONGRESS CATALOGING-IN-PUBLICATION DATA

Horowitz, David, 1939–
    The black book of the American left : the collected conservative writings of David Horowitz / by David Horowitz.
    volumes   cm.
    Includes bibliographical references and index.
    ISBN 978-1-941262-01-6 (hardback)
      1. Social movements—United States—History.   2. Radicalism—United States.   3. Anti-Americanism—United States.   4. Horowitz, David, 1939– Political and social views.   I. Title.
HX86.H788 2013
335.00973   2013000496

10   9   8   7   6   5   4   3   2   1

Contents

Introduction to *Culture Wars*

Culture Wars is the fifth volume of *The Black Book of the American Left*, and the first of three focusing on the attacks on American values that first gained traction in the 1960s. These conflicts have continued through half a century, dividing Americans more sharply than at any time since the Civil War, while re-shaping the national culture in ways that reflect the agendas of the progressive elites. "Political correctness" is the term that is widely employed to describe the changes to the cultural landscape effected by these elites, whose influence reached a critical mass in American educational and media institutions in the 1990s.

The phenomenon of "political correctness" is, in fact, an updated version of the "party line"—a stock feature of the organizations of the Communist-progressive left. The utility of a party line lies in the way it demonizes opponents, converting dissent into deviancy, while requiring its adherents to reduce complex realities to political formulas, which deprives them of the ability to learn from their experiences. The term was coined by Mao Zedong as a slogan for closing party ranks, and is integral to the left's totalitarian impulses and messianic ambitions. The radical character of the political-correctness movement has been obscured by the widespread reference to its adherents as "liberals," even as they have engaged in a relentless assault on the liberal values that are embedded in the American constitutional framework.

The cultural offensive launched by progressives was inspired by an Italian Stalinist named Antonio Gramsci, whose works became an academic fashion in the 1970s, a time when the liberal arts divisions of American universities had come increasingly under radical control. Writing in the 1930s, Gramsci had proposed an innovation in Marxist theory which sought to address the fact that the working class had failed in its historic mission as a revolutionary force. There was nothing original in Gramsci's observation, which was shared by many socialists at the time, including Benito Mussolini, a Leninist who turned to populism as a solution to the dilemma posed by the missing proletariat. What was original was Gramsci's own solution, which was to put cultural institutions at the center of the revolutionary agenda.

Marxist radicals had previously focused on taking control of the means of industrial production. Gramsci now proposed that their attention and energies should be redirected towards controlling the means of cultural production. In Gramsci's conception, this meant infiltrating and then subverting universities, churches, media and the institutions of the arts—the instrumentalities by which ideas were introduced into the general culture. In devising this strategy, Gramsci turned one of Marxism's central claims on its head. Marx had famously said that "the ruling ideas are the ideas of the ruling class," implying that the principal obstacle to social progress was a "false consciousness" imposed from above, which validated the social *status quo*. The imposition of these false ideas was accomplished through the cultural institutions which the ruling class controlled. In Gramsci's vision, radical subvention of these institutions and therefore of the culture would make radical ideas the ruling ideas, which would result in radicals becoming a political ruling class.[1]

---

[1]An unacknowledged irony of this new vision is its tacit concession to a core element of the conservative outlook. While Marxists and socialists necessarily believe that the determinant social factors are economic, conservatives recognize that culture and genes are the most important factors determining individual achievement and the success of human societies. If attempts to equalize the stores of individual wealth could lead to social equality or create economic prosperity, there would be a historical record to confirm this optimism, but there isn't. Volume VII of

The first section of this volume consists of three essays I wrote with Peter Collier that describe the spread of "political correctness" in the universities, the first stage in the left's march through the institutions of the culture. "It's the Culture, Stupid!" opens with the appointments of two academic ideologues to key roles in the newly elected administration of President Bill Clinton—an indication of how far the left's assault had advanced by 1992. The two essays that follow describe the course of political correctness as a new orthodoxy in the intellectual culture.

The next section, titled "Media Culture," examines the radical influence in the nation's media, beginning with the left's domination of the film industry, exemplified in its ability to impose the longest blacklist in American history on a political opponent. For more than thirty years Hollywood leftists were able to deny Elia Kazan, one of America's greatest directors, the honors, recognition, and opportunities his talents had earned. His crime? In the early 1950s he chose to defend his country rather than members of the Communist Party active in theater and film who were engaged in betraying their country to a totalitarian enemy. The ban on Kazan lasted longer than the blacklist of any of the famous targets of the McCarthy era, and, unlike theirs, his exile was not enforced by a handful of studio heads but by the creative film community as a whole. Consequently, his blacklisting reveals far more about the dominance of the entertainment media by a political orthodoxy than anything McCarthy and his supporters achieved.

"Up From Multiculturalism" examines an ideological centerpiece of the left's offensive. Previously, Americans had shared a common culture that was rooted in America's constitutional framework. This constitutional republic was a multi-*ethnic* society whose success could be attributed to its distinctive and *unitary* culture of individualism and equal rights under the law. A national identity was created by the commitment of a diverse cit-

---

this series, *The Left in the University*, addresses in detail the transformation of the universities into a political instrument of the left and the base for this new strategy of revolution.

izenry to these basic values held in common. Multiculturalism in its very inception, on the other hand, was an assault on the idea of a singular, shared culture or a set of dominant values.

While multiculturalists presented their agenda as a program of equality and inclusion, it was in its conception and implementation a movement aimed at deconstructing the American identity and the culture that sustained it.[2] To accomplish this deconstruction, the American narrative of freedom was systematically rewritten as an unrelenting history of racism and oppression. "Up From Multiculturalism" describes the institutional mechanism by which this radical departure from Americans' traditional view of themselves was imposed on a university culture whose institutional base was so decentralized as to seem immune to the imposition of an orthodoxy, and a change in perspective so sweeping and profound.[3]

Three essays in this volume tell the story of my encounters with Steve Wasserman, a veteran radical who in 1996 became the editor of the *Los Angeles Times Book Review*.[4] Since Wasserman's election was not untypical of other national media institutions, and would not have been possible if the *Times* itself had not undergone a cultural change, this story may be said to be emblematic of the wider transformation. Similar stories could easily be told about the new cultural arbiters at *The New York Times*,

---

[2]For a sustained critique of this intention, see Arthur M. Schlesinger, Jr., *The Disuniting of America: Reflections on a Multicultural Society*, 1992
[3]Leftists will maintain that the traditional view was also an orthodoxy. However, no one was punished or harassed or systematically excluded from faculties for intellectual dissents from this view. The punishment of Communists, whether justified or not, was the result of pressure from agencies external to the university. Moreover, this punishment was meted out because of their membership in a conspiratorial party loyal to a foreign power, not their expressions of dissenting ideas. This pluralistic openness changed with the ascension of leftists to positions of power in university departments, where ideological correctness became a criterion for hiring. See Volume VII in this series, The Left in the University, for an account of these changes.
[4]Chapters 3, 8 and 9: "Karl Marx and the *Los Angeles Times*," "Calibrating the Culture Wars," and "Wasserman's Revenge"

The Washington Post and other major media institutions. The incidents recounted in these chapters speak volumes about the changes that had already taken place as the century drew to a close. The fate of my appeals to the publisher of the *Times,* recounted here, provide a textbook confirmation of Lenin's boast that Communists could count on the capitalists to sell the rope that would be used to hang them.

Several of the essays that follow—most prominently "Telling It Like It Wasn't"[5]—address the left's insistence on rewriting the past as a step towards reshaping the future. This left-wing revisionism was the work not only of journalists and polemicists but of university professors who politicized entire academic fields, including those of American history and American Studies. How far leftists have been willing to go in fabricating easily ascertainable facts to advance a political agenda is the subject of the final chapter in this section, "The Progressive Myth Machine." David Brock is the publisher of an Internet site sponsored by George Soros and the Clintons, whose proclaimed purpose is to correct misinformation disseminated by conservative media. In practice Media Matters functions as an attack site focused on discrediting opponents of the political left, by any means necessary. As one of those targets, and as a subject in Brock's book, *The Republican Noise Machine,* I was afforded the opportunity of reviewing his account of my career, and documenting the facts ignored and even inverted by him. In reviewing Brock's book, I was thus able to cast light on the methods favored by an individual who has been described *by The New York Times* as "a Democratic political operative," is the head of a major Democratic political action committee, and whose site is a key provider of talking points for the party's legislators and activists.[6]

---

[5]It was originally published as "Whitewash," but we changed the title when we anthologized it in *Deconstructing the Left.*

[6]Michael Luo, "Effort for Liberal Balance to G.O.P. Group Begins," *The New York Times, November 23, 2010; Brock's PAC is American Bridge 21st Century.*

Parts II and III of this volume focus on sexual and gender politics. These are reflections of the left's totalitarian ambitions—its desire to transform not only the political order but the entire social order and the individuals who compose it. Generally described as "identity politics," these efforts were expressions of the left's signature project of "social construction"—its determination to use social institutions and the power of the state to create "new men and new women." In other words, to reshape human nature to fit the utopian program.

Under Communist regimes, such efforts led to human disasters on an epic scale: tens of millions of deaths through politically induced famines and the systematic slaughters of individuals who refused to go along with the socialist scheme. In America, the left is still unable to marshal the full power of the state against its political opponents, but even in this democratic environment its utopian incitements and the intimidations of political correctness led in the 1980s to the greatest human catastrophe outside of war in the nation's history. As the articles in this section show, the epidemic of AIDS was fueled in the first place by the left's crusade for "sexual liberation," defined as promiscuous sex with strangers, and then facilitated by its politically inspired destruction of elements of the public health system designed to combat such contagions.

The leaders of the gay rights movement were all veterans of the radical Sixties who had gravitated to the Democratic Party, the dominant presence in the governments and public health agencies of San Francisco, Los Angeles and New York, the three urban centers from which the epidemic originally spread. Once the epidemic took root, the left then directed its political influence to disabling the safeguards of the nation's public health systems in order to protect the sexually "liberated" zones it had created, which happened to be the spawning grounds of the disease. Thanks to the left's practice of charging its opponents with "homophobia" and bigotry, resistance to its policy agendas was easily overcome. The subsequent crippling of the public health systems led to a massive expansion of the epidemic and the eventual deaths of more than

650,000 Americans, most of them homosexual and young, most of whom could have been saved if traditional public health policies had been employed.

In 1983, just before the virus was isolated, at a time when authorities were first becoming publicly concerned, Peter Collier and I wrote an article about the political forces shaping official responses in the city of San Francisco. Retitled here as "Origins of a Political Epidemic," the article was written with the help of some prominent gay leaders who had become alarmed by what they saw taking place but, because of the intimidation, were unable to oppose publicly. It was the first journalistic report to expose the destructive impact of the gay liberation activists and also the criminal negligence of local authorities, who acquiesced to their self-destructive, politically correct demands. The remaining articles in this section track the relentless path of the epidemic and the inability of the rest of the nation to wake up from its ideology-induced slumber and revive the public health policies that had been abandoned.

In my autobiography *Radical Son* I wrote about my involvement in reporting the story Collier and I had written, and also about the hostile reaction it received. At the time there had been only 300 deaths from an epidemic that was doubling every 6 months. I recalled how I had calculated that, at this rate, in 20 years there would be 200,000 people dead if nothing were done—as it turns out an understatement; how I realized that the cultural tide supporting the destructive agendas of the left was so strong that there was nothing anyone would do to stop it; and how utterly helpless I felt.[7]

The final section of this volume, "Gender Politics," deals with another destructive aspect of the cultural attitudes promoted by the left. This was an ideological feminism, which created its own party line and was used to corrupt institutional standards, demanding gender quotas in hiring and evaluations. In 1995 this

---

[7]*Radical Son*, pp. 337–349

feminist juggernaut precipitated the greatest witch-hunt in American history over a series of incidents at the "Tailhook" convention of naval aviators in Las Vegas. As a result of the feminist attacks and the purges that followed, what had been an annual event was terminated. The reputations recklessly destroyed and careers summarily ended were a national tragedy, a travesty worse than anything that had resulted from the infamous McCarthy investigations. But they received no critical coverage by media in full self-censorship mode as a result of similar feminist campaigns that had put them on notice that they themselves were not immune from similar attacks.

Part IV of this volume is also about the media culture, and focuses on one of my early concerns in creating the Center for the Study of Popular Culture in 1988.[8] This was the government's creation of what became a billion-dollar media platform for left-wing propaganda in the public broadcasting networks PBS and NPR. The authorizing legislation for this complex—the Public Broadcasting Act of 1967—specifically forbade the creation of a politically oriented network, since a party in power could potentially use such an institution to undermine the democratic system. Nonetheless, a politically oriented network was created despite the law. From its inception, public broadcasting has been managed and run almost exclusively by individuals of the left.

For several years I was actively engaged in lobbying public broadcasting officials to persuade them to observe the letter of the Public Broadcasting Act by including a diversity of views in their current affairs programming. I published a magazine, COMINT, which was distributed to 12,000 members of the public broadcasting community in what proved to be the futile hope of embarrassing them into complying with their enabling legislation. As a result of this activity, I had first-hand experience to confirm the suspicion that those responsible for programming—with the notable exception of the producers of the MacNeil/Lehrer News-

---

[8] Later renamed the David Horowitz Freedom Center

Hour—were uninterested in observing their legal mandate and were by and large fellow-traveling progressives who encouraged radicals of the Steve Wasserman type and defended them from critics when the tendentious screeds they aired were challenged.[9] The chapters in this section, originally written for *COMINT*, recount how PBS executives produced and then defended programs celebrating Communist guerrillas, terrorists and Black Panther murderers, while airing specials that treated conservatives like Ronald Reagan as traitors.[10] When confronted, public broadcasting executives regularly claimed that these political propaganda films actually met the system's quality standards, although it was not clear how this could be possible, since the Public Broadcasting Act stipulated in so many words that current affairs programming must be "strictly fair, objective and balanced."

---

[9]A partial archive of *COMINT* is available on the web at http://www.discoverthenetworks.org/viewSubCategory.asp?id=1590. A collection of *COMINT* articles, edited by Laurence Jarvik and myself, was published in 1995 by the Center for the Study of Popular Culture under the title *Public Broadcasting and the Public Trust.*

[10]"High Crimes and Misdemeanors" was the title of one of two Bill Moyers PBS specials effectively making such a claim.

PART I

The Progressive Party Line

It's the Culture, Stupid!
(co-authored with Peter Collier)

eople are aghast at the appointment of University of Wisconsin chancellor Donna Shalala to a Cabinet post in the Clinton administration, and rightly so. But the true epiphany in the pre-inaugural process preceded Shalala's ascension and might have been covered up by the compliant media if not for a story that first surfaced in *The Jewish Daily Forward*. It was the president-elect's naming of Johnnetta Cole to head the transition team's talent search in the areas of education, arts, labor and humanities. Cole is presently president of Spellman, one of the "historically black" colleges. Yet the institutions of higher education have become so subordinated to political agendas that this just opens the question. In Cole's case it is not what she is but what she has been. And thereby hangs a tale. In the early Seventies Cole was a member of the Venceremos Brigade, a New Left organization that went to Cuba to cut sugar cane for the dictatorship and wound up serving the DCI, Castro's intelligence service. By the Seventies Cole was president of the U.S.-Grenada Friendship Society, a clone of the U.S.-Soviet Friendship Societies that Stalin invented, in this instance fronting for Marxist dictator Maurice Bishop. In 1980 she was again in Havana with an elite handful of others in orbit around the U.S. Communist Party, discussing ways to help the Cubans export revolution to Central America. A year later Cole was actively involved in the Soviet front and Communist Party

Originally published in *Heterodoxy* Magazine, January 1993; http://www.discoverthenetworks.org/Articles/1993%20-%2001%20Vol%201, %20No%208.pdf

subsidiary, the U.S. Peace Council, which had been reactivated to set up a fifth column in America for the Marxists in Nicaragua and El Salvador.

We could go on. But the point is clear. This is a profile of one of those left-wing apparatchiks who spent the Big Chill rededicating themselves to the leftover left's solidarity mode. The only thing missing from Cole's dreary *curriculum vitae*, in fact, is any indication of remorse for fifteen years spent doggedly working in the vineyards of pro-Communist anti-Americanism. If it is a tragedy that such a record did not stop Cole from working her way onto an affirmative action fast track in higher education, it is a farce that Clinton should have chosen her to play a key role in staffing his administration. What was such a person doing on his short list for Secretary of Education? Why, when some of the more disgraceful episodes in Cole's background were made public, did the Clintonites merely shrug, as if collaboration with the most oppressive tyrannies of this century meant nothing at all? Did transition chairman Vernon Jordan define the new administration's idea of political morality when he said regarding Cole that all these things happened a long time ago and anyway who cares?

It would be nice to think that Cole's selection was the result of a computer malfunction, or that some sort of random dialing process inadvertently called up her name. But Cole is a protégée of Donna Shalala, whom she served at Hunter College, when Shalala was its president. It was no glitch. Nor was it merely, to turn Milan Kundera's phrase on its head, the triumph of forgetting over memory. It is hard to believe that Clinton is so disoriented by the dubious commitments of his political adolescence that he really sees no difference between trying it once while not inhaling, and sucking up to Castro for twenty years; between failing to fight for your country's cause and supporting your country's enemies. Sadly, Vernon Jordan is right. Johnnetta Cole's past commitments don't matter to the Clinton crowd; what matters is that she's on the right track now, having finally found a popular front that works in multiculturalism and radical feminism.

The media treated the Cole episode as a tiny closet drama. Yet it stands as the first stirring of the rough beast of political correctness now slouching toward Washington, a mentality that forgives America-bashing because it has been nurtured on a vision of the rampant white, heterosexual male—a synecdoche for America the bad—running roughshod over the country and the world.

In his unctuous endorsement of the Democratic ticket in *Rolling Stone*, Jann Wenner said that he supported Clinton and Gore because they had "come of age in the Sixties and [had] sensibilities and value systems" that were formed then. Right. That's exactly the problem. Probably out there this very minute buying a party hat and noisemaker for his box seat at the inaugural, Wenner thinks he is helping usher in an era of good vibes, a don't-stop-thinking-about-tomorrow view of the world. But the change about to overtake the country is less generational than ideological. And if there is an irony here it is that Clinton, more than any other politician, seemed to have understood the tragedy of the Sixties—the unloosing of a 25-year night of the long knives that allowed the Left to subvert institutions of the center like the university and his own Democratic Party. Clinton came to power, after all, by portraying himself as someone anxious to rescue the party from its ideological tar pits, rebuild the damaged center and purge it of the alienating extremism of the Left. Yet, by the first few weeks of his presidency-elect, he was already feeding the animals.

Midway through the appointment process, when half the cabinet was chosen, Clinton came under fire. He had said, after all, that he wanted a cabinet that looked like America. Where were the women? Perhaps Donna Shalala's gender didn't qualify. (Subsequently outed by Queer Nation, Shalala denied she was gay, but who knows these days except the vanguards, in their secret consistories, what is what?) In any case, the feminists felt that *they* had a right to know. Clinton responded with his jive-angry act, saying that he refused to be bound by quotas. It was a clumsy imitation of an independent politician, exactly what he had done during the campaign when he attacked Sister Souljah. At the time of the

Souljah outburst he was mortgaging his future to Maxine Waters, an L.A. congresswoman from Jesse Jackson's camp, and to the other interest groups of the rainbow who would later demand a payoff. (An early warning of the form this might take is Clinton's promise to lift the ban on HIV-infected Haitians now quarantined at Guantanamo, presumably to award them the indispensable tools of citizenship under the new dispensation: a green card, a condom, and a hospital bed.) Shortly after his démarche with the harridans of NOW, Clinton appointed a bevy of females, including some even less qualified than Shalala, for jobs. Thus, at the very moment he was complaining about quotas, he was capitulating to the quota-mongers' demands.

True, Clinton's national security apparatus is more traditional, albeit loaded with Carter retreads. But because Ronald Reagan and George Bush knitted together the damaged threads of Truman's containment policy and brought the USSR to its knees, foreign affairs, while perhaps no more manageable, is potentially less decisive—at least for a while—than before. It is the social agenda that is now at the center of American concerns, and this agenda is in danger of being handed to what we will probably soon be calling the Hillary Left. The point person is Donna Shalala, only 4'11", but so committed to the cause that even *Newsweek* had to concede her credentials as "the high priestess of political correctness." The people at Madison she bedeviled while working as chancellor of the University of Wisconsin breathed a sigh of relief at her departure. She had been a disaster there, backing hate-speech rules that the courts threw out as hateful to the First Amendment, implementing draconian Ethnic Studies requirements and hiring/admissions rules that had the feel of the Great Helmsman's Five Year Plans. Shalala avoided foreign entanglements with a far stronger denunciation of fraternities on the Madison campus who had done a tasteless skit involving Fiji Islanders. This idea of moral equivalence was one which the leftover Left had made familiar in the 80s: criticize the Soviet Union but only by coupling it with the equally culpable U.S.A.

Shalala is only one appointment, it has been said. Yes, but to an agency whose budget is larger than the national budgets of every country except Germany and Japan. There are, no doubt, other appointments to come in domestic affairs which will buttress the Left's seizure of the culture. It is rumored that Joseph Duffey, who has made appeasement of the radicals into performance art at the University of Massachusetts, is on the short list to take over USIA and thus to dictate how America is portrayed abroad; and that Catharine Stimpson, whose lugubrious advocacy of PC as head of the Modern Language Association is legend, may be given control of the National Institute of Humanities. With her connections to Hillary, Marian Wright Edelman and the Children's Defense Fund (an organization which may be a Nineties version of the Trilateral Commission), Shalala is more than a Secretary; she is a symbol. In her, the long march through the institutions is complete. No one believed it possible back in the early Seventies, when the first burned-out New Leftists re-enrolled in the universities they had spent the previous years trying to destroy, but this was always a march on Washington.

During the last few weeks before the election, some warned that we were headed for a PC administration. But they were told that Clinton himself would stand against such nonsense. That was why he had created the Democratic Leadership Council, after all. The DLC was an organization based on political common sense and devoted to re-creating the vital center. Yet, at least from the time of the Democratic convention, it has been clear that the president-elect was a paper hound dog. The convention itself had the feel of a 12-step clinic. Recovery was in the air—a psychological as well as an economic imperative. Everyone there seemed to be in recovery—from AIDS, from abuse, from harassment, from prejudice. They were overcoming co-dependency, a yuppie version of guilt, and low self-esteem, the yuppie version of sin. Everyone had a tale of how he had overcome. The robotic Al Gore had the story of his son—a nightclub imitation of a moral quickening. Clinton's self-defining vignette was doctored with a slightly different spin.

When he was presented as the boy who had stood up against an abusive stepfather, it was an attempt to replace the heroism he never achieved in war with the battleground of the dysfunctional family. The subliminal message was that this primal trauma had left a mark. No wonder that he had perhaps strayed from the course during a life lived in these psychological shadows. But the important thing was that he had seen the light and was in recovery, and the misdeeds he never admitted committing in his marriage were behind him.

Despite the clumsy attempt at premature closure, it was easy to see the subtext: Clinton had signed not just a truce with his wife but an unconditional surrender. Every marriage conceals a deal. But not since FDR has the deal had such national repercussions. It is easy to imagine the terms of it: yes, I'll stay with you despite the bimbo, but there's a price; I want a hand in it if you make it through the primaries. Her feminism had given the First Partner the insight Clinton might have learned if he had gone to Vietnam: if you have them by the balls, their hearts and minds will follow. Hillary may not be the thick-ankled virago her enemies make her out to be, any more than she is the philosopher-queen portrayed in gushing mash notes from Eleanor Clift in *Newsweek* and Susan Faludi in *The New York Times*. Garry Wills certainly flatters her by reviewing a body of work that is anorexically thin.

Like her friends Shalala and Cole, Hillary grew up in the woman's movement imbibing the clichés. The family is not the site of enduring ties, she believes, but a bloody ground of unremitting negotiation where that which is nuanced, voluntary and not immediately reciprocal is dangerous; where every duty must be defined and every right prescribed. Only such a mentality could use a depressing phrase like "cherished, albeit fantasized, family values." For Hillary and her comrades, the family is not a building block of autonomy, but an obstacle in the path of social progress and a psychological ghetto of dysfunction. What these people want to do may seem liberal: protect children from arbitrary power. But what they really want to do, as Christopher Lasch has observed, is to protect children against the family itself. The state sets children free and the family holds them back: that's their view. Children's rights is a carom shot in the struggle against patriarchy. Making children responsible is freeing them from parental authority. For Hillary's gang, a quintessential act of human liberation is a 13-year-old girl having an abortion without parental notification, much less approval.

It is not hard to see where that leads: to further enfeeblement of the one institution in our society that can stand against crime and moral decay. For all her palaver about families and children, Hillary seems not to have understood the tragic lesson of the black family, which has become a laboratory showing the evil wrought by the malign symbiosis of a devalued patriarchy accompanied by intrusions of the therapeutic state. In her view that family is best which governs least. It should be something like a round-the-clock version of day care. Any expectations for something more than this are on the one hand sentimental and on the other dangerous, because intimacy is unpredictable and carries the burden of unequal relationships. What would Hillary and friends substitute for those "fantasized" family values they claim to view with nostalgic fondness but actually scorn? Programs. Programs architected no doubt by Marian Wright Edelman and the ubiquitous Children's Defense Fund.

Hillary makes one wish for a Clintonectomy even before the administration takes power. Yet what we face now in her accession to power was bound to happen sooner or later. The culture war has been going on for a long time and the left has been winning. Yet even as they march into the nation's capital, they still like to pretend that they are a counter-culture under assault by low-browed, reactionary American nativism. This is a self-serving fantasy. The left *is* the cultural establishment. This is bad because it means they have power. It is good because it means they must defend what they do and say—defend the payoffs to interest groups, the projects in cultural deconstruction, the obscene tinkerings with sex and

gender, the quotidian inequities and spirit-killing double standards, the manufacturing of racism through the promulgation of
rules about blood quantum and background that resemble the
Nuremburg Laws. All these things they have hitherto done by hidden agenda in the mad laboratories of the university—those
islands of repression, in Jeane Kirkpatrick's phrase, existing in a
sea of freedom. Now the sea has shrunk and the islands have
grown larger, becoming a land bridge stretching all the way to
Washington.

The culture war is this generation's Cold War. In the formative
period of that other conflict there was much discussion of what
strategy to use against totalitarianism: containment or rollback—
with the left, of course, pushing a minority position for capitula-
tion. As it worked out, through a combination of luck and
fortitude, containment turned out to be rollback. As those present
at the creation saw, if the West had the courage to hold the Soviet
Union in check, it would eventually collapse of its own hideous
internal contradictions. The same is true of the empire of political
correctitude. It seems like a formidable juggernaut. But, like Communism, it is against nature as well as equity; and the people of
this country, who might not have been able to prevent it from taking over the academic culture, will not tolerate it as a national
regime. Those of us linked only by a mutual loathing of the smelly
little orthodoxies are now the real counter-culture, and we had
better start acting like it.

2

The PC Cover-Up
(co-authored with Peter Collier)

T he annual convention of the Modern Language Association last December in San Francisco presented the usual menu of cognitive dissonance. An observer could sample the trendy vaunt and display of professing neo-Marxists sauntering through the Hilton hotel in their $300 pleated trousers; and of lesbians sidling out to erudite discussions dressed in janitor-chic with key rings dangling from their belt loops. There were the usual hallway conversations in which "race/class/gender" was repeated metronomically, as if constituting a compound noun. And of course there were the papers and panel discussions with weird titles and contents that have made the MLA one of the great targets of opportunity for journalists over the past decade. This year's efforts were particularly concerned with what one participant called (in a modish neologism that drew looks of puzzlement and then of approval) "people of gender." One professor contributed "Techno-Muscularity and the Boy Eternal." Another did some academic outing in "Hollywood and the Butch Femme Fatale: A Love Letter to Jodie Foster." There was also a session on the burning question, "Is Alice Still in Phallus Land?"

This glorious hugger-mugger has come to be expected of MLA meetings. What was unusual about this year's pow-wow was the frisson of seriousness. The literature professors acknowledged that

---

This was the editorial essay that launched *Heterodoxy* magazine, appearing in April 1992. *Heterodoxy* was a publication of the Center for the Study of Popular Culture that Peter edited. http://www.discoverthenetworks.org/Articles/1992%20April%20Vol%201,%20No.pdf

something big had happened over the past year. It was not the fact that Saddam Hussein had been bombed back to his bunker, or that the Soviet Union had at last cried Uncle Sam; these events were regarded either as irrelevant by most of those who had come to San Francisco or simply as irritating reminders of their country's continuing power and resolve. What agitated the conventioneers was the growing awareness on the part of the American public during 1991 that the collection of pathologies known as "political correctness" was spreading like an airborne toxic event through the groves of academe.

This is not to say that there was an open debate about the issues that had caused such an outpouring of national concern and revulsion in previous months—the double standards and race preferences of affirmative action which manufacture racial competition and hostility; the invidious codes against "hate speech" that attack the First Amendment; the mandatory racial sensitivity training sessions that smack of the political reeducation camp; or even the use of the hiring committee as an outreach for the radicalization of the university. No, political correctness was not even granted the mystical status of those forms of sexual harassment which are said to exist even if they only exist in the eye of the sufferer. The subject of PC was approached at this meeting only by bristling denial. Claiming that professors were being made into "scapegoats" for national economic problems, MLA President Houston Baker lectured one reporter, "Never before has the profession of literature and culture studies been more democratic and open." Catherine Stimpson, the saturnine dean of the graduate school at Rutgers University, added that the real problem in higher education was that conservatives and Bush administration officials were "cluster-bombing" the university with criticism.

The status of victims was irresistible to these left-wing academics because victimology has become so great a part of what they teach. But, as Stimpson's metaphor indicates, there is something more to the current furor than mere low self-esteem; there is indeed a nasty little war brewing in the university and in the culture at large. When the history of this war is written, it is safe to say the opening chapter will indicate that, until the last year or so, it was a low-intensity conflict. The origins of this guerrilla campaign can be traced to the 1960s. Back then, radicals wanted to burn the university down; it was the enemy not because it had real power, but because it was a pillar of liberal society—open, pluralistic, and committed to objective intellectual process. Denied success in the wider society, the left could always count on being able to throw its weight around in the university; and the university, for its part, did not resist. A pathological symbiosis had developed. As the radical project dead-ended in histrionics and self-immolating violence at the end of the Sixties, the discredited New Leftists realized that the university did not hold a grudge. In fact, it might be a place of comfortable exile and regrouping. They put away their Molotov cocktails and resubmitted their applications. The liberal values that had previously made the university so abhorrent to them now made it accept them without questioning their motives. As they gradually moved onto the tenure track, radicals were beginning what German radical Rudi Dutschke had in mind in 1969 when he called on his comrades in America and elsewhere to quit the barricades and begin "the long march through the institutions."

The seeds of the 60s bore strange fruit in the 80s as the immune system of the university, already battered by nearly two decades of violent confrontation, was subjected now to a series of new intellectual viruses. Feminism pressed a claim to equality, which once granted became a demand for dominance. Heidegger and Althusser, representatives of German Nazism and French Stalinism, took their place among the new household gods of the academy. Deconstruction, one of those intellectual innovations that seemed amusingly eccentric and stylish in French hands, became a blunt instrument when it reached these shores: Monsieur Hulot transformed into RoboCop. By the time it was revealed that its chief American apostle, Paul de Man, had been a crypto-Nazi and anti-Semite with a vested interest in the indeterminacy of his own life's meaning, deconstruction had already been wedded to overtly propagandistic race/class/gender agendas. As critic John Ellis would note later on, this alliance between deconstruction and Marxism had all the integrity of the Hitler-Stalin Pact, and like that agreement had a common enemy in the "bourgeois" status quo.[1]

The marriage of nihilistic intellectual styles to a politics of resentment created the order of battle for the guerrilla war of the 80s, as radicals who had gained tenure with the assistance of old-fashioned liberals now closed ranks behind their new power to ensure that faculty diversity ended with them. The assault on higher education advanced by way of a two-pronged offensive which sought to destroy the ideal of scholarly objectivity and disinterested knowledge and substitute in its place an ideology which was defined not by what it was for but by what it was against—Western values, democratic traditions, and most of all America itself. Under the guise of being about "diversity" and "multiculturalism" (two lies in one word, since what the radicals envisioned was neither multi nor cultural), political correctness, as it came to be called, aimed to prove that America was the Great Satan and aimed also to use the university to undo American evil.

Arguments about invisible structures of oppression broke down institutional resistance to the radical message. Psychological sanctions involving allegations of racism and sexism (and eventually homophobism), the most powerful of all sanctions in a liberal society, broke down the resistance of the individuals. These words were used not to identify pathology but to bludgeon potential critics of the new radical project into silence. More anxious to prove itself free of imagined sins than to protect the integrity of its institutions, the academic center could not hold. With a few exceptions, it caved in. By the end of the Eighties, the radical guerrillas had reached their objectives not only with virtually no opposition, but also without attracting much notice. But just as the

---

[1]John M. Ellis, *Against Deconstruction*, Princeton University Press, 1990

revolution that spread political correctness had come from above—from the faddish administrators and the tenured radicals on the faculty—not from below in the student body, so now opposition to political correctness began to develop largely from outside the campus community rather than from the hostages within. As concern mounted that American universities were becoming "islands of repression in a sea of freedom," in Jeane Kirkpatrick's phrase, *Newsweek* printed a story on the new "thought police." There followed similarly concerned articles in *Time, New York Magazine,* and *The New York Review of Books. The New Republic* did a special issue on the abuses of political correctness, and Ted Koppel explored the problem on ABC Nightline. Most of all there was Dinesh D'Souza's *Illiberal Education,* a book published last year which came to stand in the same relation to the campus crisis as Rachel Carson's *Silent Spring* had stood to the crisis in the environment thirty years ago.

Largely because of the persuasiveness of D'Souza's book and the furious debate it engendered, the advocates of political correctness found themselves on the defensive in 1991 for the first time since beginning their war. Used to bullying the academic community into frightened acquiescence, they at first were uncertain about how to deal with the resistance they now encountered. But during the summer of 1991 the PCers began to regroup. By September 1991, Houston Baker, Stanley Fish and others had formed Teachers for a Democratic Culture to promote curricular reform and respond to "misleading charges about political correctness." In November, the ubiquitous Baker and others met at the University of Michigan for a council of war they called "The PC Frame-Up."[2]

It was fitting that such an event should have been held on the campus where Jeane Kirkpatrick and George Bush had been shouted down by radicals during the 1980s, where a student

---

[2]I attended this conference and appeared on one of its panels as a lone dissenting voice.

lounge is named for the Communist hack Angela Davis, and where the first attempt to legislate against free speech on campus, a statute since ruled unconstitutional in a federal court, had been put into effect. It was typical that many of the 400 students who made up the core of the audience for the three-day event were there not by choice, but by compulsion—their professor, one of the organizers of the event, made attendance count for one-third of their grade. Houston Baker told them that the fear of political correctness was a "moral panic fueled by large sums of money" supplied by conservative foundations run by the new bête noire—white males. Baker's words were echoed by University of Michigan Law Professor Catharine MacKinnon, who interrupted her ritual demonization of the white males present in the audience to attack the press for reporting the phenomenon of political correctness. The slip of her contempt for the First Amendment showed again later on when she suggested to her audience that the works of Kipling should be locked away from the public to protect the sensibilities of groups they offended, with access allowed only to government-approved scholars.

It was left to two former New Leftists-turned-professors, however, to define the character of the PC cover-up. Todd Gitlin, a one-time leader of Students for a Democratic Society who teaches sociology at UC Berkeley, told the Ann Arbor audience that what appeared to be political correctness was merely an illusion, a manifestation of America's paranoid need for external enemies which was especially acute now that the end of the Cold War had robbed it of the Communist bogey. He was followed by Jon Weiner, a 60s activist who now teaches at UC Irvine. Without disagreeing with Gitlin, Weiner said that the new radical orthodoxy was good and that we needed more of it. In other words, political correctness doesn't exist, but if it does exist it is good. This message was cognate to the response of a prior generation of radicals who had also infiltrated liberal institutions: there are no Communists here, they had said then, but if there are, they are only working for human freedom and dignity. Back then the effort had been to protect communism as it subverted the political process; at Ann Arbor the effort was to protect political correctness as it subverted the cultural process.

By the time of the MLA convention in late December, the PC cover-up was at full steam. The MLA's executive committee produced surveys to prove that the classics were indeed still taught and that the panic over "de-canonization" was therefore illegitimate. No corresponding data were adduced, of course, to show *how* they were taught—how the classics, especially in American literature, had become voodoo dolls into which radicals stuck their own ideological pins; and how writers like Melville, Hawthorne and Henry James and characters like Lewis Carroll's poor Alice were forced to submit to unnatural acts in the radical classroom. Members of the MLA told each other that their only crime was opening up the American Dream and letting in the dispossessed and intellectually homeless—people of color and people of gender. But if they themselves were blameless, the university nonetheless faced a dire threat. It came from the onslaught of politicians and critics like D'Souza who were funded by the nefarious right-wing foundations and who had mounted a PC "scare" to take people's minds off the horrors of life in Reagan-Bush America.

Shortly after the MLA convention, journalist Paul Berman put the finishing touches on the cover-up in an article in the left-wing journal *Tikkun*. What appeared to be a totalitarian mentality in the university, Berman said, was mere intellectual friskiness inspired by the French thinkers of the late 60s. Berman himself was a stranger neither to the totalitarian mentality nor to its frisky manifestations, having spent 10 years defending the Sandinista dictators in Nicaragua as "New Left" pioneers seeking only to provide their people with "an alternative route to modernization." What was now being called political correctness in the university was under attack, he wrote, merely because it represented "the heritage of democratic openness and social reform that dates from the radical 60s." And so, by the beginning of 1992, the response of the PC elite to concerns raised about its takeover of the university was clear: to generate an intellectual fog that would hide the abuses of reason, due process, fairness and simple common sense that comprise the intellectual repertory of the tenured radicals; to transform their own desecration of the academic process into nothing more than a paranoid projection of others' dark imagining. It was the same old radical vaudeville act that had played intermittently for the past 75 years: "Ain't nobody here but us chickens, boss."

Covering up PC is waging the cultural war by other means. The irony is, of course, that these academic guerrillas are the same people who've been wrong about everything important that has happened since 1917 and who have now lost the political struggle everywhere but in the university. The collapse of communism and triumph of democracy has left them without a larger objective and without the other half of the equation for the theorems of moral equivalence they propounded so long. They are a vanguard that has become a rearguard. The ironic fact that Marxism, dead all over the world, still thrives among the dilettantes of the humanities has been frequently noted. It is as if geography departments had been taken over by flat-earthists, biology departments by disciples of Lombroso, or astronomy departments by the persecutors of Galileo. The result is intellectual backwardness. Women's studies, for instance, has been possessed by a kind of sociological Lysenkoism, which allows ideologues like Catharine MacKinnon to teach their students that the category *female* is an artifact that owes nothing to biology and everything to society. And as the reactionary state has "created" gender distinctions, so the revolutionary state can legislate and enforce new definitions of sex and sexuality, of what is politically correct and therefore permissible. We have heard all this before.

These tenured radicals hold onto the university as desperately as the Sandinista *comandantes* hold onto the confiscated luxuries that are the only memorial to their dead revolution. The paradox is that, while the advocates of political correctness are discredited and isolated in society at large, their ideology nonetheless seeps into popular culture in a process resembling the epic spread of dullness through society which Alexander Pope, one of those dead white European males out of fashion these days, describes so well in *The Dunciad*, a work that suddenly seems filled with contemporary resonances.

The spread of political correctness to Hollywood has been obvious since the mid-Eighties, when Daniel Ortega was served up at show-biz cocktail parties like an exotic *hors d' œuvre*. PBS has become the spokesman for political correctness on television. But PC has also spread to what our Frenchified academics might call the basic structures of our life. When, during the Clarence Thomas-Anita Hill spectacle, Catherine MacKinnon appeared on ABC Nightline as an "expert" on sexual harassment and was even named the ABC News "Person of the Week," it showed exactly how far PC dullness has gotten MacKinnon's "theory." An outgrowth of her gender Marxism, the theory holds that heterosexuality is rape, an exploitation of women in the same way that wage labor is (for Marx) the exploitation of a class. "Rights" is a male concept. When the law is concerned with rights in cases of sexual harassment, therefore, it is merely the instrument of women's subjugation. Since women live in a "male-constructed" reality, making them feel environmentally uncomfortable can be a criminal assault. Since men control women within patriarchies, intention and consent are no longer acceptable defenses against charges of sexual harassment. It is possible to be guilty without intending to do anything; it is possible to be blameless even when complicit in the crime.

ABC's acceptance of this looniness is bad enough, but far worse is the fact that it was also accepted by the Supreme Court in 1986 as the basis for the case of *Meritor Savings Bank v. Vinson*. After hearing that verdict, MacKinnon said, "What the decision means is that we made this law up from the beginning, and now we've won." Making up things from the beginning, of course, is what PC is all about.

The ideology of anger and resentment so prevalent on the campus today has also spilled out into our political culture. The politically correct line is that David Duke was created by the Willie Horton Republican campaign ad. The fact, however, is that David Duke was created by the inequities of affirmative action and the racism it manufactures. Duke is a Frankenstein built by these politically correct engineers of human souls. And, despite what they say, it is not at all certain that they are displeased by their frightening creation.

Until this last year, radicals believed that they could get away with McCarthyite thuggery on campus and that their fellow citizens would not be offended by the muffled sounds of free inquiry being strangled and destructive ideologies being jammed into place. They were wrong. Political correctness is now a national concern and their recent attempts to contrive a cover-up will not make it go away. The war over political correctness has been joined, and it must be fought to a conclusion. If the radicals succeed, they will use their version of history to determine what kind of a country America was and their version of politics to determine what kind of a country it will become. If they are defeated, they will lose their last redoubt.

Treason of the Clerks
(co-authored with Peter Collier)

A few years ago Houston Baker, current president of the
Modern Language Association, was negotiating with
administrators at the University of Pennsylvania over the
conditions under which he would remain at Penn. Regarded as one
of the eminences of Afro-American literature, Baker had staked
out his political pretensions in a speech to a rally of the left at the
University of Michigan: "My generation of black students never
considered ourselves political in any quotidian image of that
word.... When we were moved to social action, we knew by every
look, word and gesture of the dominant culture that we would
never enter the American political process.... *Man, like, we
couldn't even vote!* Hence we decided to skip politics altogether
and move directly to revolution." In fact, middle-class blacks like
Houston Baker, who lived in cities outside the segregated South,
could of course vote—though the 20-year-olds at the Michigan
gathering were perhaps too young and uninformed to be aware of
this. Moreover, while the 60s revolution was erupting in the U.S.,
Houston Baker was living in fair comfort in the British Isles, where
he was writing his doctoral thesis. In retrospect he might have
come to believe that he was a victim of American oppression or
even an invisible man; but in 1969, when the revolution back
home was reaching its crescendo, Baker was actually being

Originally appeared in *Heterodoxy Magazine*, September 1992;
http://www.discoverthenetworks.org/Articles/1992%20September%20
Vol%201,%20No4.pdf

assiduously wooed by Maynard Mack, the celebrated expositor of Swift and Pope and one of the most prestigious names in the academic firmament, who had come to England to secure the young black scholar for the English department at Yale.

Merely being in New Haven at the same time that the Black Panther Party was an "on-campus reality" (as Baker puts it), torturing and then murdering comrade Alex Rackley, does not qualify someone as a revolutionary, of course.[1] But even if Baker missed the action in the 60s, he made up for it in the 80s, "moving directly to the revolution" of political correctness. He is the author of a few scholarly works but more importantly of casual provocations which, somewhere along the line, have become as important as literary output in awarding status in today's academy. The difference between Shakespeare and Virginia Woolf, according to a famous Bakerism, is the difference between a Hoagie and a pizza. Rap music, he avows in another *bon mot*, is the great art form of the 20th century.

Such statements, showing a fashionable contempt for the canon and for the claims of high culture, have gilded Baker's résumé and made him into the academic equivalent of those prized free agents who have altered both the economics and the morality of professional sports. Sought by Stanford and other schools while teaching at Penn, adeptly playing the new suitors off against his current employer, Baker was able to punch his own ticket. His wish-list did not include demands for the admission of

---

[1] Alex Rackley was a member of the New York chapter of the Black Panther Party, accused of being an informer. He was brought to the New Haven chapter for a Panther trial. With national Panther leader Ericka Huggins present, Rackley was tortured and then taken into a field to be executed. Panther supporters at Yale, including future First Lady Hillary Clinton, demonstrated in support of the accused Panthers and assisted in their trial defense. The trial of Huggins and Panther leader Bobby Seale ended in a hung jury. Warren Kimbro, the Panther who had shot the 19-year-old Rackley in the head, was convicted of second-degree murder and given four years. He later became a college dean. See Paul Bass and Douglas Rae, *Murder in the Model City: The Black Panthers, Yale and the Redemption of a Killer*, 2006.

more black students or the hiring of more black professors, or for another load of diversity. He was interested in something else altogether—a piece of turf, a building, an *edifice* that would symbolize his growing power in the academic world. The new institution was to be known as the Center for the Study of Black Literature and Culture.

The bargain was sealed when the Penn administration agreed to eject the adult education program from one half of the building it shared with Psychology and give Baker the space. Shortly after the Center moved in, the staff of the Psychology Department received a memo from their chairman asking if they minded giving up use of the bathroom on the first floor, which was situated on the Baker side of the building. The psychologists were an amenable group and eager to be seen as good neighbors. But since there was no other first-floor toilet, they invoked their bowels and bladders as arguments for the *status quo*. The bathroom, in fact, had always been shared and in asking that it continue to be so they were not disturbing the natural order of things. After some parleying, and appeals to the administration, the parties arrived at a solemn compact which recognized the right of Psychology to use the bathroom facilities on the first floor. Wishing to encourage the amicable settlement, the administration had the bathroom remodeled, which the people in Psychology regarded as an impressive testament to Houston Baker's new *cachet*, especially when one of the new appointments turned out to be a shower.[2]

For a few weeks, the pact held. Psychology staffers engaged in bathroom politesse with employees of the Center for the Study of Black Literature and Culture. Amity reigned. Integration was in the air. But soon this *glasnost* began to evaporate when the chairman of the Psychology Department started getting letters of complaint from the Director of the Center for the Study of Black Literature and Culture. A dog from Psychology had somehow been

---

[2]These and other details of the negotiations are from the authors' interview with psychology professor Martin Seligman.

allowed to stray into the bathroom. A wrapped sandwich had been placed in the refrigerator which Baker had situated outside the bathroom at his end of the building. The chairman of the Psychology Department made apologies to the Director. But the complaints kept coming. Then, one day, members of the Psychology department came to use the bathroom and found that it was locked. All efforts they made to negotiate a key were rebuffed. In desperation, the Dean was brought in to continue the negotiations. But his efforts failed too. Soon the negotiations were taking place between Houston Baker's lawyer and the University counsel, who confided to a faculty member that this was not the only issue under negotiation and that, in fact, a fifth of his retainer was spent on matters pertaining to Houston Baker.

It was eight months before an agreement was finally reached that would allow the irredentists in Psychology to have access to the bathroom on the first floor of the building. Even this new truce was swiftly broken, however, when Houston Baker interpreted the agreement as affording access only between the hours of 9 and 5, Monday through Friday. What were they to do, the psychologists asked, when nature called after banking hours or on weekends? Baker let them know that was *their* problem. The conflict continued. Finally, the administration intervened. The passageway connecting the two parts of the building would be sealed. In addition, a new bathroom would be built for Psychology at a cost of $20,000. This was exclusive of the money it cost to seal off the two sides of the building. The new psychology bathroom didn't have a shower, of course, but it was on the first floor and it was theirs. In what might under other circumstances be called black humor, the psychologists put up a plaque commemorating their struggle and naming the new space: the Houston Baker Bathroom.

Say what you will about Karl Marx, at least he thought of the revolution as an enterprise involving nobility and risk. Prometheus stealing fire from the gods: this was Marx's image of the revolutionary hero. The possible punishment for failure was eternal obloquy; the potential reward for victory was the salvation of humankind.

For the enforcers of political correctness—people who natter about Marx and clutter his name with *post-* and *neo-* and *actually existing* and other prefixes—the revolution they wage is guilt-free and no-fault and about as heroic as visiting an automatic teller machine. Political correctness is not the revolutionary's sword but the bureaucrat's *Diktat.* It is less about the things it claims to be about than it is about nest-feathering careerism and opportunistic ambition. In one of those delicious ironies that waft through the groves of academe, *actually existing* capitalism is employed every day in the academy by those who deny the claims of property and markets at the same time that they avidly seek titles to others' buildings and strive to privatize previously communal bathrooms.

All the vulgar Marxisms emanating from the university are right about one thing: power is the essence of this political culture. PC is not about culture or knowledge. It is about power. It is about the strivings of a new class of academic bureaucrats who have sought to harness the theoretical moral authority and real power that flows from the categories of race/class/gender as a way of seizing perquisites and terrain inside the ivory tower. Free speech and free inquiry as well as the notion of objective truth are not values worthy of respect but merely obstacles standing in the way of their acquisitive push. Under the reign of the commissars of PC, concepts like diversity are kicked around like hacky sacks, while the academy is now a narrower place intellectually, morally and spiritually than it has been at any time since it was an appendage of the church. In the last two decades the American liberal arts university has become more politically correct and less intelligent, sinking to the lowest level in its three-hundred-year history. And the blame rests with the big enchiladas of political correctness, who must be considered in the same class as the televangelists who pretend to gather millions for Jesus which they use for their own debaucheries, debasing the very currency of the doctrines they preach.

Who are the Lenins of this revolution, the Trotskys, Mao Zedongs, and Castros? Well, Houston Baker, for whom the private bathroom is equivalent to the sealed railway car hurtling toward the Finland Station, is one. A far more alert and therefore more wasted talent is that of Stanley Fish, a name almost synonymous with the PC phenomenon now that he has completed his dog and pony show with Dinesh D'Souza. Of all the big enchiladas of political correctness, Fish is the most liberated from conventional expectation, the least perturbed by appearing the fool. The legends of his posturing proliferate. On one celebrated occasion, for instance, he was scheduled to give a seminar at Temple University for high-powered academics only. When he arrived for the seminar, he had a fawning graduate student in train and a tape recorder to document the occasion. Whenever he himself began to speak, he would turn on the tape recorder. When someone else spoke, he would turn the tape recorder off if their comments did not pass muster—a sign, in that semiotically-enriched atmosphere, that the speaker did not exist. And whenever someone asked a question Fish did not believe would stretch his intellect, he would turn the question over to the graduate student for a response.

This is what PC is all about: preening display, fatuous narcissism, petty power games. If Fish is interesting at all, it is because he does not bother to hide his distaste for the idealism that some of his colleagues claim as their motivation. He cops to his opportunism, acknowledging that the primary appeal of categories like race/class/gender is that they are above all *useful* to him. (As one colleague notes, "Stanley would just as cheerfully follow the tenets of Allan Bloom if he could get personal mileage from them.") Whatever the game, Fish acknowledges that power and money are the ways you keep score. He refers to a certain talk as his "Porsche lecture" because that is what its repeated delivery bought him. He makes no bones about his miniaturized Nietzscheanism. "I want to be able to walk into any first rate faculty anywhere and dominate it, shape it to my will," goes one of his more notorious pronouncements. "I'm fascinated by my own will." If this were not so impotent and self-parodying, it might be called a fascist yearning.

Some people got upset when it was revealed a year or so ago that Fish had written a letter to the administration at Duke regarding the formation of a campus chapter of the conservative National Association of Scholars, in which he urged that members of the organization not be allowed to sit on important university committees. It was, in fact, an attempt to see how far he could get— taking a bite out of an academic Sudetenland, rather than any passionately held agenda. When he was rebuffed he merely went on to the next thing, looking for another place to work his pipsqueak will. This is what it is all about. Fish's vaunted "theorizing" makes sense only in the hall-of-mirrors world of the university, where the institutional immune system has been destroyed by a series of opportunistic intellectual diseases. It is no accident that people like Fish believe everything is determined by language. Guess who controls the language in an academic setting? He has carried his dada from literature to the law, arguing that the cop and even the judge use the force of law in a way that is indistinguishable, say, from the force used by a mugger. ("There's always a gun at your head.") Conversely, the rapist is as much an exponent of "principled force" as the legislator or district attorney. One would like to sentence this Gucci revolutionary to an afternoon in the tenderloin of some big city and videotape him expounding his theories to the citizens of the street as they circle around and eat his lunch.

For someone like Stanley Fish, the chaos caused in the academic world by the bulldozers of PC on which he hitchhikes is not a moral crisis but a personal opportunity. Most of his comrades on the ramparts are less candid and more confused about what they are doing. Gerald Graff, for instance, professor of English at the University of Chicago and founder of the Teachers for a Democratic Culture, appears to have convinced himself that he is fighting back barbarians of the right who are banging on the gates of the new Eden created by the radical elite. If Fish is the revolutionary cynic, someone like Graff is the revolutionary surfer obsessed with catching the next wave. At the beginning of the vogue for deconstruction and other French ticklers, he wrote about how literature makes real assertions about the world and thus must be viewed in biographical and social contexts. While to the untutored this might seem a sensible position, it was regarded as a conservative one by those who were beginning to determine academic futures. And to be conservative, of course, is to be excluded from the new diversity. Soon Graff had become full of cheery *homage* to Derrida. The change took place with all the force of a conversion experience just at the moment that the truly chic radicals were leaving deconstruction. "I think Gerry was buying at the top," says Professor John Ellis, a faculty friend. "He really wasn't thinking. He just didn't want to be lonely." Graff embodies the malaise of literature professors who like to think they are dealing with big truths nobody else appreciates and who are gripped by two powerful emotions at the same time—megalomania and self-contempt—a chemistry creating what the French call *ressentiment.*

In time, Graff would make his peace with the new orthodoxies by floating what Camille Paglia might call junk bonds of his own. This was his notion of "teaching the conflict." When dealing with *Heart of Darkness*, for instance, the enlightened professor should explore the issue of whether or not Conrad was a racist and his work a text of colonialism. Of course, the "issue" is not an issue until the professor makes it so; no student would come up with something so peculiar. And to teach the conflict—a phrase that somehow echoes the nasty notion of "fight the power"—is a way of smuggling political correctness into discussions under the cover of an even-handed activity, an approach that allows an intellectual like Graff to do politics without seeming to be a mere political hack. Some observers regard Graff's new political organization, Teachers for a Democratic Culture, as little more than a press release and a rolodex. But the TDC gives Professor Graff an opportunity to be a public figure and to stir the debate, an arena to teach the conflict and show that he is on the right side. Being on the battlements, however, carries certain risks. It is necessary to make hortatory statements of intent. And, for sheer flatulence, it is hard to beat one of Graff's pronouncements: "Speaking as a leftist, I too find it tempting to turn the curriculum into an instrument of social transformation." In the breathtaking narcissism and silliness of this statement lies the problem of academic culture in our time: the vengeful clerks who insist on being relevant, and will destroy anything, even a venerable institution like the American academic tradition, to make it happen. Years ago, Gerry Graff wrote an essay about his infantile leftism of the 60s in which he concluded: "My politics had reality only within the political arena of university one-upmanship and careerism." He had seen the enemy and now, more than ever, it is him.

Stanley Aronowitz, a 60s "labor organizer" and now an academic entrepreneur, is head of the Union of Democratic Intellectuals, a group which proposes itself as an ally for Graff's Teachers for a Democratic Culture but by common report has even less reality. Before acquiring an academic institute, Stanley was known in the left as "the prophet of the next"—the next revolutionary theory, the next revolutionary class, the next revolutionary party, the next personal incarnation. As a younger man he became labor organizer-in-residence at *Studies on the Left*. As an aging new leftist he got a Ph.D. from an Antioch extension school where credit was given for "life experience"—apparently in Aronowitz's case his street theater as a 60s radical. Fellow socialist die-hard Bogdan Denitch brought him to the Graduate Center at City University, where Denitch is a professor of sociology. In an act of entrepreneurship even Houston Baker might have envied, Aronowitz not only managed to stay at CUNY by organizing a student demonstration when his tenure was denied, but acquired the academic equivalent of a room of his own—the so called Center for Critical Studies, which soon became a funded stop on the tour for tenured radicals.

The studies and conferences to emanate from the Center have naturally been critical of the capitalist order. Stanley's major work, *Science as Power*, advances the Stalinist proposition that science is just an instrument of class oppression. After reading it, the distinguished historian of science Daniel Kevles wrote in the *Times Literary Supplement:* "If the author knows much about the content or enterprise of science, he keeps the knowledge well hidden." Aronowitz is also the author of *The Crisis in Historical Materialism*, explaining that his use of the preposition 'in' is intentional, because in his opinion there is no crisis of "historical materialism"—a concept codified by Stalin which is still as good as ever if the *glastnostians* would stop meddling. A more proletarian version of the Teachers for Democratic Culture, the Union of Democratic Intellectuals may be a rolodex of second-raters. But at least it has the honesty to admit, which Graff's organization does not, that it is involved in an assault on the university, rather than a response to right-wing attacks. "Safeguard and extend the cultural gains we have made"—this is how the Aronowitz group describes the tasks ahead.

Laboring in the trenches like Graff and Aronowitz is just one half of the PC Mutt and Jeff act. The other half is represented by people like Professor Catharine Stimpson. She cultivates a cultured reasonableness that is a step away from the PC bully, yet her version of sweetness and light has a Transylvanian shadow across the visage and a smudge of blood at the corner of the mouth. It was the lugubrious Stimpson who stepped into the lists to condemn conservative academic Carol Ianonne for lacking credentials during the struggle over Ianonne's nomination to the National Endowment of the Humanities. According to Stimpson, Ianonne's appointment was purely political. Yet Stimpson herself, though president of the MLA at the time, was not exactly George Lyman Kittridge. The author of a sappy (and Sapphic) *Bildungsroman* one of whose most memorable moments has the female protagonist recalling how she was beat up by her brother because she had prevailed in a game of basketball, Stimpson's *œuvre* is almost entirely composed of feminist tracts. No president of the MLA was ever a more political appointment than she.

This Mother Hubbard lives in a shoe full of clichés. She affects a wounded tone when asking questions such as why we cannot be students of Western culture and multiculturalism at the same time, shaking her head in perplexity at the political stubbornness of *some people.* "The PC phenomenon, not hyped up, will eventually dry up," she says. What she means, of course, is that, unattended by the media and the American public, the PC phenomenon will win on the campus and then everything will be all right. Stimpson calls the 60s her "salad days." To see how full the salad bowl was of locoweed, it is necessary only to consider the prestige accorded to Fredric Jameson, the prince of academic Marxists. No one in the literature racket is more cited than this Duke professor of what Frederick Crews has called "dialectical immaterialism," and no one is accorded more respect. Yet this Marxist pedant, ever more committed to his ideological fixation during the period of its long twilight struggle, is in reality the Doctor Demento of the politically correct text.

His signature phrase is "always historicize." How does he himself do this? In *Ideologies of Theory,* he talks about the "problem" of Chairman Mao, a figure whom he regards with awe: the problem is that Mao stopped too soon in prosecuting the bloodbath known as the cultural revolution—"drawing back from the ultimate consequences of the process he had set in motion, when, at the supreme moment of the Cultural Revolution, that of the founding of the Shanghai Commune, he called a halt to the dissolution of the party apparatus and effectively reversed the direction of this collective experiment as a whole..." The translation for this malevolent "analysis" (in a book published 25 years after the fact, certainly long enough for the historicizing process to take effect) is that Jameson, who is still more Mao than thou, believes that China was better off when it was "experimenting" with human lives (an estimated 70 million were killed) even more destructively than it does now.

More Jameson historicizing occurs in thoughts about Castro (he was outraged when the networks' coverage of Gorbachev's visit to Cuba resulted in comparisons between Fidel and Ferdinand Marcos) and the misunderstood Joseph Stalin. "Stalinism is disappearing," Jameson has written, "not because it failed but because it succeeded and fulfilled its historical mission to force the rapid industrialization of an underdeveloped country. . . " The mass murder, starvation, lunatic engineering of human souls and actual economic bankruptcy of the Stalinist "development" slips right by the sophisticated armchair revolutionary, who would be only too happy to see it happen again in some other Third World place. Why is this man teaching our children? Why is Duke paying him a six-figure salary? What has this tranquilized totalitarianism got to do with literature, Jameson's alleged field of expertise?

When Jameson applies his theory to actual texts the result is usually opaque. When it is clear it is usually banal, as when he criticizes *The Godfather* as "American capitalism in its most systematized and computerized, dehumanized, multinational, and corporate form," in a sentence that reprises the rhythms and contents of the defunct *New Masses*. Jameson does not involve himself in the quotidian battles that obsess people like Graff, Aronowitz and Stimpson. His work has done it for him. His theorizing ("everything is in the last analysis political") has helped give currency to the current vogue for race/class/gender polemics. His hatred of capitalism and democracy has helped underpin the current academic transformation. This may help make up for the lamentable failure of communism.

As we look at the big enchiladas we understand that they are not titans of intellectual or political achievement but what Trotsky used to deride as the "epigones" of an already bankrupt totalitarian tradition. They could succeed only within the hermetic seal of the university where they have managed to destroy the laws of supply and demand for ideas. In advancing their lucrative professional careers and in trying to cobble together personal authenticity, they have made American universities into an intellectual wasteland and a standing joke among the hundreds of millions of people recently liberated from the former Soviet bloc by real revolutionaries against the very ideas and heroes America's PC academics cherish the most. Woytech Romachevski, a young Pole who came to America hoping to study at Stanford, spent time on the campus and came away reconsidering his ambition. "Back home these people would have been called *social parasites,*" he says. "Here they are a privileged class. Under Communism the *nomenklatura* is at least able to build the hydro-electric plants."

PART II

Media Culture

The Longest Blacklist

At a time when its latest cinematic heroes are a fascist (Eva Perón) and a misogynist (Larry Flynt), it is perhaps not surprising that Hollywood is experiencing a crisis of conscience in finding a place in its heart for a patriot like Elia Kazan. Last month the American Film Institute and the Los Angeles Film Critics Association denied Kazan a lifetime achievement award, thereby continuing to shun one of cinema's most accomplished artists. Even the subsequent defenses of Kazan that appeared in *Variety*, *The New York Times* and the *Los Angeles Times* lacked true conviction. Not one managed a forthright defense of Kazan for what he is: the longest-standing victim of Hollywood's McCarthy-era blacklists. I use the plural in speaking of blacklists advisedly. For, as Kazan himself observed in defending his decision to testify before the House Committee on Un-American Activities, the Communists in Hollywood were the first to blacklist artists, and they did so in any organization and on any project they happened to control. Thus one of the questions Kazan had asked himself was, "Why should I defend people like this?"

Elia Kazan is probably Hollywood's greatest living legend, and yet the director of *A Streetcar Named Desire* and *On the Waterfront*, the man who launched the careers of James Dean and Marlon Brando, the first artistic choice of Tennessee Williams and Arthur Miller, cannot get an award from his own creative community

Monday, February 10, 1997, http://archive.frontpagemag.com/Printable. aspx?ArtId=24418; http://www.salon.com/1997/02/10/horowitz970210/

because of the unforgivable sin of appearing as a friendly witness before the House Committee on Un-American Activities more than 40 years ago. Perhaps the most puzzling aspect of the recent spate of articles about the Kazan affair is the amount of print the defenders of Kazan have spent on the attempt to justify the extension of "forgiveness" to him after all these years. Why does a man have to be forgiven for defending his country? The question seems not to have occurred to his public champions. Perhaps most flagrant in this regard was a piece by the theologian Martin Marty, which appeared in the "Opinion" section of the *Los Angeles Times*. Marty noted that a usual prerequisite for forgiveness was repentance, and that Kazan had not repented. He nonetheless called for a "creative forgetting" to allow the 87-year-old artist to be readmitted into decent society.

To many, no doubt, the gesture appeared gracious. But to others this call for repentance had a hollow ring. What about all those Communists in Hollywood who betrayed their country, its democratic ideals and human decency itself in order to support a mass murderer like Joseph Stalin and to lend a hand to an empire that destroyed the lives of millions? Did anybody demand that the Hollywood Reds repent *their* sins in order that *they* be forgiven? Were they required to put on sackcloth and ashes before the entertainment industry presented them as improbable heroes of free speech in films like *The Front, The Way We Were* or *Guilty by Suspicion*? In fact, no such humility was required of *them*. As Marty noted, the treacherous code of E.M. Forster prevails: It is better to betray your country than your friends. But even if one were to accept the debased ethic of an alienated writer like Forster, who said that the people Kazan named were his friends? In his autobiography *A Life*, Kazan makes very clear that the Communists whom he named had not only betrayed his country, they betrayed *him*, as an artist and a man.

The release of the Venona transcripts and other Soviet documents makes clear beyond any doubt that American Communists were part of a conspiracy to betray their country and were in fact engaged in acts orchestrated by the Kremlin to undermine its security and render it defenseless in the face of its totalitarian adversaries. Propaganda, which was what Hollywood excelled in, was no small national asset to the Russians. If Hollywood's Communists have no need to make apologies for their role in trying to deliver America to its enemies, why should Kazan apologize for defending America against them? If the opponents of the blacklist argue that it is an evil in itself, why then is it acceptable to blacklist Kazan? Unless one insists on a double standard—one rule for Communists, another for patriots—only one conclusion is possible: It is time to lift Hollywood's longest-standing blacklist and honor Elia Kazan not only as one of its greatest living artists, but as a man who stood up for what he believed, and who braved years of persecution to defend his ideals.

2

Up From Multiculturalism

Like most of the destructive -isms of the 20th century, multiculturalism is an invention of well-fed intellectuals. It did not well up from the immigrant communities and ethnic ghettoes of America as an expression of their cultural aspirations or communal needs. In fact its primary sponsor and most effective agency has been the Ford Foundation, a ten-billion-dollar tax dodge created to protect the fortune of America's leading industrial bigot. Henry Ford published the *Protocols of the Elders of Zion* in the 20s and influenced Adolf Hitler's anti-Semitic crusade, winning himself an Iron Cross in the process. After his death, his foundation passed into the control of the intellectual left and its fellow travelers, the bureaucratic mandarins and parlor socialists of the moneyed elite.

Multiculturalism as we know it would not have been possible without the catastrophe that has befallen our colleges and universities in the post-60s era—the politicization of the academy and the debasement of the curriculum. The transformation of the liberal arts divisions of the academy into crude indoctrination platforms and recruiting centers for the crypto-Marxist left has been described bluntly by Harold Bloom as "Stalinism without Stalin." All of the traits of the Stalinists in the 1930s, observed Bloom "are

This article originally appeared in *Heterodoxy* magazine, January 1998. It is adapted from a speech delivered at the Seventh National Conference of the National Association of Scholars in New Orleans, December 12–14, 1997. http://www.discoverthenetworks.org/Articles/January%201998.pdf

being repeated ... in the universities in the 1990s."[1] Bloom is correct that the mentality is Stalinist, but it is the particular Stalinism of Antonio Gramsci.

The American system of higher education is remarkably diverse. There are more than three thousand institutions of higher learning, occupying a variegated cultural geography. There are public and private colleges, technical institutes and schools of the arts, land-grant schools and schools with denominational affiliations, and many others besides. It is almost inconceivable that all these institutions would adopt a single party line like "multiculturalism," and would do so within the space of a decade or two. How, then, was this possible?

Well, it is possible because behind it was a pile of money larger than the discretionary disbursements of the federal government in regard to culture and education; while, unlike federal monies, philanthropic investments are viewed as a benign force by the academic community itself. Moreover, the power of the Rockefeller, Carnegie, and Ford foundations to shape America's institutions of higher learning is nothing new. At the beginning of the era of the modern university Andrew Carnegie decided that it would be a good idea to give college teachers pensions. A college president was pretty hard-pressed to refuse such a gift, if he wanted to retain the best faculty available. Accordingly, the Carnegie Foundation attached conditions to its grants, and it is these conditions that served to define the entire educational era that followed.

The Carnegie Foundation announced that only colleges—as defined by itself—would be eligible for the grants. Carnegie then defined a college as requiring so many hours of secondary school education (which are still known as Carnegie Units); as possessing an endowment of at least $500,000; and as having at least eight departments, with each department headed by a Ph.D. That, in fact, was how the Ph.D. became the key to the academic kingdom.

---

[1] Harold Bloom, "Authority and Originality" in Mark Edmundson, ed., *Wild Orchids and Trotsky*, NY Penguin, 1993, p. 213

Acquiring a Ph.D. meant that university intellectuals had to earn the approval of their betters for the decade that shaped their professional life, a credentialing system that has been more effective than a Central Committee in creating ideological conformity. The Carnegie Foundation also announced that it would not fund pension programs for denominational institutions, which is how Brown, Drake, Wesleyan and many other colleges gave up their denominational affiliations, and how the secularization of American higher learning began. As a congressional commission asked at the time: If a college will give up its religious affiliation for money, what will it not give up?

Since Carnegie's day, the power of the foundations has only grown. A crucial flexing of their financial muscle with ramifications for the present directions of the university came during the Second World War. America's spy agency, the OSS, needed "area specialists" for its intelligence operations. The department system that the Carnegie Foundation had created was not functional in creating intellectual specialists for military intelligence, which had more specific agendas than the existing disciplines could service. The OSS had no use for historians, political scientists or economists as such. It wanted specialists in the particular geographical areas and national units it had targeted for attention. For efficiency reasons it wanted these specialists to have an interdisciplinary approach to the targets in question, a demand that the university as then constituted could not fulfill.

The solution was to re-shape the university, for which the OSS turned to Rockefeller and later, as the CIA, to Ford. Grants were offered for the creation of "area studies" programs and area specialists. The Russian Institute at Columbia and the Asian Studies Center at Berkeley were prototypes of the new academic curriculum. Naturally there was powerful resistance from the existing departments and the scholarly disciplines, which regarded this as an abusive intrusion into academic concerns and a debasement of their intellectual pursuits. But, just as naturally, the money provided by Rockefeller and later by Ford overrode these objections and the new interdisciplinary area studies programs flourished in schools all over the country.

Like the spy chiefs of the Central Intelligence Agency, Marxists also favor an interdisciplinary approach. Marxism was never about "economics" but always about "political economy," a theoretical agenda embracing all aspects of society and culture in the service of giving birth to a new human cosmos. That is because Marxism and all species of post-modern radicalism are totalitarian in their epistemologies and political agendas. Nothing escapes their political imperatives. Like all Gnostics, Marxist radicals are confident that they possess the theoretical key that will unlock the mysteries of man and society. Like Marxists, post-modern radicals don't believe in immutable realities like human nature, which in the preposterous view now orthodoxy in the university is "socially constructed." Their agenda, like that of Lenin and Hitler, is to reconstruct the world and create new men and new women who will inhabit it, and also think just as they do. Such an enterprise requires an adolescent credulity and amnesia towards the past, but also an interdisciplinary "knowledge."

When their revolution in the streets came up empty, the radicals of the 60s turned to a vulnerable, open, and essentially defenseless institution for their next acts of desecration and conquest. They began colonizing the university with spurious intellectual projects that looked a lot like the CIA area-studies program: Black Studies (now "African American" of course), Women's Studies, Queer Studies, Cultural Studies, and even American Studies (but with a Marxist compass). Unlike the CIA prototypes, these politically charged new disciplines did not target foreign adversaries but the indispensable enemy of the left-wing imagination, America itself.

What made the routine violations of academic norms required by the new discipline was millions upon millions of dollars in bribes in the form of grants, subsidies, and other awards to administrators and faculties by the Ford Foundation and its satellite donors. It is no exaggeration to say that without the financial intervention of the Ford Foundation there would be no African American Studies, Women's Studies, or Queer Studies as we know them.

As even Arthur Schlesinger recognizes, the goal of the multiculturalists is to deconstruct the very idea of American nationality, whose theme is *e pluribus unum*—out of many, one. From its inception as a nation of immigrants 200-odd years ago America has been an inclusive multi-national, multi-ethnic society, integrating diverse communities on the basis of an ideal of equality before the law. This success has been predicated on a specifically *American* culture that makes the integration possible. Multiculturalism is a head-on challenge to the very notion that there *is* an American culture, that this culture is superior to others in precisely its ambition to be inclusive and equal, and to its formula for achieving that. If there is no cultural melting pot, then the ethnic, and racial and gender pieces become the irreducible elements of the social contract and the theme is reversed: out of one, many. This is the idea behind "identity politics."

The multicultural assault first on the academy and then on society at large is a plan the Left developed following its failures to launch a "revolution in the streets" in the 60s. Its author is Antonio Gramsci, one of the many disreputable Communists who have been enshrined as intellectual icons by the academic left. Gramsci's contribution to Marxist theory was to suggest that by seizing control of the culture you could extend that control to the rest of the social order as well. Never mind that the Gramscian revision, suggesting that the ideas that rule society may not be the ideas of the ruling class, destroys the entire edifice of Marxist theory; logic was never the Left's strong point. The real beauty of Gramsci's strategy was that it allowed its radical practitioners to forget economics (which they never understood anyway) and the failures of actually existing socialist experiments, while continuing their adolescent hatred for America and its immense good works.

Over the last several decades, even as the star of the left has ascended in the academic firmament, it has become obvious to ordinary mortals that its intellectual tradition, which currently embraces Marx and Foucault, Heidegger and Derrida, Angela Davis and Catherine McKinnon, is bankrupt. Socialist economics, "critical theory," and progressive loyalties have produced the worst atrocities, the most gruesome suffering, and most crushing oppression in human history. But not for a moment in the nearly 10 years since the Berlin Wall fell has the left been ready to confront its failure or figure out what happened to its impossible dreams. It has simply moved on to another trench in its permanent war against the capitalist democracies of the West. In the course of this transition, it has degenerated from a Stalinist universalism to a neo-fascist tribalism, which is what multiculturalism and "identity politics" are really about.

It is not too difficult to locate the antecedents of this development. At the time of the First World War, it had become apparent to socialists like Lenin and Mussolini that something in their expectations had gone seriously awry. On the way to the war, the proletarian international was supposed to enact Marx's universalist vision. The workers of the world had no country to lose, and the war could not be carried on without them. But when it came down to the actual moment, the socialist parties of Germany and France decided they did have more to lose than chains and voted to support their national governments and the war budgets that made the conflict possible. The socialist idea had collapsed.

In response to this debacle of Marxist theory, leftists did not decide to take the honorable course, pack up their bags and go home. Like today's radicals, they wanted to continue their own war against the societies they inhabited. Two paths lay before them, whose avatars were Mussolini and Lenin. Lenin decided that conspiratorial vanguards were necessary to ensure that next time the working classes would behave as they were supposed to. He created the Communist International to crack the whip of theory over the proletarian masses. But the human components of the "International" also stubbornly obeyed the dictates of reality rather than theory and, instead of acting as an international vanguard, quickly became an organization of frontier guards for the Soviet Union.

Mussolini, who had been a Leninist until then, chose the other course. He decided that the true revolutionary agency was not an international class of workers but the nation itself. Fascism in fact was a socialism of the nation, an identity politics *avant la lettre.* This is the real intellectual heritage of today's post-modern, politically correct, ethnically obsessed multicultural left, which owes more to Mussolini than to Marx. "Every anti-liberal argument influential today," writes the political scientist Stephen Holmes, "was vigorously advanced in the writings of European fascists [including the critique of] its atomistic individualism, its myth of the pre-social individual, its scanting of the organic, its indifference to community ... its belief in the primacy of rights, its flight from the political, its decision to give abstract procedures and rules priority over substantive values and commitments, and its hypocritical reliance on the sham of judicial neutrality."

Gene Vieth has made the same observation: "Cultural determinism, the reduction of all social relationships to issues of sheer power; the idea that one's identity is centered in one's ethnicity or race; the rejection of the concept of the individual ... all of these ideas are direct echoes of the fascist theorists of the 1930s." In short, multiculturalism and "identity politics"—the politics of radical feminism, queer revolution, and Afro-centrism—are forms of an intellectual fascism which, if coupled with actual state power, can be counted on to produce similar results.

3

Karl Marx and
the Los Angeles Times

"The opening statement of Marx's famous *Manifesto*, that the history of mankind is the history of class struggle, is really the essence and sum of its message. This message is above all a call to arms. According to Marx, democratic societies are not really different in kind from the aristocratic and slave societies that preceded them. Like their predecessors, liberal societies are divided into classes that are oppressed and those that oppress them. The solution to social problems lies in a civil war that will tear society asunder and create a new revolutionary world from its ruins. This idea of Marx has proven to be as wrong as any idea ever conceived, more destructive in its consequences then any intellectual fallacy in history. Since the *Manifesto* was written 150 years ago, more than a hundred million people have been killed in its name. Between ten and twenty times that number have been condemned to lives of unnecessary misery and human squalor, deprived of the life-chances afforded the most humble citizens of the industrial democracies that Marxists set out to destroy. Marx was a brilliant mind and a seductive stylist, and many of his insights look reasonable enough on paper. But the evil they have wrought, on those who fell under their practical sway, far outweighs any possible intellectual gain. It would be a healthy development for everyone, rich and poor alike, if future

February 16, 1998, http://archive.frontpagemag.com/Printable.aspx?ArtId=24345

generations put Karl Marx's manifesto on the same sinister shelf as *Mein Kampf* and other destructive products of the human soul."

The above paragraph was written for the 150th anniversary of the publication of *The Communist Manifesto* in response to a request by Steve Wasserman, the editor of the *Los Angeles Times Book Review*. Wasserman was an old radical friend from Berkeley who had been a political protégé of Tom Hayden and Robert Scheer, two comrades who at the time were quoting Mao and Kim Il Sung, and attempting to organize guerrilla fronts in American cities, with which they hoped to launch a "war of liberation" in America. Inspired by texts like the *Manifesto*, Hayden's troops practiced with weapons at local firing ranges and planned for the day when they would seize power, abolish private property and take over the means of production. It was therefore of some interest to me how Wasserman would treat the *Manifesto* now that he was an editor of one of the largest metropolitan newspapers in America. After the failure of the revolutionary hopes the 60s had encouraged, Wasserman had entered the literary world to become the editor of *Times Books,* and then of the *L.A. Times Book Review.* I kept in touch with him from a distance over the years, and knew him to be of the same mind as many other radicals, chastened by the failures of that revolutionary and destructive left but not willing to give up the intellectual traditions and political ambitions that had given it birth. So I was both curious and ready to respond when he called me to this task.

Wasserman requested a piece assessing the *Manifesto* and its impact in 250 words. "Yours will be one of six such statements," he explained. "Well that's a challenge, Steve," I said to him half-jokingly. The article I actually wrote and submitted was 255 words, just five over his specification. But in the meantime Wasserman had changed his mind and cut the first 126 words of the piece, so that that the finished copy available to one million *Times* readers began with the sentence in the middle paragraph that reads, "Since the *Manifesto* was written 150 years ago, a hundred million people have been killed in its name." The first part of the paragraph, which described the sinister message of the *Manifesto* as a call to war, and therefore why so many people had been killed, did not appear.

When the actual newspaper copy appeared, however, I saw the extent of Wasserman's betrayal of our friendship, such as it was, and also of his readers. The "symposium" of the six mini-pieces, of which mine was one, was actually appended to a two-page spread with a picture of Marx, a poem by the German Communist Bertolt Brecht, and a fatuous 3,000-word lead essay by the unreconstructed Marxist Eric Hobsbawm, a man who had joined the British Communist Party in the 1920s and remained a member through the 1960s and all the slaughter of innocents along the way. This was the impression of the Marx's *Manifesto* the *Times* editor really wanted to make on his readers.

For leftists like Hobsbawm, my comments about the hundred million people the Communists killed were beside the point, even though Marxists like Hobsbawm did the killing or justified it to fellow travelers and credulous audiences in the West. For Hobsbawm, the *Manifesto* was not a historical document nor a wrongheaded and destructive one. It was a living prophecy. According to him, it correctly analyzed the dynamics of industrial capitalist societies and provided a vision of the social future. The one concession he was willing to make to what actually had transpired in the last 150 years was that it did not correctly predict that the proletariat would be the carrier of its revolutionary truth: "However, if at the end of the millennium we must be struck by the acuteness of the *Manifesto*'s vision of the then remote future of a massively globalized capitalism ... it is now evident that the bourgeoisie has not produced 'above all, its own gravediggers' in the proletariat."

But for Hobsbawm this error was of no consequence since the *Manifesto*'s central theme is correct: democratic capitalism must be destroyed or it will destroy us. According to Hobsbawm, even Communism's failure only strengthens this Marxist idea: "The manifesto, it is not the least of its remarkable qualities, is a document that envisaged failure. It hoped that the outcome of capitalist development would be 'a revolutionary reconstitution of society at large,' but, as we have already seen, it did not exclude the alternative 'common ruin.' Many years later another Marxian rephrased this as the choice between socialism and barbarity. Which of these will prevail is a question which the 21st century must be left to answer." In this Marxian fantasy the democratic postindustrial society we inhabit, with living standards higher and living conditions better for the mass of its citizens than available to any other people since the beginning of time, is no more than "barbarity," a "common ruin." And the only alternative is the socialism that Marx envisioned.

This, in 1998, is what for the *Times* editor—and in fact the academic establishment that has showered Hobsbawm with its highest honors—is the epitome of progressive thought. Of course the slogan "socialism or barbarism" was coined by Rosa Luxemburg at the end of the First World War, when Communists like Hobsbawm set out to destroy the liberal societies of the West and to create a Marxist utopia in the ruins of the Russian empire. Seventy years and 100 million deaths later, Eric Hobsbawm and Steve Wasserman have learned little from the experience. Steve Wasserman may not be ready to mount the barricades tomorrow and attempt to implement the vision laid out in this intellectual trash. But many, younger than he, will.

I did not call Wasserman when the *Times* symposium appeared; I wrote him a note instead.

February 16, 1998
Dear Steve,
    The 75th anniversary of *Mein Kampf* is coming up. It's too bad that Heidegger and Paul de Man are dead, but I'm sure you could get David Irving or David Duke to come up with a 3,000-word spread telling us why, even though it was written so long ago and has resulted in nothing but human misery ever since, it is still one of the most prescient and indispensable works for under-

standing western civilization and the Jews. You might also try that French Holocaust denier whom Chomsky likes so much. For my part, I'll be glad to provide you with 250 words of balance again. Of course, if you should need more room for the fascists, feel free to cut whatever I send you in half.

How embarrassing, my friend.

Letters to the Publisher of the Los Angeles Times

[The letter that follows wasn't merely revenge for the treatment my review of Marx's Manifesto *received. When Wasserman was first hired to edit the* Book Review, *he had asked me to write a letter defending his appointment, since an interview I had given which mentioned his youthful radicalism caused him some trouble. I did so and we then had a lunch at which I expressed my concerns about the virtual exclusion of conservative viewpoints from the* Times. *I hoped I had persuaded him of the merits of a pluralism of views, particularly in an institution like the* Book Review. *I was sorely disappointed in these hopes, and was not really prepared for the degree to which Wasserman actually turned the* Review *into an ideological journal of the left. The* Manifesto *episode was the final straw, prompting me to take my concerns to the* Times' *new publisher, Mark Willes, a former CEO of the Kellogg Corporation. As a very infrequent* Times *op-ed page contributor, I had been invited to a Christmas Party at the op-ed editor's house where I was one of only two conservatives present. I cornered Willes and told him my concerns and said that I would write to him. The futility of this exercise became evident when Willes turned my letter over to Wasserman for a reply]*[1]

Dear Mark Willes,

I would like to share with you my recent experience with the *Sunday Book Review* section of your paper. I am writing this in the spirit of our earlier conversation, and my understanding that

March 29, 1998, http://archive.frontpagemag.com/Printable.aspx? ArtId=22629; Mark Willes was formerly CEO of the Kellogg Company.

the *Times* aspires to be the voice of the entire Los Angeles community, including those of us who are politically conservative. I am taking the liberty of copying this letter to Michael Parks and Leo Wolinsky, with whom I have shared my concerns on this or parallel matters.[2]

On this particular Sunday, I open my *Book Review* and typically find four of the six major reviews identified on its cover to be written by leftists: Scheer, Davidson, Breines and Langer. For the purposes of this discussion, I will define "leftist" as someone who either writes regularly, or could write comfortably, for *The Nation*, the *Village Voice* or the *LA Weekly*. The same person probably is suspicious of the economic market and believes that real socialism hasn't yet been tried, and that, while Bill Clinton should be defended against Republicans, he generally has "sold out" to the "corporate ruling class." Thus, in this Sunday's *Book Review*, Bob Scheer claims that the professional journalists of the *Times* itself have "career needs and class ambitions" that "coincide with the moneyed interests of the conglomerates and privileged families who pay their salaries." I'm sure this will come as news to you (and to Michael and Leo). And I wonder how the *Times* can have such confidence in an insider [Scheer was a national correspondent for the *Times*] who should know better, yet who can write such stuff with a straight face. A conservative writer, by contrast, would be someone who writes regularly (or comfortably) for *National Review*, *The American Spectator* or *The Weekly Standard*.

The first thing I note is that there are *no* reviews by conservatives in today's issue of the *Los Angeles Times Book Review*. Nor are there likely to be any such reviews on any given Sunday. Last December, the *Review* ran a feature on the 100 best books of the *Times* for the year. It was a selection from actual reviews that had appeared in the *Times* during 1997. There were 87 *Times* reviewers represented in the feature, some having reviewed more than one book on the list. There were many, many left-wing reviewers represented, including far-left propagandists like Saul

---

[2] Parks was the editor of the *Times* and Wolinsky the managing editor.

Landau, a lifetime flack for Fidel Castro. On the same list, however, I was only able to locate one reviewer, Walter Laqueur, who could reasonably be defined as conservative, although he is an academic writer rather than a political author in the sense I defined above. Laqueur writes for *The New Republic* and *The New York Review of Books*, rather than the three conservative publications, but also, if I'm not mistaken, has written on occasion for *Commentary*. Though I should probably know better, I find this virtual exclusion of political conservatives shocking and, if not calculated, inexplicable. At the same time, this exclusion is very much the policy, conscious or otherwise, of the *Times Book Review*, which is currently being edited as though it were *The Nation*, rather than one of America's most important journalistic institutions.

I had my own unhappy experience with the *Book Review* in February, when its editor Steve Wasserman asked me to write 250 words as part of a seven-article symposium on the 150th anniversary of *The Communist Manifesto*. As edited by Wasserman, my piece and two others that were harshly critical of the *Manifesto* became mini-appendages to the 3,000-word feature by Eric Hobsbawm, a lifelong Communist and unreconstructed Marxist. Hobsbawm, who joined the Communist Party in the 1920s and stayed for nearly half a century, celebrated Marx's text as a brilliant and prescient analysis not only of 19th-century capitalism (which would have been bad enough) but of contemporary society as well. His preposterous thesis was supported by another 500-word contribution Wasserman solicited from an East German Marxist, who made similar claims. In his feature essay, Hobsbawm exempted Marx from responsibility for the epic crimes that Marxists had committed, and that he had dedicated his own intellectual life to defending. Hobsbawm concluded his article by proposing that the choice facing Americans now—a choice, in his view, foreseen by Marx—was 'barbarism or socialism.' This is exactly how Lenin sold Bolshevism in 1917. How embarrassing for the *Times* to have featured such a claim. How odd that the *Times*, a product of American capitalism and its First Amendment freedoms, should construct a symposium not just to include this point of view but to promote it.

"I am enclosing a correspondence between Wasserman and myself about this symposium. I think it is clear from this exchange that Wasserman has an agenda in defending Marx, and does not have much respect for a perspective that regards these views as bankrupt, and that is pretty much accepted not only among conservatives but across the spectrum outside the left. I have known Steve for thirty years and our relationship has been perfectly cordial. But my experience with the symposium and our letter-exchange leaves me with the strong feeling that people with views like mine are not really part of the *Times'* community—certainly not in the sense that the school of neo-Marxists like Hobsbawm, Scheer, Landau, Davidson, Breines, Langer, Christopher Hitchens, and a host of others who appear regularly in its book pages, are. Nor would it be reasonable for conservatives like me to expect that except on rare and idiosyncratic occasions the *Book Review* would either include our views in its ongoing dialogue or treat them with the regard they deserve. This is regrettable and hardly in keeping with what ought to be the standards of a great metropolitan paper.

Sincerely,
David Horowitz

[Instead of answering my first letter, Mark Willes washed his hands of the problem and turned the letter over to Wasserman about whose editorial policies I was complaining. I should have washed my hands of the matter, too, but instead made another futile stab at opening a discussion.]

[Second Letter]

Dear Mark Willes,

I have received a response from Steve Wasserman to my letter, which he wrote at your request. I have already had a correspondence with Steve that makes clear his unwillingness to acknowledge the problem. It is hardly surprising then that his response is not really a reply to the issue I raised. Moreover, its central argument is incomprehensible.

What can it mean to say, as he does, that the "categories of Left and Right have been rendered hollow and meaningless by the human experience of the recent past?" If that is so, why does the *Times* print a "Column Left" and a "Column Right" on its op-ed page? Does he really think that the views expressed in *The Nation* and *National Review*—my specific points of reference for the terms "left" and "right"—are wildly unpredictable, or indistinguishable from one another? Are there not generally recognizable "left" and "right" views of the role of government in the economy, of affirmative action, of school choice, in fact of virtually every issue the *Times* treats daily? Of course there are, and the *Times* editors not only know it but report it that way. Why does the *Times* print polls categorizing respondents as "liberal" and "conservative" if these categories are meaningless? Why, then, is it so difficult to recognize these divisions in the editing of the *Times Book Review*?

My issue, of course, was not "to weigh up the anti-Communist credentials of our occasional contributors as the chief criterion of their right to be published," as Wasserman disingenuously suggests. Such a position would indeed be "vile and shameful," but it has nothing to do with anything I wrote to you, to Wasserman, or at any time in my long public career. In fact, I raised no objection to *any* particular author being published, not even Eric Hobsbawm. I have not proposed *any* political litmus to be applied to contributors to the *Review*, as Wasserman implies. On the contrary. I am *objecting* to the political litmus that is presently being applied by Wasserman himself.

Nor is it "bean counting" or asking for "quotas," as Wasserman suggests, to point out that only one writer for the *Review* out of eighty-seven represented in the year-end issue can reasonably be called conservative. I have not asked for absolute balance or strict equality of representation, or anything remotely resembling that. The issue I have raised is the overwhelming weight given to one side of the political argument in the selection of contributors and the presentation of points of view. I am concerned about the systematic bias in the editing of the *Book Review*, which minimizes one side of the national debate, and makes the *Review* a merely partisan publication—uninteresting to those outside the choir, and unworthy of the *Times* and its ambition to serve the entire community.

In his letter, Wasserman does not respond to the issue I raised, nor does he explain the policy of the *Book Review* that would lead to the kind of imbalance I pointed out (or the *Review*'s embarrassing celebration of Marxism in the year 1998). Nor does he provide an intelligible explanation for ignoring this problem. I hope, therefore, that this is not the end of the dialogue. I would be happy to discuss this further with you or with your editors at your convenience.

Sincerely,
David Horowitz

[To this second letter I received no reply.]

4

Intellectual Dishonesty and Ideological Lock-Step

In the April *Esquire* and countless television interviews David Brock, the slayer of Anita Hill and relentless scourge of sanctimonious liberals, has gone down on his knees to plant an unlikely kiss on the presidential posterior. In an "Open Letter to Bill Clinton," Brock apologized for not having been interested in good government when he wrote the story of the former governor's sexcapades in Arkansas and repeated the state troopers' allegations they were used to pimp his scores. This particular Brock production—which the author modestly claims is the true origin of the present presidential crisis—he now reveals was motivated by a more primitive ambition than getting at the facts. "I wanted to pop you right between the eyes." This is but the latest chapter in Brock's odyssey from right to left. Chapter one appeared in the July 1997 *Esquire*, under the headline "I Was a Right-Wing Hit Man." Illustrating the article was a staged photo of Brock tied to a tree, one nipple seductively exposed. The editors didn't say whether he was waiting to be shot, or to nurse.

"Writer Tells Truth, Conservatives can't Handle It" is the way Brock would like to spin the story of his exit from the political right. He has already been hailed by left-wing hit men like *Slate's* Jacob Weisberg, who followed Brock's *mea culpa* with an obituary for conservatives he wittily called "The Comintern: Republican

Published as "The David Brock Affair: Murder or Suicide?" April 1, 1998, http://archive.frontpagemag.com/Printable.aspx?ArtId=24330; *Sex, Lies & Vast Conspiracies*, Center for the Study of Popular Culture Books, 1998, pp. 31–38

Thought Police." As in all such capers, however, there is the "story" and then there are the facts.

David Brock first made a name for himself as the only reporter who bothered to track down the details of Anita Hill's life and career, while the rest of the journalistic community lazily accepted her own heroic version of herself. In *The Real Anita Hill*, Brock gathered enough evidence to blow a barn-sized hole through the principal claims that had made Hill's case against Clarence Thomas seem credible: that she had no ulterior agenda in pressing her charges; that she was a put-upon, apolitical, possibly conservative victim; and that she was too shy, too timid or too unsophisticated to have pressed sexual harassment charges when the incidents allegedly took place 10 years in the past. Brock showed the reality to be quite different. Hill was, in fact, an aggressive climber, fashionably steeped in left-wing feminism, with an established penchant for lying when faced with adversity. Asked to leave her first Washington legal job at Wald, Harkrader and Ross for reasons of incompetence, she struck back using the leftist victimology she had picked up at Yale. Ironically, it was by claiming she had been sexually harassed at Wald that she originally won the sympathy of Clarence Thomas, who generously gave her a job in his Civil Rights Commission office. Brock also convincingly established a pattern of petty ambition and spiteful revenge in Hill's previous career that put a very different color on her celebrated performance in front of the Senate Judiciary Committee opposing Thomas' nomination to the Supreme Court.

For his journalistic discoveries Brock was pilloried mercilessly in the liberal press. In a typically overheated attack, *New York Times* columnist Anthony Lewis characterized the book as "sleaze with footnotes," only to confess privately afterwards that he had "breezed hastily" through it before writing his condemnation. In other words, he hadn't really read it. Joining Lewis, Garry Wills contemptuously dismissed Brock as "not only a sleazebag but the occasion in others for sleaze-baggery." Like other liberal writers, Wills didn't find sleazy the ransacking of Thomas's garbage, video-rental lists and divorce papers by Hill advocates, or the questionable nature of an accusation based on events that took place 10 years previously with no witnesses but Thomas and Hill. In another gutter attack, Frank Rich of *The New York Times* accused Brock of hating the entire female sex, while not so subtly outing him as a homosexual in the process.

Contrary to the overheated imaginations of these leftists, Brock's outing had no adverse effect on his reputation in conservative circles. On the contrary, his star kept rising as someone who had single-handedly accomplished what a decent, non-partisan press should have done in the first place—check out the story of a character assassin. When Brock's next story featured interviews with Arkansas troopers who told him stories of their moonlighting as panderers for the governor in Little Rock, his stock among conservatives soared even higher. New York's only conservative publisher, Adam Bellow at the Free Press, offered Brock a $1 million advance to do an investigation of the career of Hillary Clinton. Given what already was known about Hillary's extraordinary luck in the commodity markets and obstructions of justice blatant enough to make Nixon's transgressions look tame, expectations about a Brock investigation were predictably high. A first printing of 200,000 copies was announced. *Newsweek* arranged to run an excerpt and a major book tour was planned.

But somewhere along the way Brock re-set his compass. When the book was finally delivered, none of the expected goods came with it. Instead *The Seduction of Hillary Rodham* was another in a long line of mash notes to the First Lady. *Newsweek* withdrew its offer to run an excerpt: "The editors are in tears that you don't have Hillary in bed with Vince [Foster], or at least someone." So disappointing was his version of Hillary's Whitewater dealings that the *New York Times* reviewer, James B. Stewart, chided him for bending over backwards to defend the First Lady on points that were indefensible. The attack dog had become a lap dog. Network appearances and scheduled interviews for Brock were canceled, and his book tour was aborted before it started. Fans of Brock expecting an exposé felt let down by his kid-glove treatment of a woman they despised. Fans of Hillary, who despised Brock for exposing Hill, couldn't care less that he was now willing to give another feminist icon a pass. Neither audience bought the book. Within two weeks of its publication, stacks of Brock's book with "50 percent off" stickers were piled four feet high in Barnes & Noble and Borders. *The Seduction of Hillary Rodham* had been remaindered as soon as it was published.

But David Brock was surprised, or so he now alleges. According to the new Brock, conservatives were punishing him because he had "told the truth." He was disinvited to parties. He was no longer a hero. Conservatives could not forgive him, as he put it, for being "somewhat sympathetic" to Hillary. Brock opens his kiss-off to conservatives in the current *Esquire* by telling how he was disinvited to an A-list party of Washington conservatives and congressional staffers. "Given what's happened," Brock quotes a voice-mail message the hostess left him, "I don't think you'd be comfortable at the party." The impression left is that because Brock was soft on Hillary he was no longer welcome among the intolerant conservatives who had once been his best friends.

What Brock omits from his *Esquire* account is that the anger directed at him came from congressional staffers who had helped him in writing his book on the understanding that he would not reveal his sources. Brock had reneged on the agreement and blown their cover. In other words, it was the betrayal of confidences and friends rather than political correctness that was the source of their ire.

David Brock is evidently incapable of facing up to his shortcomings for which he has only himself to blame. Egged on by his grandiose self, he has transformed his personal failings into an epic case. "The age of reporting is dead," he writes as though his journalist persona were on a par with William Randolph Hearst, who could resonate with the *Zeitgeist* itself. And then: "My side turned out to be as dirty as theirs," as though a team of conservatives had written his articles and book. And then this self-serving absurdity:

"There is no liberal movement to which [liberal] journalists are attached and by which they can be blackballed in the sense that there is a self-identified, hardwired conservative movement that can function as a kind of neo-Stalinist thought police that rivals anything I knew at Berkeley."

But Brock can't even keep from exposing his own mendacity. After all, his conservative publisher Adam Bellow accepted the final Hillary manuscript with all its liberal trappings. "With my publisher's blessing, I was faithful to my reporting," Brock reports without noticing the implication. Bellow then printed 200,000 copies of a book that didn't sell, adding hundreds of thousands in costs to the million-dollar royalty loss. At the time his *Esquire* article was published, moreover, Brock was still the journalistic star of the political right's most Clinton-antagonistic magazine, with a half-million-dollar contract in his pocket to show for it. In fact, the managing editor of *The American Spectator,* Wlady Plesczynski, had passionately defended Brock's Clinton book to this very writer six months before Brock's article, and had done so at a "Dark Ages Weekend," the big conservative New Year's bash to which the supposedly ostracized Brock was an invited panelist. David Brock's problem is not conservatism, it is narcissism.

Which is a principal problem for the left as well. In a lead article in *Slate*, its editor Jacob Weisberg used Brock's accusations to deliver what he probably regarded as a deathblow to any further intellectual pretensions by conservative intellectuals. Weisberg is the man who once wrote a cover piece for *New York* magazine featuring headshots of six prominent conservatives under a screaming three-inch headline labeling them "UN-AMERICANS." In his *Slate* article, Weisberg upped Brock's ante: "The party where humorless thought police work to enforce a rigid ideological discipline isn't made up of Democrats. It comprises Republicans.... Brock portrays a political subculture in which loyalty to the cause means everything, truth very little." Weisberg is confident, of course, that he is under no obligation to check Brock's slanders before repeating them. "The treatment of Brock has no parallel among liberals. A few left-wing journalists, such as Nat Hentoff and Christopher Hitchens, have caught flak for dissenting from the conventional liberal position on abortion. But...."

Weisberg's distortion is one that I take personally. Peter Collier and I were once editors of the largest magazine of the left, best-selling authors and sought-after writers, until we strayed from the party line that Weisberg-Brock pretends doesn't exist. My books were no longer reviewed and it was more than ten years before an invitation came to write for a non-conservative magazine again. For criticizing the Sandinista dictatorship, our mutual friend, Ronald Radosh, was literally banned from writing on the subject of Nicaragua while still a masthead editor of the socialist magazine *Dissent*, a ban that was imposed by the magazine's founder and icon of democratic socialism, Irving Howe.

But this is far from only a personal story. If journalists on the left lack a party line, perhaps Weisberg can refer us to the brave souls who did not go along with the wolf-pack that descended on Judge Bork and Clarence Thomas, or who may have suggested in some overlooked venue that the Clinton obstructions of justice and the White House abuse of governmental agencies might meet the Watergate standard. Perhaps he will let us all know the names of those progressives who dissented from the politically correct line on the AIDS epidemic, which led to the unnecessary deaths of so many young gay men.[1] Perhaps he will give us the honor roll of those progressives who broke ranks to deplore the feminist witch-hunt in America's military.[2] Or perhaps he can refer us to a liberal journalist who exercised his profession's legendary skepticism in writing about the recent release of the sociopath, killer, and former Black Panther Geronimo Pratt.

As for the conservative lockstep, in the last six months conservative pundit Arianna Huffington has attacked every conservative leader Weisberg could name without causing any noticeable

---

[1]See Part II of this volume.
[2]See Part III of this volume.

diminution in her invitations to parties or service on the boards of conservative think tanks.[3] *Weekly Standard* editor William Kristol is regularly slammed by Republican leaders, and Pat Buchanan was labeled a "fascist" by both *The American Spectator* and Bill Bennett without diminishing his presence at conservative conferences. Newt Gingrich has been viciously caricatured on the covers of *National Review* and *The Weekly Standard,* which announced his "meltdown" and ran an article pillorying him as "Political Road Kill." In a survey of *l'affaire* Brock for *The Washington Post,* Howard Kurtz managed to get three major conservative journalists, Robert Novak, William Safire and William Kristol, to complain on the record and in the liberal press about other conservatives, while conceding, "The idea that conservative journalists have always marched in lock-step with their ideological brethren is something of a myth." So much for Weisberg's "Comintern."[4]

As a former partisan of the left, I can testify to how exhilarating it is to breathe the conservative intellectual air. Conservatism is a tent so big that the conventional wisdom is to doubt its coherence as a political movement. The impending breakup of the right in the post-Communist world—because there will be nothing now to hold the squalling wings of conservatism together—is almost a journalistic cliché. Today, in the pages of the conservative magazines that Weisberg describes as under party discipline, conservatives war over immigration, abortion, drug policy, homosexuality, openings to China, the place of religion, the credibility of supply-side economics and the sanity of Jude Wanniski and Jack Kemp (for embracing Louis Farrakhan).

By contrast, if liberals are at war with each other it is over how to position themselves to get elected. How many serious clashes of values are there in liberal ranks? Are there liberals who view the ending of welfare as a positive good, who would like to see the

---

[3]Huffington subsequently joined the left-wing ranks.
[4]http://en.wikipedia.org/wiki/Comintern

non-defense budget cut, who want to reduce the capital-gains tax to zero? Consider a more volatile issue like affirmative action. Is there a single prominent liberal who has dared to remain publicly faithful to the civil rights principle of a color-blind standard as enunciated by Martin Luther King, or who has had the courage to denounce racial preferences in the Nineties in the same moral voice that liberals used to denounce racial preferences in the Sixties? If so, this writer certainly missed it.

Consider the parallel case to Brock's Anita Hill book. Two left-wing reporters, Jane Mayer and Jill Abramson, followed *The Real Anita Hill* with a counter-volume about Clarence Thomas called *Strange Justice.* It turned out to be an unoriginal, unerringly sordid personal attack on the only Supreme Court justice who is also an African American, a man who rose against extreme odds of poverty and racial oppression to achieve high office, and who has only a single blemish attached to his entire public career—and how many public figures can say that? This blemish, moreover, is the result of an unproven claim about alleged events in a distant past, coming from an embittered, unreliable, partisan source whose gripings never should have been given a public platform in the first place. *Strange Justice* was promoted and celebrated by the same shameless chorus that prevented Brock's own investigation from being taken seriously outside the ghetto to which conservatives have been consigned. Was there a single liberal journalist or reviewer who broke ranks to condemn the atrocity the left committed on the public reputation of Clarence Thomas or deplore the character assassination of an African-American jurist?

Or, consider the other side of Weisberg's equation: In the wake of the partisan lynching of Justice Thomas, Senator Orrin Hatch accepted, without demurral, Clinton's nomination of Ruth Bader Ginsburg, a long-time ideological leader of the feminist left. Was Hatch read out of the conservative movement for this political surrender? Did any conservative journalist rummage through Ginsburg's garbage and personal secrets in order to smear and taint her, as liberals did Thomas and Bork? Was there a relentless

Republican interrogation at the hearings aimed at ferreting out her ideological commitments? Did conservatives join in any effort to destroy her ability to be a role model to women, in the way liberals closed ranks to destroy Thomas's public persona and keep him from becoming an inspiration to his community?

The media are so utterly and pervasively dominated by the left-wing culture that liberals have lost the ability to see who they are and what they do. Or to care about fairness and the pluralism of ideas. We are all driven to some extent by the sense of our own righteousness. But normally others are around to keep our *hubris* in check. When ours is the only voice audible, *that* becomes the only truth we hear. In his new *Esquire* "Open Letter" Brock writes: "If sexual witch-hunts become the way to win in politics, if they become our politics altogether, we can and will destroy everyone in public life." Given the context if this warning, it is little more than an attempt to smear the conservative witch-hunt style without, once again, offering any supporting evidence. And who is Brock's new mentor now that he has joined the left? Why, if it isn't Sidney Blumenthal, the Svengali behind the First Lady's "vast right-wing conspiracy" hysteria over her husband's infidelities, and also behind the very real sexual witch hunts against the staff of her husband's prosecutor Ken Starr.[5]

---

[5]Brock subsequently became the publisher of MediaMatters.com, a multi-million dollar website whose *raison d'être* is witch-hunting conservatives and Republicans.

5

Warren Beatty's Socialist Agitprop

Just when you thought the old socialist left was dead and buried it is sprouting across the cultural landscape like a spring weed on Viagra. Last week Warren Beatty's terminally silly agitprop, *Bulworth*, opened in theaters nationwide. The premise of the film—hold your breath—is that a liberal politician has to first suffer a nervous breakdown in order "to speak truth to power." Notwithstanding its fundamental absurdity, or perhaps because of it, the film manages to be quite funny—a tribute to Beatty's comic talent as writer, actor and director. Moreover, its critique of political hypocrisy and cant is often telling. But the "truth" that it proposes as its main thesis is unintentionally funnier still.

According to *Bulworth*, all liberal politicians are bought by "big rich guys" in order to keep them from publicly identifying the real solution to society's problems, which is *socialism*. (This will earn particularly big guffaws in the newly liberated countries of Eastern Europe.) Even more bizarrely, Bulworth, the film's liberal politician hero played by Beatty, tells us that Black Panther criminal Huey Newton is oppressed America's lost leader. I am not making this up. According to the pop Marxism that underlies the film's message, the "deindustrialization of urban America" has deprived minority communities of champions like Newton, who in real life was a cokehead gangster, a murderer, an extortionist and a rapist. Newton's message, as his cohort Eldridge Cleaver told

Originally published as *Bul*****, June 1, 1998, http://www.salon.com/ 1998/06/01/01horo/; http://archive.frontpagemag.com/Printable.aspx? ArtId=22653

a "60 Minutes" audience shortly before the latter's death last month, was a summons to war that would have created a "holocaust" in America if enough people had heeded it.[1]

Bulworth attacks the media for being corrupted by the same rich guys who buy politicians like him. But this begs the real-life question: how could a right-wing media billionaire like Rupert Murdoch, who owns 20th Century Fox, drop $30 million on a left-wing bomb-thrower like Beatty to promote this subversive claptrap? When asked in TV interviews whether he actually knew any corrupt politicians, the aging matinee idol—who has been close to most significant liberal Democratic legislators over the last 30 years—said he did not.

Bulworth belongs to the Oliver Stone School of Conspiracy-Mongering. But where Stone's JFK was harshly criticized by liberal centrists who were among its targets, Beatty's film has been given a free ride, its Marxist message trumpeted as a rediscovered gospel. "It may be the most keenly astute and honest film about politics ever," gushed a Los Angeles critic. Others have coyly endorsed the movie's wisdom. According to New York magazine's David Denby, Bulworth is a "thrillingly dangerous political comedy" and Bulworth a "holy fool," i.e., an idiot who tells the truth.

Bulworth would be a less significant barometer of the Zeitgeist if it were not accompanied by another effusion of reactionary sentiment on the occasion of the 150th anniversary of the Communist Manifesto. Since we are also approaching the 10th anniversary of the fall of the Berlin Wall, one might have expected the Manifesto, along with its bloody incitements, to be consigned to a shelf of poisonous tracts alongside Mein Kampf and the Protocols of the Elders of Zion. But two of the nation's preeminent journalistic institutions, the Los Angeles Times and The New York Times, celebrated the commemorative edition published by New Left Review as a tribute to Marx's sociological "masterpiece." While

---

[1]June 15, 1997; Cf. "Eldridge Cleaver's Last Gift," in Vol. 2 of this series, Progressives, Part II, chapter 9.

the reviews lamented that Marx had overestimated the revolution-ary fervor of the proletariat, they both treated it as an insightful analysis for his time and ours. *The New York Times'* homage, writ-ten by an English professor, suggested that the Manifesto could hardly be faulted as "a classic expression of the society it anato-mized and whose doom it prematurely announced." Prematurely indeed.

The *Los Angeles Times* reprinted the worshipful 3,000-word introduction to the new edition by historian Eric Hobsbawm, for 50 years one of Communism's chief intellectual spear-carriers. According to Hobsbawm, the *Manifesto*'s brilliance lies in its recognition that the future for 1998 America, as for 1848 England, is a choice between "socialism or barbarism." Hobsbawm and Sen-ator Bulworth clearly have a lot in common. In a correspondence with me about this tribute, *Los Angeles Times Book Review* editor Steve Wasserman, a former Berkeley radical, explained that, "much of what [Marx] wrote about capitalism remains as penetrat-ing as the day he penned his polemics." To which I replied: "Like what for instance? The labor theory of value, the reserve army of the unemployed, the rejection of the market, the reduction of political and historical issues to issues of economic class, the pre-diction of increasing class polarization, the prediction of increas-ing misery, the prediction of a falling rate of profit, the prediction of capitalism's collapse?"

There was no answer because there could be none. Marxism is mythology. The failure of progressive intellectuals like Wasser-man and Beatty to understand this, coupled with their enormous influence in the culture, is actually one of the main obstacles to progress. Progressives cling to a welfare system that has destroyed families in America's inner cities. They have taken the core mes-sage of the *Manifesto*—an incitement to civil war—and trans-formed it into a summons to gender and racial confrontation that makes any coming together to solve problems in these areas next to impossible. To the extent that their reactionary message exerts even greater influence through films like *Bulworth*, it will make the more pragmatic liberalism of centrist Democrats harder to implement, and the election of conservative majorities that much more inevitable.

6

A Proper Love of Country

It is just a little over two years ago that I wrote my first column for *Salon*, a piece about Elia Kazan in which I called for an end to America's "longest blacklist." I did not say so at the time, but I felt a kinship with Kazan because the invitation to write for *Salon* ended my long exile from the literary culture, the result of a graylist in force for ex-radicals like myself.[1] I had no idea the shunning of Hollywood's greatest living film legend would come to an end only two years later, or that it would come as a result of an honor bestowed on him by the Academy of Motion Pictures itself. The honor was presented in the face of a continuing and very vocal resistance protesting the informal blacklist of Communists introduced into the film industry by the Hollywood studio heads some fifty years ago. Abe Polonsky and Bernard Gordon, two minor film professionals who organized the protest, were among those blacklisted at the time.

Allow me to clarify my own views of congressional investigations. Their purpose is to inquire whether there should be legislation to deal with certain problems and to provide information useful for designing it. Given this mandate, it was as legitimate for Congress to hold hearings inquiring into the influence of the

---

March 26, 1999, http://archive.frontpagemag.com/Printable.aspx?ArtId=24274
[1]My grace period lasted a little longer than two years (February 10, 1997 to November 25, 2002). When *Salon* began charging subscriptions, its editors informed me that their audience would not pay for a magazine that included columns by David Horowitz, and I was dropped.

Communist Party in an important industry like film as it was to inquire into the influence of organized crime in the labor movement. The Communist Party was conspiratorial in nature and orchestrated by Moscow. It systematically infiltrated unsuspecting organizations, intending to control them in the interests of a hostile foreign power. Kazan deeply resented the way the Communist Party had taken control of the Group Theater, where he was an actor and director, and exploited it for its own political ends.

What was not legitimate was for legislators to use congressional hearings to attempt to expose the influence of Communists or gangsters to the public at large. Such public hearings became in effect trials of those summoned before them, without the due-process protections that would have been afforded in a court of law. The committees became juries, judges and executioners all rolled into one. The mere charge of being a gangster or a Communist was enough to ensure punitive consequences.

By this standard, all legislative investigations that are open, whether they are of organized crime or of Communists or of executive branch misdeeds, as in the Iran-Contra Hearings, potentially qualify as witch-hunts. Like the Communists, Oliver North, a target of the Iran-Contra hearings, had no constitutional protections when he appeared before a senate investigating committee. He had to sit in the dock while senators, who enjoyed legal immunity, denounced him as a liar and traitor to the entire nation. I don't remember protests from liberals over the public hanging of North and the other Iran-Contra figures. Yet the only way to avoid such abuses of congressional power is to require that congressional hearings like this be closed.

There were other aspects of the Hollywood investigations and Kazan's role in them that were obscured during the award controversy. Every one of the Communists Kazan named had already been identified by other witnesses. None of those he named worked in the film industry but were theater professionals in New York. Kazan's testimony destroyed no Hollywood careers. It was not Congress that imposed the blacklist but the film industry itself. This little-known fact was dramatized by the way the black-list finally came to an end. It was accomplished through the act of a single individual, Kirk Douglas, who decided to give the black-listed writer Dalton Trumbo a screen credit for the film *Spartacus.* What made the blacklist possible, in other words, was the Holly-wood community, the collusion of all those actors, writers, and directors (some of whom sat on their hands and scowled for the cameras the night Kazan's own exile ended) who went to work day in and day out during the blacklist years while their friends and colleagues languished out in the cold.

Ultimately, the anti-Kazan protest was an attempt to re-fight the Cold War, which is why the anti-Kazan forces lost. Suppose the studio heads who met in 1951 to ban Communists in Holly-wood had instead announced that they were not going to employ Nazis and racists, or members of the Ku Klux Klan. Would Abe Polonsky and Bernard Gordon and the other progressives have come out to protest this blacklist? Would they have regarded friendly witnesses against the Nazis and racists as betrayers of friends? Or would they have welcomed them as men who had come to their senses and done the right thing?

Many of those who defended the Kazan award invoked the quality of his art to overlook what he did politically. The director Paul Schrader was typical. Artistically, he told the *LA Weekly,* "Kazan is a giant. [But] that does not mitigate the fact that he did wrong things. I think evil things. But at the end of the day, he's an artist, and his work towers over that." Schrader explained that say-ing Kazan shouldn't get an honorary Oscar was like saying Leni Riefenstahl shouldn't be acknowledged because she worked under the heel of Hitler's propaganda machine. What Schrader (and oth-ers) conveniently overlooked was that it was Kazan's antagonists who volunteered to work for Stalin's propaganda machine, while Kazan went to the mat for America, for the democracy that had given him refuge, freedom, and unparalleled opportunity.

I had the occasion to raise this issue, on a talk show, with Vic-tor Navasky, editor of *The Nation* and author of a book on the

McCarthy period that established him as the most articulate defender of the Old Left. When I asked Navasky if he would have similar objections to a blacklist of Nazis, he said, "The difference is the Nazi Party was illegal. The Communist Party was legal." This was an odd position for a New Left radical. Would it have been all right to inform on members of the civil-rights movement because they broke laws? Should the Communist Party have been outlawed to make the hearings legitimate? In fact, one of the purposes of the congressional hearings, as Navasky well knows, was to see if such legislation was warranted. If Congress had decided to outlaw the Communist Party, wouldn't Victor Navasky and other progressives be pointing to this as an example of witch-hunting, and evidence of an incipient American fascism at the time? Of course they would.

In fact, Navasky draws a sharp distinction between Communists and Nazis that has nothing to do with legalities. In a *Newsweek* column, he wrote that, unlike Nazis, "the actors, writers, and directors who joined the Communist Party ... in the 30s started out as social idealists who believed that the party was the best place to fight fascism abroad and racism at home." But this is not a plausible argument for anyone familiar with the political realities of the time, and in particular of the left. There were many organizations other than the Communist Party where one could fight fascism abroad and racism at home if one so desired. Indeed, during the Nazi-Soviet Pact, the Communist Party was hardly the place to fight fascism abroad at all. What made the Communist Party distinctive for those who joined was its belief that the Soviet Union was the future of mankind, and that loyalty to the Soviet Union and preparation for a Bolshevik-style revolution in the United States were appropriate politics for progressives. People who joined the Party were given secret names so they could function in the underground when the time came for such tactics; they were introduced into an organization that was conspiratorial in nature because it fully intended to conduct illegal operations. That was what the revolution required as they understood it.

One of the famous incidents of the blacklist period was the Peekskill riot, where anti-communists broke up a public concert by Paul Robeson, the most famous figure associated with the Party at the time. The occasion for the riot was a public statement Robeson had made that blurted out what every Communist secretly felt: in the Cold War with Stalin's Russia, he was actively pulling for the other side. What Robeson said was that American Negroes would not fight in a war between the United States and the Soviet Union. This was a crude attempt to exploit the racial feelings of black Americans, but it accurately reflected the sentiments in Robeson's own heart and in the hearts of his comrades.

This is the missing self-perception that underlies the odd postures of the left during the Kazan affair and indeed the postures of many post-Communist leftists when they reflect on the Cold War years. Another missing self-perception is the failure to acknowledge that those who protested the Kazan honor were actually the aggressors in the affair, while presenting themselves as victims. Imagine what would have happened if a group of Hollywood conservatives had organized a protest over the honorary Oscar the Academy gave to Charlie Chaplin some years ago earlier because he was a Communist fellow-traveler. Suppose they had done so because forty years earlier Chaplin had given money and support to the Stalinist cause. Can it be doubted that cries of "red-baiting" and "witch-hunting" would be heard from the left? Why was Kazan's case any different? Why didn't they see their own protest as a witch-hunt to deny an honor to someone who was on the other side of the political battle fifty years ago?

I have been reading a recently published book called *Red Atlantis* by the film critic of the *Village Voice*, J. Hoberman. Its concluding chapter is about the Rosenberg case.[2] As in the Kazan affair, the passions over the Rosenbergs still run high despite the fact that here too the historical record is conclusive. Just as there

[2]http://www.amazon.com/exec/obidos/ISBN=1566396433/centerforthest 01A/

is no secret anymore that virtually all the victims of the blacklist were also defenders of a monster regime that was America's sworn enemy, so it is clear that the Rosenbergs were spies for Stalin's Russia. Hoberman does not deny either fact, but so minimizes them that they become insignificant to his argument. The climactic passage of his text contains these judgments:

Q. WERE JULIUS AND ETHEL GUILTY?
A: AFFIRMATIVE. GUILTY OF WANTING THE BETTER WORLD.
Q. DOES THAT MEAN THEY WERE TRAITORS?
A. NEGATIVE. NEGATIVE. NEGATIVE. NEGATIVE. NEGATIVE.... NEGA....

"How could the Rosenbergs be traitors? Traitors! To whom?" asks Hoberman. "The Rosenbergs never betrayed their beliefs, their friends. They kept the faith. They sacrificed everything, even their children. In a time when turning state's witness was touted as the greatest of civic virtues, the Rosenbergs went to their deaths without implicating a soul."

Here is the mentality that underlies the Kazan protest and the left's defense of itself. The argument proposed by Hoberman is absurd to anyone not so committed to the progressive faith. isn't it the case that even Nazis think of themselves as wanting a better world? Don't we all? Do good intentions exculpate all sins? If Hoberman's logic is accepted, doesn't wanting a better world become a license to tell any lie, perpetrate any crime, commit any betrayal? But how could he have overlooked the real-world betrayals that the Rosenbergs did actually commit? If they sacrificed their children, as they did, surely this was a betrayal. If they maintained their innocence to friends and comrades, as they did even though they were guilty, surely this was a betrayal. If they pledged their faith to Stalin's evil regime, was not this a betrayal of their own ideals of peace and justice? If they spied for the Soviet government, as Hoberman concedes they did, is there any question that they betrayed their country and their countrymen?

It is above all their country and its citizens who are the missing elements in the consciousness of progressives like Hoberman, Navasky and the anti-Kazan protesters. For them, collaborating with their own democratic government as it tried to defend itself against a mortal Communist threat is more culpable than serving a totalitarian state and aiding an enemy power. What is missing from these progressive hearts, after all is said and done, is a proper love of country, and therefore a sense of the friends, neighbors and countrymen they have betrayed. A proper love of country does not mean the abandonment of one's principles or the surrender of one's critical senses. It means valuing what you have been given, and sharing the responsibility for nurturing and defending those gifts, even when you dissent. The Old Left, the Stalinists, the people whom Kazan named, betrayed their country and the real people who live in it, their friends, their neighbors, and ultimately themselves. They may have betrayed them out of ignorance or misplaced idealism, or because they were blinded by faith. But they did it, and they need to acknowledge that by showing humility towards those, like Kazan, who did not.

7

Calibrating the Culture War

A critical attack on neo-conservative authors Norman Podhoretz and Hilton Kramer reveals how the culture war has become a dialogue of the deaf. Writing in the *Los Angeles Times Book Review*, the author of the attack, Russell Jacoby, identifies his problem with these neo-conservative writers, as "less their positions than their delusions about them; they seem to think they represent lonely and beleaguered outposts of anti-Communism." How could conservatives be beleaguered in an American culture that is itself conservative, Jacoby wants to know, inadvertently revealing how far to the left his own views are. Reviewing Kramer's *Twilight of the Intellectuals*, he comments: "Kramer refashions reality.... [He] writes as if he were a denizen of the former Soviet Union, where the party controls intellectual life and only a few brave souls like himself risk their lives and careers to tell the truth." Jacoby particularly rejects Kramer's lament that "it was not the Western defenders of Communist tyranny who suffered so conspicuously from censure and opprobrium in the Cold War period but those who took up the anti-Communist cause." Jacoby asks: "What could he mean?"

What he does mean is obvious to any attentive reader of Kramer's book not blinded by an ideological bias. He is writing about the emblematic figure of Whittaker Chambers, the subject

---

May 24, 1999, http://archive.frontpagemag.com/Printable.aspx?ArtId=24279; http://www.salon.com/1999/05/24/books/; *Hating Whitey and Other Progressive Causes*, Spence, 1999, pp. 184–198

of the first two essays in book. For Kramer, Chambers is the arche-typical ex-Communist whose treatment in "the court of liberal opinion" was a reflection of the attitude of the literate culture towards the anti-Communist cause. Chambers risked his life and career to expose one of the top Soviet spies in government, yet his status in the culture represented by influential media like the *Times* was not that of a hero but of a renegade and snitch. As a direct consequence of his patriotic deed, Chambers was fired from his position as a top editor at *Time* and brought to the brink of per-sonal ruin. Despised for the remaining years of his life, he has since become a forgotten man outside the circles of the right. Forty years after his death, I had the occasion to ask some senior honors students at the University of California whether they had ever heard of Whittaker Chambers. They said they had not, but they knew who his adversary, the Soviet agent Alger Hiss, was: he was a "victim of McCarthyism."

In contrast to Chambers's fate, the convicted perjurer Hiss emerged through his ordeal a political martyr to the liberal cul-ture, and a *cause célèbre* among *Nation* leftists who continued to champion his "innocence" long after his guilt had been estab-lished. The traitor Hiss even has an academic chair named in his honor at Bard College, a distinguished liberal arts school. At his death in 1996, Hiss was eulogized in progressive magazines and by liberal TV anchors as an "idealist" and a long-suffering victim of the anti-Communist "witch-hunt." As Kramer frames this parable of the Cold War in America, "Hiss—convicted of crimes that showed him to be a liar, a thief, and a traitor—was judged to be innocent even if guilty, while Chambers—the patriot who recanted his treachery—was judged to be guilty even if he was telling the truth. For what mattered to liberal opinion was that Hiss was seen to have remained true to his ideals—never mind what the content of these 'ideals' proved to be—whereas Cham-bers was seen to have betrayed them."

Here Kramer identifies a central paradox of the Cold War: the survival among Western intellectuals of the very ideals—socialist

and progressive—that led to the catastrophe of Soviet Communism. As Kramer puts it: "Liberalism, as it turned out, was not to
be so easily dislodged from the whole morass of illiberal doctrines
and beliefs in which, under the influence of Marxism, it had
become so deeply embedded, and every attempt to effect such a
separation raised the question of whether ... there was still something that could legitimately be called liberalism." Yet, Jacoby's
only response to these seminal chapters on Whittaker Chambers
and the questions they raise is that they make the book seem
"musty"—in other words, a relic. He concludes this even as
Chambers' final vindication is as recent as the release three years
ago of the Venona transcripts of Soviet intelligence communications, which definitively establish Hiss's guilt.

Whittaker Chambers is a hero of the anti-Communist cause.
But it took forty years for the publishing world to produce a biography of the man who defined an epoch.[1] Chambers, on the other
hand, stands virtually alone among anti-Communist heroes of the
Cold War in finally receiving his biographical due. Elizabeth Bentley, Louis Budenz, Bella Dodd, Frank Meyer, Walter Krivitsky, Victor Kravchenko, Jan Valtin—once large figures of the cause, along
with countless less well-known others— are more typical in having been virtually disappeared from cultural memory.[2]

By contrast, for example, Abbie Hoffman, a political clown of
the 60s, was already the subject of three biographies within a
decade of his death, not to mention a book-length exposition of his
political "philosophy." There can be no question that the nostalgic
glow around Hoffman's memory and the interest in his life are
integrally connected to the fact that he was a stalwart defender of

---

[1]Sam Tannenhaus, *Whitaker Chambers: A Biography,* Random House,
1997
[2]A biography of Elizabeth Bentley by Kathryn Olmsted finally appeared in
2002 under the title *Red Spy Queen,* along with Kevin J. Smant's *Principles and Heresies: Frank S. Meyer and the Shaping of the American Conservative Movement,* Intercollegiate Studies Institute, May 1, 2002.

Communist tyrannies in Cuba and Vietnam, and thus of the shared ideals of progressives like Jacoby who now dominate the literary culture and shape its historical judgments.

Russell Jacoby acquired his credentials by writing a book called *The Last Intellectuals*, which bemoaned the vanishing "public intellectual." This was a label he gave to intellectuals who worked outside the academy, wrote lucid (instead of post-modernist) prose, and influenced the public debate. The very title of Jacoby's book, however, is an expression of progressive arrogance and the unwillingness of leftists like Jacoby to acknowledge their cultural success. What Jacoby really mourned was the disappearance of the *left-wing* public intellectual, a direct result of the political conquest of the liberal arts faculties of American universities and their conversion into platforms for the left. Jacoby is well aware that an important consequence of this takeover is that almost all contemporary conservative intellectuals are (of necessity) *public* intellectuals and not academics. Indeed, this fact is regularly used by leftists in their *ad hominem* attacks on conservative intellectuals who, they claim, are "bought" by their institutional sponsors. Jacoby himself cannot even mention Kramer's magazine *The New Criterion* without adding that it is "funded by a conservative foundation." Of course *The Nation*, for which Jacoby himself writes regularly, is funded by rich leftists and leftist foundations. So what?

The reason conservative intellectuals gravitate to think tanks like Heritage, American Enterprise, and Hoover, and to magazines like *Commentary* and the *New Criterion*, is *because* of their *de facto* blacklisting by the leftist academy. Jacoby's real lament is over the public influence exerted by these conservative intellectuals. Academic intellectuals, he complains, write for a professional coterie instead of a broad public. Yet the pull of the institutional security academia affords is so great that Jacoby himself has since succumbed to its lure. Since writing his assault on the "obscurantist" university, Jacoby has given up his own independent existence, swallowed his critique, and accepted an appointment from his political comrades in the history department at UCLA. While lack of self-reflection and self-irony seem to be indispensable traits of progressives generally, Jacoby's *Los Angeles Times* attack is extraordinary in its abuse. Not only is his attack directed at two intellectuals who, for political reasons, were denied a platform in the *Los Angeles Times*, but were also denied the very academic patronage that Jacoby himself enjoys. *"What can he mean?"* indeed.

Jacoby's attack was actually one of four non-fiction reviews the *Los Angeles Times Book Review* chose to feature on its cover in this issue. Three were reviews of conservative books, all attacks from the left. The fourth was a review of two books on Clinton, both written by leftists, both praised by the reviewer whose sympathies were with the left. This issue of the *Times* happened to be May 9, 1999, but it could have been any date. In December 1997, the *Book Review* ran a year-end wrap-up of the *Times'* 100 Best Books compiled from previous *Times* reviews. Because some had written more than one notice, there were 87 reviewers in all. They were a familiar sampling of the literary left, and even of the true-believing left (Saul Landau, Martin Duberman, Robert Scheer and Ellen Willis, for example). Among all the names, however, the only reviewer I could detect with the slightest claim to a conservative profile was the academic Walter Laqueur.

I learned how the "100 Best Books" were picked shortly after the issue appeared, when I had lunch with Steve Wasserman, the newly appointed *Review* editor. I knew Wasserman as a former Berkeley radical and protégé of *Times'* contributing editor Bob Scheer, who was promoting the party line of Korean dictator Kim Il Sung at the end of the 60s and plotting to overthrow the American empire as a member of the Red Family commune. Scheer's current politics were still to the left of Senator Bulworth, in whose eponymous film he had made a cameo appearance courtesy of Scheer's friend Warren Beatty. After the Sixties, Scheer had ingratiated himself with Hollywood's Bolsheviks, married a top *Times* editor and become a figure of influence in the paper's hierarchy, which enabled him to secure Wasserman his job along with 11 Pulitzer nominations.[3]

As it happens, I had defended Wasserman's appointment at his own request, when journalist Catherine Seipp attacked him in the now defunct *Buzz* magazine. In my letter to *Buzz*, I praised what I thought were Wasserman's good intentions of fairness, despite our political differences. The lunch we had arranged was an attempt to rekindle the flame of a relationship; and the fact that he would agree to have a civil contact with me, a political renegade, seemed an auspicious sign. Such gestures of civility had been rare. His led me to assume (falsely, as it turned out) that he had some respect for my own odyssey. In fact, in our correspondence he had praised my autobiography *Radical Son* and even thought said the critical portrait I drew of Scheer in the book was "charming" and "accurate."

Within the stringent boundaries the left normally set for itself, Wasserman could even be an artful critic of his comrades. I have sometimes been accused of lumping leftists together and ignoring the spectrum of progressive opinions. The reverse would be more accurate. I have often given too much benefit of the doubt to people like Wasserman, in recognition of mild deviations they have been willing to risk, and have failed to see the hard line coming before it smacks me in the face. When I raised the issue of conservatives' exclusion from the pages of his magazine, Wasserman dismissed my concern out of hand as "bean-counting." He compared it to feminist complaints of under-representation, even though there were plenty of feminists and feminist sympathizers among the *Review*'s contributors. I found myself wondering whether a leftist writer with a reputation comparable to mine would have been invited to lunch by Wasserman and *not* asked to write a review for his magazine.

---

[3] See "Scheer Lunacy at the *Los Angeles Times*" in *Progressives*, Volume 2 of this series for an examination of Scheer's journalistic work.

I should have known at the time that this was not going to be a long-lived reunion. It came to an end almost a year later when Wasserman finally did ask me to write for the *Review*. As I have written elsewhere, he wanted me to join a "symposium" about the 150th anniversary of the publication of *The Communist Manifesto*. My contribution was to be 250 words (which he promptly cut to 125). I made the mistake of assuming others' would be equally brief. When the symposium appeared, it opened with a 3,000-word illustrated spread by unrepentant Communist Eric Hobsbawm, celebrating Marx's genius and contemporary relevance. In featuring this travesty, Wasserman had revealed the standard by which he lived (and his real opinion of me). Why not ask David Duke to write a paean to *Mein Kampf* on *its* anniversary, I asked, in an acid note I sent him.

But I could not let the matter rest there, and decided to take it up with the top editors at the *Times*. Both of them were men of the left, who listened politely and ignored my concern. I also wrote a letter to the *Times'* newly appointed publisher and CEO, Mark Willes, previously an executive at General Mills. I had met Willes at a *Times* Christmas Party which was held at the Hancock Park mansion of its editorial-page editor, Janet Clayton, an African-American woman whose living room was tellingly adorned with an iconic portrait of Jesse Jackson. Except for the passage of thirty years, the *Times* party could have been organized by *Ramparts*, the radical magazine I had once edited. Clayton's living room soon filled up with the intellectual and political leaders of the Los Angeles left. Scheer was there, gnashing his teeth at me because of what I had written about him in *Radical Son*, along with Tom Hayden, ACLU head Ramona Ripston, and black radical (and *Times* contributor) Earl Ofari Hutchinson. In fact, the only person not of the left I encountered that whole evening, in a room with over a hundred people, was Paula Jones's spokeswoman Susan Carpenter McMillan.

It occurred to me to make an appeal to Willes because he had already made a few gestures that seemed to indicate his intention to introduce some balance at the *Times*. He had even demoted several left-wing editors who had climbed the affirmative-action ladder to the top of the paper, among them Scheer's wife. In my letter, I challenged the rationale behind pitching the book section of a major metropolitan newspaper to what was essentially a *Nation* audience. I made it clear that I had no problem with the representation of left-wing authors in the paper. It was the exclusion of conservatives that concerned me. But I had misjudged Willes, whose reason for demoting the editors was related more to the *Times'* poor economic performance than its sometimes extreme political postures. Like many businessmen, Willes showed little political sense when it came to the issues of left and right. Shortly after this episode, Willes was publicly embarrassed by a leaked internal memo in which he demanded that *Times* reporters include ethnically diverse sources in all articles, regardless of subject matter or context. This was too much even for the quota-driven *Times* staff and its politically correct editors. Instead of answering my letter, Willes handed it over to its target, Wasserman, whose reply was understandably terse and revealed that our relationship was effectively over.

In my discussions with Wasserman and the *Times'* editors, I had raised another issue—the exclusion of conservative writers from the annual *Los Angeles Times* Festival of Books. This was an event normally attended by 100,000 readers and five hundred authors flown in from all over the country, eager to show up because of the opportunities for publicity and validation that an appearance for the *Times* entailed. At the previous festival, however, the only conservative authors I had been able to identify besides myself were Charlton Heston and Arianna Huffington. I was made aware of the festival as a result of my own exclusion when my autobiography *Radical Son* was published. Like any author of a new book, I had been looking for venues to promote it. Given the liberal bias in the general media, securing an audience was already problematic for me. Although I had co-authored bestsellers with Peter Collier, and in *Radical Son* had told a dramatic story of murder and intrigue, I found my book blacked out in the review sections of most of the major metropolitan papers. A chance to have "60 Minutes" do a segment on the book was blocked by its chief investigative producer, Lowell Bergman, a veteran Berkeley radical. I had enough experiences like this to welcome the possibility of an appearance at the book festival. As a somewhat well-known author based in Los Angeles, I found it odd that I should not be invited. When I brought this up to Wasserman at our lunch, he had just brushed me off. "There are lots of authors," he said. To his credit he didn't believe his own brush-off and did try to get me invited, unsuccessfully, because my request for inclusion had come too late.

That was last year, before the Marx fracas. This spring I answered my phone and to my surprise Wasserman was on the other end, inviting me to the Festival. We had not spoken for nearly a year and his voice sounded strained and not particularly friendly as he made the offer. "I want to thank you, Steve," I said, accepting. "I know how hard this must be for you." The conversation was so short I never found out exactly how I had earned the invitation, or exactly who had decided I should get it—certainly not Wasserman. The Festival was held on the UCLA campus and was a capsule demonstration with a cast of thousands as to why conservatives like Hilton Kramer and Norman Podhoretz could harbor the "delusion" that the culture was controlled by the party of the left, and that they were marginalized, beleaguered, censured outsiders.

As in previous years, the Festival headliners were leftists like Alice Walker and Betty Friedan, and even Sister Souljah, who had drawn thousands of their dedicated fans to the event. There was no Tom Clancy, no Tom Wolfe, no Thomas Sowell, and no Robert Bork to draw a parallel conservative crowd. Among the hundreds of authors, in fact, I counted only a handful (actually five) who were conservative, all locals. None had been flown in like Walker, Friedan, and Sister Souljah as marquee attractions. As a tribute to his own lack of self-irony, Wasserman had appointed himself chair of a panel on "The Ethics of Book Reviewing."

I amused myself by walking around and bumping into former comrades, who seemed omnipresent. Among them were *Nation* editor Victor Navasky and *Nation* writers Todd Gitlin and Bob Scheer. I especially enjoyed the encounter with Scheer, who made an end run around the other two in order to avoid having to shake my hand. Later I came on Christopher Hitchens showing his in-laws the event. Christopher greeted me cordially and thanked me for defending him in *Salon* when he had come under attack from the left.[4] When I told him how Scheer had run away, he smiled and said. "Yeah, he's not speaking to me either."

I had been scheduled for the second of three serial panels on the 60s, called "Second Thoughts," although in fact I was the only panelist who had had any. The panels were recorded for later showing on C-SPAN and were held in Korn Auditorium on the UCLA campus. When I arrived, the room was packed with 500 graying and scraggly-faced leftists, many in message T-shirts and *Nation* baseball caps. I counted thirteen panelists in all for the three 60s discussions, every last one but myself a loyalist to the discredited radical creed. Tom Hayden and Scheer were on a panel together. Russell Jacoby was there too.

The other panelists at my event were Maurice Zeitlin and Sara Davidson. A third leftist had failed to show. Davidson was the author of a 60s memoir of sexual liaisons called *Loose Change* and the chief writer for the PC television series "Dr. Quinn, Medicine Woman." Her 60s roots were on display in her latest book, *Cowboy,* about her affair with a man whom she described as intellectually her inferior, and whom she had to support with her ample television earnings, but who gave great sex. She celebrated the affair as a triumph of feminism. The panel moderator, Maurice Zeitlin, was a sociologist at UCLA and had written books with titles like *America Incorporated* and *Talking Union.* Maurice and I had been friends in Berkeley at the beginning of the 60s, when

---

[4] See "The Secret Power of the Leftist Faith," in *Progressives,* Volume 2 of this series.

the two of us, along with Scheer, were part of a radical circle that produced one of the first magazines of the New Left called *Root and Branch*. Maurice and Scheer had co-authored one of the first favorable books on Fidel Castro's Communist revolution, which I had edited. Although we lived in the same city, I had seen Maurice only once, by accident, in the last thirty-five years.

While waiting for the panel to begin, I thought about the dilemma the whole scenario presented to me. I owed Wasserman a thank-you for being there at all, but at the same time I could not ignore what was happening in front of my nose. A leftist political convention was being held under the auspices of one of the most important press institutions in America, and was being promoted to a national TV audience under the pretense that such select and resentful voices somehow represented American culture. I resolved the dilemma by thanking Steve and the *Times* editors "for allowing me to crash this party," and then said that it was a "national disgrace" that a major press institution would stage a symposium on the 60s stacked 13-1 in favor of unrepentant radicals. Later in the discussion, I pointed out that the UCLA faculty reflected exactly the same bias. A politically controlled hiring process had resulted over time in the systematic exclusion of conservatives from the liberal arts programs at UCLA and most other schools. In contrast, even non-academic leftists like Russell Jacoby were regularly appointed to university faculties by their political cronies. Another was Scheer, who had been made a professor of journalism at USC's Annenberg School by its dean, Jeff Cowan, a former Clinton administration official.

In my remarks, I focused on the way 60s leftists had betrayed their own ideals by doing an about-face on civil rights and supporting race preferences; by abandoning the Vietnamese when they were being murdered and oppressed by Communists; and by helping to crush the island of Cuba under the heel of the Castroist dictatorship. I also described my experiences with the Black Panther Party, a gang led by murderers and rapists whom the left had anointed as its political vanguard and whose crimes leftists continued to ignore. I thought it interesting that a left that had supported international criminals during the Cold War was now supporting criminals like Mumia Abu-Jamal and the inhabitants of what one of their leaders, Angela Davis (a "distinguished professor" at UC Santa Cruz), called the "prison-industrial complex" at home. These crusades against law enforcement, so characteristic of the left, hurt the poorest and most vulnerable citizens of our cities, particularly blacks, who were the chief victims of the predators the left defended. While the ideas and programs of leftists were seductive, their implementation had been an unmitigated human disaster—which is why I had become a conservative. There was not much enthusiasm from the leftist audience for my comments.

As was common in my experience on similar platforms, the debate turned out to be a non-event. Adopting a standard tactic of the left I had encountered in the past, Sara Davidson simply ignored the challenge implicit in my remarks and opened hers by saying that she saw the 60s "in a wider, bigger context than just the Black Panthers." Then she commented: "My challenge is not to revise the 60s, to re-analyze and reinterpret it, but to get back in touch with the essence and the spirit of that time." This was the kind of thoughtless arrogance one could expect from people inhabiting a cultural universe that they effectively controlled, in which no challenge could threaten their perch or require a serious reply.

Zeitlin then gave a speech that could easily have been made in 1964 about the "silent generation" and American imperialism in Vietnam. He concluded with a flourish about the Movement and how it was inspired by the idea of social justice. Maurice's eloquence about this commitment and about Vietnam was not tempered by a single fact that the post-war Communist occupation had revealed—neither the two-and-a-half million Indo-Chinese slaughtered by the Communists after America's forced withdrawal, nor the interviews with North Vietnamese leaders that showed how the support of American radicals for the Communist cause had helped to prolong the war and make the bloodbath possible. Nor did he bother to explain the silence of the crusaders for social justice during the long night of Vietnam's oppression by its leftist liberators.

During the rejoinder period that followed, the audience got into the act and the discussion heated up. There was lots of heckling, making it difficult for me to complete a sentence. Shouts of "racist" were audible. A member of the audience rubbed his fingers in the air as though holding a wad of bills, while he and several others accused me of selling out for money. It was a moment familiar to me from almost all my university appearances, when the risks of being a "public intellectual" and conservative were made eminently clear. If I had been an employee of an academic institution and dependent on it for my livelihood, my career would certainly have been destroyed if I had expressed the views I had.

Name-calling and *ad hominem* assaults were indispensable weapons in the arsenal of the left, and really their only weapons. Fear was what kept everyone in line. "Over the whole of this worthy enterprise," Hilton Kramer wrote sarcastically of modern liberalism, "there hovered a great fear—the fear of being thought 'reactionary,' the fear of being relegated to the right.... The very thought of being accused of collaborating with 'reaction,' as it was still called, was a liberal nightmare, and there was no shortage of Stalinist liberals (as I believe they must be called) to bring the charge of 'reaction' ... at every infraction, or suspected infraction, of 'progressive' doctrine." That was why at universities like UCLA, while private professional polls showed faculties to be evenly divided over race preferences, only a handful of professors on either campus had dared to publicly voice their opposition.

Zeitlin was embarrassed by the heckling and to his credit spoke up in my defense. He recalled how, as a young teaching assistant at Princeton at the end of the Fifties, his own students had signed a petition to get him fired because of his views on the Vietnam War. He told the UCLA audience that they were engaged in the same type of behavior. Referring to me as "one of the most trenchant critics of the left," he advised them that when they were groaning at my remarks they couldn't hear what I had to say (as though that would bother them). "It is precisely this," he added, "that David turns into a characterization of The Left, as though there really is such a monolith." Here Maurice had exposed the blind spot (in this case also his own) that kept the left innocent of its effects. If there was no left, then how could it do any of the things conservatives accused it of doing? How could it dominate the culture or exclude conservatives even more effectively than McCarthyism had excluded leftists in the past? Obviously it could not. This assumption (that there really was no left) was why Jacoby and so many others could think such an idea incomprehensible.

Of course the left is not a monolith. But then it never has been—not even in the days of Lenin and Stalin. Today, the left includes civilized exponents like Zeitlin, but also ideological fascists who will shout down a conservative speaker and threaten opponents with verbal terrorism, and even physical violence. Ward Connerly, a trustee of the University of California who has led the fight against racial preferences, has been prevented from speaking at several major universities by leftist gangs. These acts of incivility have been abetted by cowardly administrators who do not share the witch-hunting mentality of the demonstrators but are unwilling to stand up to them. There is not a conservative faculty member lacking tenure at an American university who does not live in fear of possible professional ruin for holding politically incorrect views. While Zeitlin can admirably chastise uncivil passions at a public forum, he nonetheless acquiesces in a political hiring process at his own university that ensures that conservatives will be virtually non-existent. Steve Wasserman may be a nuanced radical whose socializing sometimes includes political pariahs like myself, but he will still enforce their marginality in the pages of his own magazine, or at festivals he organizes. And Russell Jacoby may be capable of composing book-length critiques of his fellow leftists but, writing in the pages of the *Los Angeles Times*, he will casually dismiss as a paranoid delusion the testimony of one of America's leading conservative thinkers that he inhabits a culture controlled by hostile forces.

8

The Army of the Saints

The other day I picked up a phone message on my answering machine that concerned a charity event for homeless youngsters I was organizing with some relatively un-political Hollywood liberals. The voice was female and said she had found a friend who was willing to volunteer her home for a fundraiser we had planned for the children, then paused—"but not if Charlton Heston comes." Then she paused again. "In fact," she said, "none of my friends' homes will be available if Charlton Heston comes." It was unnecessary for her to tell me, as she did under her breath, that "they murdered those kids," to alert me to the fact that this was about the Columbine tragedy in Colorado, where two sociopathic teenagers had barged into a high school and ambushed their classmates, killing thirteen before turning their weapons on themselves. Nor did she have to connect the dots and say that the passions Heston provoked as head of the National Rifle Association, which had thwarted the passage of gun-control legislation in the aftermath of these events, was the cause of her friends' determination to shun him and make him a social pariah.

Accustomed as I am to such intolerant reflexes in people who think of themselves as "liberal," this one drew me up short. Consider, reader, the people you know and call your friends. How many individuals could you name, whom these friends would want to bar from a social gathering whose sole purpose was to

July 6, 1999, http://archive.frontpagemag.com/Printable.aspx?ArtId=24286; http://www.salon.com/1999/07/06/guns_4/

raise money for homeless children? David Duke? O. J. Simpson? Slobodan Milosevic? For myself, I don't have a single conservative friend or acquaintance who would say: "If Barbra Streisand wants to help us raise money for poor kids, I don't want her in my house." Charlton Heston is no conservative troglodyte. He is a New Deal Democrat, the former chair of the Hollywood committee for Martin Luther King's march on Washington, a lifelong champion of civil rights and artists' rights (he was a staunch defender of the National Endowment for the Arts) and generally a decent, humane, and ecumenical soul. Of course, such facts are irrelevant in this matter because the hatred liberals obviously bear towards Heston has no real-world referent in terms of who he actually is. Even Heston's role as spokesman for the NRA doesn't make their passion any more intelligible to someone outside their ideological bubble. Do the three million, mainly lower-middle-class and working-class, members of the NRA want to see children die? Would the legislation they defeated have indisputably saved those children, or others to come?

The fact is that there are 20,000 gun laws already on the books, seventeen of which were violated by the Columbine killers. What would one more law accomplish that the other 20,000 could not—especially one that would merely mandate background checks on buyers at gun shows? Is there any evidence that these shows are the sites of a significant number of criminal purchases, or that such legislation would have any effect on armed crimes? The Brady Bill has been violated on 250,000 occasions, according to police records, but not a single violator has been punished. Is there any correlation at all between stringent registration laws and a low number of gun deaths? Social scientist John Lott has just published a study showing that communities in which citizens are armed have lower incidences of gun violence than communities where guns are relatively absent. In places where gun violence has actually been reduced, like New York, where the murder rate has been cut by a phenomenal 60 percent, the reason appears to be aggressive police methods, which have come under fire from many of these same liberals who think gun control is the answer. Do the people who hate Chuck Heston adore Mayor Rudy Giuliani? Hardly.

I do not intend this as an argument for or against the gun legislation that was proposed and failed in the wake of Columbine. It is merely a case for sobriety in assessing the issues that make up the dispute. The gun legislation in question may have been worthy or not. The point is that any difference it might make is so insignificant that it could not justify the foam-at-the-mouth response of its proponents or the stigma they have attached to people, like Charlton Heston, who disagree with them about it.

Why are liberals so compulsively bigoted? It is not a question that can be casually dismissed. After all, those conservatives who might shun a Barbra Streisand make no fetish out of diversity the way liberals do, nor do they wave the bloody shirt of past witchhunts whenever they come under attack, as liberals do as well. Moreover, the little *auto da fé* over the possibility that Chuck Heston would materialize at a charity event is no aberrant case. George Stephanopoulos's recent memoir captures a parallel moment at the very center of the political process. Before impeachment irretrievably embittered the atmosphere of the Clinton White House, Stephanopoulos and the president were discussing an open congressional seat and the prospect of an upcoming special election. "It's Nazi time," Clinton remarked to Stephanopoulos, meaning time to get back to campaigning against Republicans. Two years later, at the outset of another campaign, Clinton told Dick Morris: "You have to understand, Bob Dole is evil, what he wants is evil"—this of a war hero who had played the role of consensus-builder in his years as Senate majority leader. Nor is Clinton alone in expressing a rabid hatred of the Republican opposition. Congressman John Lewis, the Democrat from Georgia, publicly referred to House Republicans as "Nazis" merely for proposing to keep the expansion of Medicare within the rate of inflation, lest the whole system go bankrupt as a presidential commission indicated it would. Other Democrats, like Charles

Rangel, referred to Republicans as racist for similar disagreements on budgetary allocations. As in the case of gun-control legislation, there is no perceivable connection between these offenses and the demonization of the offenders by liberals.

And this not a trope deployed only by politicians of the left. In his last book, the academic philosopher Richard Rorty lavished extravagant praise on left-wing academics and political correctness for ending what in his view was "sadism" in the verbal treatment of minorities in universities. Yet, in the spring issue of *Dissent*, Rorty describes the Republican House members who thought the president had committed perjury and obstruction of justice "greedheads" and "hypocrites of the Christian Right (sometimes known as cultural conservatives)" which is only somewhat more tolerant than Paul Berman's description of the same group as "crazed reactionaries." Outside the KKK-Farrakhan hate fringe (which embraces bigots on the left and right), there is no conservative analog to this liberal paranoia. Conservatives with intellectual credentials comparable to Rorty's—Irving Kristol, Norman Podhoretz, William F. Buckley, Jr. and James Q. Wilson come to mind—do not normally (or even rarely) indulge in the kind of *ad hominem* name-calling that seems second nature to Rorty when he is writing about his political opponents. As for politicians, perhaps there is a Republican office-holder who every now and then does enter the electoral cycle with the war cry, "It's commie time!" But I certainly haven't met him. The current Clinton security leaks are grave enough to have generated a hundred Joe McCarthys, but not one has yet appeared. There is just no analog to the liberal passion for conservative-bashing, which has unfairly stained the reputations of figures as disparate as Bork, Thomas, Gingrich, Barr, Connerly, and now DeLay. Conservatives who have not even laid a glove on such obvious targets (and rhetorical terrorists in their own right such as Barney Frank and Maxine Waters) tend to think of their opponents as benighted, or irresponsible, or simply misguided. But they do not treat them as agents of the devil, as liberals often do.

But then Republicans are political amateurs. They leave a business in the private sector to fight city hall over practical matters. They want to restrain the government leviathan that is suffocating enterprise. Or, less nobly, they want to harness it to some self-interested goal. Liberals have a grander design. Their interest in politics is missionary. They see government as a means of social redemption, to change the world. They're not there to tinker with gun-control laws. They're there, as Hillary Clinton put it, "to define what it means to be human in the Twenty-first century."[1] In the nightmares of NRA opponents, this means to do whatever it takes to reform the people, and probably to trample over any rights necessary to remove all 240 million guns from public possession, in quest of a utopia where violence no longer exists.

The reason liberals are so bigoted lies in a vision that has ancestral roots in the Puritan origins of the American new world. They see themselves as soldiers in the army of the Saints—a vision incomplete without the opposing army of Satan, the dark adversary corrupting the innocent and blocking their path to progress. People like Charlton Heston stand in the way of their impossible dream. In the fantasies of these liberal Lenins, all the little dead children killed in drive-bys across America could be walking the safe streets of the 'hood if only the Chuck Hestons of this world would disappear.

---

[1]Michael Kelly, "Saint Hillary," *The New York Times,* May 23, 1993; http://www.nytimes.com/1993/05/23/magazine/saint-hillary.html?pagewanted=all&src=pm

9

Wasserman's Revenge

The September 27, 1999 issue of *The New Yorker* features a politically motivated caricature of myself ("The Cold War Thrives in Sunny California") by Jane Mayer, co-author of the diatribe against Clarence Thomas (*Strange Justice*) that was recently made into a film for TV.[1] When Mayer called to interview me for *The New Yorker*, I told her my low opinion of her journalism and suggested that, in light of the Clinton-Lewinsky follies, an apology by her to Clarence Thomas was in order. She pretended not to understand what I had said. I cooperated with her anyway, not because I had expectations that she would report fairly but because I didn't want to give her the opportunity to print a caricature of myself and punctuate it with the statement, "Horowitz would not answer my calls." Since I knew that Mayer was incapable of reporting a story accurately, and that she was only going to use the occasion to write a political smear, I was hardly surprised by the result when it appeared. There is thus no reason to write this response at all, except that it affords me the opportunity to throw light on the techniques by which a great American jurist was tarred and feathered by a dishonest and mean-spirited political hack posing as a journalist.

Mayer's column purports to inform *New Yorker* readers of a vendetta I am alleged to have carried out against Steve Wasserman,

---

September 24, 1999, http://archive.frontpagemag.com/Printable.aspx?Artld=24312
[1] http://archive.frontpagemag.com/readArticle.aspx?ARTID=22600

the book review editor of the *Los Angeles Times*, and against the *Los Angeles Times* itself. The impression it leaves is pretty much summed up in the snide comment from Wasserman she reports: "It's very tedious to deal with what should rightfully called by its proper name: Red-baiting." While Wasserman's words and opinions inform 90 percent of the *New Yorker* article's perspective on me, not a single statement of mine made during a long interview with the author is quoted in the published piece or informs its contents. Mayer should have saved the *New Yorker's* dime and my time, and just taken down Wasserman's whine and left it at that.

The story Mayer tells is uncomplicated by the facts, as she intended it to be. Steve Wasserman came to Los Angeles to edit the *Los Angeles Times Book Review*. An ex-radical named David Horowitz, who (unlike the rest of us) has not yet gotten over the Cold War, was lying in wait for Wasserman when he arrived. The minute the unsuspecting fellow settled into his editor's chair, Horowitz pounced on him, accusing him of making bombs, attacking him for publishing a review of *The Communist Manifesto* by a "Marxist historian" and then writing "vitriolic columns in *Salon* accusing the *LA Times* of harboring leftists ..." Not only is the reality pretty much the opposite of the picture Mayer presents, but the facts are all in print, so that even if Mayer didn't believe a word I said in my lengthy interview with her, she could have referred to the documentary record to check her opinions with the evidence if she had cared to.[2] Obviously this was not on the list of things that interested her.

If she had actually looked at the files of the *Los Angeles Times*, she would have noticed a lengthy, nasty, politically motivated profile of David Horowitz that shortly preceded the arrival of Steve Wasserman and any vitriolic columns David Horowitz might have written about Wasserman in the *LA Times*.[3] The section of the

---

[2]See the articles, "Karl Marx and the *Los Angeles Times*," above.
[3]Michael Y. Ybarra, "Radical Reborn," *Los Angeles Times*, February 28, 1997

paper where the hit-piece appeared was edited by Narda Zacchino, Robert Scheer's wife. Would this attack from the left in the pages of a major metropolitan newspaper qualify as carrying on the Cold War? Or is it only conservatives who can be guilty of this offense? Other salient facts are these: When Steve Wasserman arrived at the *LA Times*, Catherine Seipp, a reporter for *Buzz* magazine, called me for my opinion on his appointment and for any Wasserman anecdotes I might share with her. In the 60s, Wasserman and I were members of the New Left. When I first met him he was a youthful follower of the Red Family, a group of Berkeley urban guerrillas that included Bob Scheer and Tom Hayden. They even had an official "Minister of Defense," named Andy Truskier, who trained them in weapons as they plotted to initiate "wars of liberation" in American cities. Hayden wrote about their plans in a book called *Trial*, which he went about removing from libraries when he ran for public office as a Democrat later on. Scheer was Wasserman's mentor and Wasserman even ghosted one of his books. Scheer, whose views have only marginally adjusted to the changing times, is now a "national correspondent" for the *Los Angeles Times* and was responsible for the recruitment of Wasserman.

I told Seipp that I thought it was both culturally indicative and somewhat comical that a major newspaper like the *Los Angeles Times* was beginning to look editorially like *Ramparts*, the radical magazine Scheer and I had edited in the 60s. I told Seipp what I knew about Wasserman, both the good and the not so good. I noted that Wasserman was a protégé of Scheer's. I recalled someone telling me in the 60s that Hayden had taught Wasserman, who was then a high-school student, how to make explosives. I thought it was an interesting oddity (and a colorful anecdote) that a would-be bomber was now a literary editor. I then spent a considerable amount of time describing my impressions of Wasserman since the 60s and why I thought he had shown himself to be fair-minded for a leftist, and might do a creditable job. I have not called Catherine Seipp to see if she has a tape of our interview or has retained the notes she may have taken at the time, which would confirm this memory. But that is not necessary in order to know how I actually responded to the editorial appointment of Steve Wasserman. When the *Buzz* article appeared, it was quite negative and Wasserman called me in extreme pain to beg for my help in protecting him from any damage the story might do to him. He asked me to write a letter to the editor of *Buzz*. Since I had no ill-feelings towards Wasserman or his appointment—quite the contrary—I gladly agreed to do so.

Mayer was not unaware of these facts since I brought them up in our interview. I described the contents of the letter in detail and offered to provide her with a copy. In the September 27 *New Yorker*, Mayer writes of me: "Horowitz's attacks began almost as soon as Wasserman took over the book-review section." In fact, as my letter to the editor shows, my *defense* of Wasserman began almost as soon as he took over:

April 18, 1997

Editor
Buzz Magazine
Los Angeles, California

Dear Editor,
I want to thank Catherine Seipp and *Buzz* ("Media Circus," May 1997) for noticing the malicious personal attack on me posing as a profile in Narda Zacchino's Style section of the *L.A. Times* and for recognizing my unflattering portrait of Zacchino's husband Bob Scheer in *Radical Son* as a probable inspiration for the hit. However, as the source of the anecdote about Steve Wasserman being taught how to make bombs by Tom Hayden, I have a correction to make. I told the *Buzz* fact checker at least three times to check the story with Steve because I had heard it second-hand at least twenty years ago. Steve now informs me that the story is untrue and I have no reason to disbelieve him. Moreover, although Steve is indeed an old friend of Scheer's, it is wrong to suggest that Scheer's partisan malice has rubbed off on

him. I have kept in contact with Steve over the years and have found him to be gracious and fair-minded in my dealings with him. As editor of *Times* Books, Wasserman was the publisher of Newt Gingrich's *Contract with America* and bought an important project on the Black Panthers (as yet unpublished), which will confirm the allegations made in *Radical Son* about their criminal activities.[4] Under Wasserman's direction, the *Times' Book Review* is already an improved section of the paper, and this conservative wishes him well.

Sincerely,
David Horowitz

Obviously I had given Wasserman too much benefit of the doubt on too little evidence. An honest reporter might have concluded that it was these high expectations I had of him, and the fact that he soon disappointed them, that led to the tensions between us. The mere fact that Steve was a leftist didn't bother me any more than the fact that my *Salon* editors were. I welcome dialogue on political issues. Indeed, it would be odd for a "red-baiter" to be a regular columnist for a leftist magazine like *Salon*. But acknowledging this would also be inconvenient for Mayer's purposes and Steve's.

My defense of Wasserman led to an invitation to lunch and even greater expectations that he might end my literary isolation, along with that of other conservatives who were excluded from powerful literary institutions like the *Los Angeles Times Book Review*. I imagined Wasserman would invite me and other conservatives to write in his pages and to engage in a robust political dialogue with his friends. Alas, it was not to be. When it became clear to me that Wasserman had no interest in developing such a dialogue, and had contempt for me and for my work, I gave up my expectations and began a public criticism of his performance. I

---

[4]*Long Time Gone: A Black Panther's True-Life Story of His Hijacking and Twenty-Five Years in Cuba*, Steve Wasserman editor, Crown, 1996

wrote two articles in *Salon* describing the progressive stages of my disillusionment—the so-called "vitriolic columns" that Mayer refers to, one of which ("Karl Marx and the *Los Angeles Times*") summarizes what happened.[5]

My real battle with the *Times*, as anyone reading my columns could see, was not an effort to purge the Reds but to get Wasserman to live up to the standard of fair-mindedness I had mistakenly ascribed to him in my letter defending him. In particular, I wanted him to open the *Times Book Review* section to conservative viewpoints, which had been virtually excluded, and not only by Wasserman. There is one redeeming aspect of Mayer's cynical fiction, which is contained in its conclusion. Here she refers to a study that Carlin Romano, a literary critic for *The Philadelphia Inquirer* and a *Nation* contributor, made of my charges. Romano examined 194 issues of Wasserman's *Book Review* and came to the conclusion that Wasserman's regular reviewers "are almost uniformly writers identified with the left." But, Romano added, this bias only balances that of *The New York Times*, which "favors neo-conservatives." Now if a man who writes for *The Nation*—as Carlin Romano does—and who is under the misapprehension that *The New York Times* has a neo-conservative bias, comes to the conclusion that Wasserman's reviewers are almost uniformly to the left, you know who's keeping the Cold War going.

---

[5] See chapter 3, above.

10

Intellectual Class War

Afew years after the fall of the Marxist utopias, I found
myself on a sofa in Beverly Hills, sitting next to a man
who was worth half a billion dollars. His name was Stanley Gold and he was chairman of Diamond Shamrock, a holding
company that was the largest shareholder in the then-largest
media corporation in the world, Disney. Since I was working on a
conservative project in the entertainment community and the
occasion was a cocktail reception for Senator Arlen Specter, a
Republican, I quickly moved the conversation into a pitch for support. But I was only able to run through a few bars of my routine
before Gold put a fatherly hand on my arm and said, "Save your
breath, David. I'm a socialist."

I recall this story every time a leftist critic assaults me with the
charge that I have "sold out" my ideals to corporate America, or
suggests that an opinion I have expressed can be explained by the
"fact" that somewhere a wealthy puppet-master is pulling my
strings. I am not alone, of course, in being the target of such
attacks that are familiar to every conservative who has ever
engaged in a political debate. Of course, those who traffic in
socially conscious abuse have a ready answer for anecdotes like
mine, namely that it is an isolated and aberrant case. Even if it's
true, in other words, it's false. That is because there is a larger

January 24, 2000, http://archive.frontpagemag.com/Printable.aspx?ArtId=
24358; http://www.salon.com/2000/01/24/gold/; *The Art of Political War
and Other Radical Pursuits*, David Horowitz, Spence, 2000, pp. 115–122

Marxist "truth" that trumps little truths like this. This larger truth is that conservative views express the views of corporate America, serve the status quo, defend the rich and powerful, and legitimize the oppression of the poor. Whereas leftist views, however well paid for, are inherently noble because they oppose all the injustice that corporate America, the status quo, and the rich represent. The "truth" is that conservative views *must* be paid for one way or another because they could not possibly be the genuine views of any decent human being with a grain of integrity, an ounce of compassion, or even half a human heart.

In the fantasy world of the left, the figure of Stanley Gold can only be understood as an oxymoron: a uniquely good-hearted capitalist who is a friend to humanity and a traitor to his class. But, then, so are such famous left-wing billionaire and centi-millionaire moguls as Ted Turner, David Geffen, Oprah Winfrey, Steven Spielberg, Michael Eisner, and a hundred others less famous but equally well-heeled. In fact, the only exceptional thing about Stanley Gold's politics is that he is also a witty and candid fellow. For, unlike the publicly self-identified progressives named above, the CEOs of most major corporations studiously avoid ideological politics whether left or right because such politics are not in the corporate interest. To become identified with a hard political position is to become a sitting target for opponents who may control the machinery of regulation and taxation and exert life-and-death power over their enterprises. Not to mention the potential for alienating customers.

From a business point of view, politicians are fungible. For the kinds of favors businesses require, one can be had as easily as another. It is safer to stay above the fray and buy influence with Republicans or Democrats as necessary. Money, not ideological passion, is the currency of corporate interest; power rather than ideas its agenda. Therefore, politicians rather than intellectuals are the usual objects of its attention. There is an exception to money's rule of political neutrality, as when a political administration for whatever reason chooses to declare war on a wealthy individual or a corporate entity, or even an entire industry. An attack will simplify political choices and make embracing the political opposition seem the best available option in an already bad situation. Big Tobacco, Microsoft and Michael Milken were all assaulted by government and adopted a defensive strategy by embracing the political opposition (Tobacco and Microsoft went strongly Republican, Milken became a Democrat).

Another exception can result from the shakedown of large corporations by political activists, an opportunity that is almost exclusively a province of the left. Under attack from radical environmentalists, for example, major companies like ARCO have become large subsidizers of the environmental movement. Through similar extortion efforts, Jesse Jackson's Rainbow/Push coalition has received more corporate underwriting than any dozen conservative groups put together. But the norm for corporate interests remains the removal of themselves and their assets from any ideological politics, which can only damage them in the long run.

Foundations are more insulated from the vicissitudes of public passions, and conservatives have a base of support in a core group of like-minded philanthropies. But in this area, too, the fevered imaginations of the left have created a wildly distorted picture of well-funded Goliaths on the right overwhelming the penurious Davids of the left. The Arab-American leftist Edward Said, for example, used the platform of the once-distinguished Reith lectures to attack Peter Collier and me over the "Second Thoughts" movement we had launched as a critique of the left: "In a matter of months during the late 1980s, Second Thoughts aspired to become a movement, alarmingly well funded by right-wing Maecenases like the Bradley and Olin Foundations." Some years later, a liberal group published a report appeared on "The Strategic Philanthropy of Conservative Foundations," which surveyed the annual disbursements of what it described as the key conservative grant-giving institutions. It calculated the annual sum of the subsidies to conservative groups from twelve foundations as $70 million. This may seem a large sum until one looks at the Ford Foundation, which dispenses funds to left and liberal groups from a disbursement of more than $900 million per year, or more than ten times as much. Ford is the principal funder of the hard-left Mexican American Legal Defense Fund (MALDEF), for example, which lacks any visible root in the Mexican-American community but has been the principal promoter of illegal immigration and the driving force behind the failed multibillion-dollar bilingual education programs. Ford created MALDEF and has provided it with more than $25 million. Ford has also been the leading funder of left-wing feminism and black separatism on American campuses, and of the radical effort to balkanize the national identity through multicultural curricula throughout the university system.[1]

In these agendas, Ford is typical of the large foundations. In fact, the biggest and most prestigious foundations, bearing among the most venerable names of American capitalism—Ford, Rockefeller, Mellon, Carnegie, and Pew—all skew left, as do many of the newer but also well-endowed institutions like the MacArthur, Markle and Schumann. MacArthur alone is three times the size of all "big three" conservative foundations, Olin, Bradley and Scaife, combined. Moreover, these foundations do not even represent the most important support the "corporate ruling class" and its social elites provide to the left. That laurel goes to the universities which were traditionally the preserve of the American monied aristocracy and now—as Richard Rorty has happily pointed out—are the "political base of the left."[2] With its multibillion-dollar endowment and unmatched intellectual prestige, Harvard provides an exemplary case, its relevant faculties and curricula reflecting the hegemony of left-wing ideas. The Kennedy School of Government at Harvard is arguably the most prestigious and important reservoir

---

[1]Cf. Horowitz and Laksin, *The New Leviathan*, Crown, 2012
[2]Richard Rorty, *Achieving Our Country*, Harvard University Press, April 15, 1998, p. 128

of intellectual talent and policy advice available to the political establishment. Cabinet officials are regularly drawn from its ranks. Yet of its 150-plus faculty members only 5 are identifiable Republicans, a ratio that is extraordinary, given the spectrum of political opinion in the nation at large, though it is typical of the university system. The institutional and financial support for the left, through its dominance in the universities, the book publishing industry, the press, television news and the arts, is so overwhelming it is hardly contested. There are no prestigious universities where the faculty ratio in the liberal arts and social sciences is 150 Republicans to 5 Democrats or even close to parity. There is not a single major American newspaper whose features and news sections are edited and written by conservatives rather than liberals, and this includes such conservative-owned institutions as *The Wall Street Journal*, the *Los Angeles Times*, the *Orange County Register* and the *San Diego Union*.

Some may object that the definition of "left" is overly broad in this analysis. They will argue that, because Noam Chomsky is regarded as a fringe intellectual by segments of the media, the media cannot be dominated by the ideas of the left. But this supposes that Chomsky's exclusion is ideological rather than idiosyncratic—because he is an insufferably arrogant and difficult individual. After all, Peter Jennings is a fan of Cornel West, who is a fan of Chomsky. Christopher Hitchens is a fan of Chomsky and a ubiquitous presence on the tube and in print. But assume that it is true anyway. The fact remains that an America-loathing crank like Chomsky is an incomparably more influential intellectual figure in the left-wing culture of American universities than any conservative one could name.

The left, it can hardly be disputed, is funded and supported by the very ruling class it whines is the sponsor of the right and the oppressor of minorities, the working class and the poor. Moreover, institutional support and funds provided to the intellectual left by the greedy and powerful rulers of society far exceed any sums they provide to the intellectual right, as anyone with a pocket calculator can compute. How is this possible? Could it be that the Marxist model is a myth? Marxists claim that the interest of the corporate rich lies in preserving the *status quo*. But if the Clinton years did nothing else, they should certainly have served to put this canard to rest. The Clinton administration's most important left-wing projects were the comprehensive government-controlled health care plan that failed and the effort to preserve racial preferences that succeeded. Both agendas received the enthusiastic support of corporate America—the health care plan by the nation's largest health-insurance companies, and racial preferences by Fortune 500 corporations across the board.

Or take another measure: In this year's presidential primary campaign, Bill Bradley is the Democratic candidate running from the left. The chief points of Bradley's platform are plans to revive the comprehensive Clinton health-care scheme that was rejected, and to press left-wing racial grievances. Bradley's most recently acquired African-American adviser is the anti-Semitic racist Al Sharpton, who has become a black leader of choice for Democratic Party candidates. But despite these radical agendas, "Dollar Bill's" $30 million-plus campaign war chest was largely supplied by Wall Street, where he himself had made millions as a stockbroker after his retirement from the New York Knicks.

The explanation for these paradoxes is this: Unless one is taken in by the discredited poppycock of radicals, there is no reason that the rich should act out the roles that Marxists ascribe to them. Only if the market were a zero-sum game as Marxists believe—"exploited labor" for the worker, "surplus value" for the capitalist—would leftist clichés make any sense. But they don't. The real-world relationship between labor and capital is quite the opposite of what the left proposes. Entrepreneurs generally want a better-educated, better-paid, more diverse working force, if only because that means better employees, better marketers, and better consumers of the company product. That is why, historically, everywhere capitalism has been embraced, labor conditions have improved and worker benefits expanded, whether there has been a strong trade-union presence or not. That is why the capitalist helmsmen of the World Trade Organization are better friends of the world's poor than any of the Luddite demonstrators in Seattle who claimed to be protesting on their behalf.

The 21st-century political argument is not about whether to help the poor, or whether to include all Americans in the social contract. Republicans embrace these objectives as firmly as Democrats, conservatives as well as liberals. The issue is how actually to help the poor, and how best to integrate the many cultures of the American mosaic into a common culture that works. Twenty years after the welfare system was already a proven disaster for America's inner-city poor, Democrats and leftists were still demanding more welfare and opposing significant reforms. Clinton himself vetoed the Republican reform bill twice and only signed it when he was told he could not be reelected if he didn't. Welfare reform has liberated hundreds of thousands of poor people from dead-end dependency and given them a taste of the self-esteem that comes from earning one's keep. If the left were serious about improving the lot of the poor, it would pay homage to the man who made welfare reform possible, the despised former Republican Speaker Newt Gingrich. If hypocrisy weren't their stock-in-trade, self-styled champions of the downtrodden like Cornel West and Marian Wright Edelman would be writing testimonials to Gingrich as a hero to America's poor. But that won't happen. Instead, the left will go on tarring Gingrich and his political allies as "enemies of the poor" and lackeys of the rich. Such witch-hunts are indispensable to the left's intellectual class war. The dehumanization of one's opponents is a better option than attempting to construct an argument based on the facts.

Although it is described as "progressive," the left is really the party of reaction, given its resistance to change and its rear-guard battles against the market and free trade. But the left controls the culture, and with it the political language. Therefore, in America, reactionaries will continue to be called "progressives" and reformers will be labeled conservative.

America Defamed

The confluence of the Fourth of July weekend with the release of Mel Gibson's *The Patriot* provides an opportunity to reflect on the way America's heritage is under continuous assault by the determined legions of the political left. The assault has been mounted by an intellectual class based in America's politically correct educational institutions with branches in the media and other professions. Its inspiration is a set of discredited 19th-century dogmas masquerading as progressive "solutions" to age-old problems that are rooted in an intractable human nature that every human society reflects. Not even the collapse of Communism has been able to reconcile the alienated psyches of progressives to the cause of the most democratic multi-ethnic society on record. Elsewhere around the world, the national identity consists of common bonds of blood, language and soil, not a set of abstract principles and ideas. But the singular American identity has been forged through a conscious commitment to what until recently was still referred to as an "American way of life"— beginning with the declaration of a new nation dedicated to the proposition that all human beings are equally endowed with a natural right as individuals to pursue life, liberty and happiness. To be anti-American is to reject this heritage, and consequently a future that is American as well.

July 10, 2000, http://www.salon.com/2000/07/10/patriotism_2/; http://www.newsrealblog.com/2010/12/16/david-horowitz%e2%80%99s-archives-the-smearing-of-the-patriot/print/

One measure of how widely this anti-American sentiment has spread is the critical reaction to the release of a film that reassembles the elements of the national myth into a powerful homage to liberty and to the American colonists who gave their lives and their fortunes to its cause. The film has been attacked for its alleged anachronisms, in particular its projections of contemporary attitudes towards slavery and race into 18th-century South Carolina. Professor David Hackett Fisher, a distinguished Brandeis historian, put it this way in a *New York Times* op-ed piece that appeared two days after the opening: "Mr. Gibson plays a reluctant hero named Benjamin Martin, a widower with seven perfect children, a 'Gone With The Wind' plantation and a work force of free and happy Black Folk who toil in his fields as volunteers." Fischer then dismisses the film as being "to history as 'Godzilla' was to biology."

But it is a historical fact that there were thousands of free blacks in the antebellum United States and eventually 500,000 all together. Their presence in the film is not a fantasy born out of ignorance but a legitimate reflection of the facts. *The Patriot* forcefully employs these free blacks to dramatize the idea that the American Revolution and black freedom make up one continuum. In the story, a black slave signs up with the rebel force because he is promised freedom after twelve months' service. But after the twelve months are up, he decides to continue with the rebels of his own free will because he understands (as these critics apparently do not) that in the conception of a new nation based on the proposition that all men are created equal lies the possibility of freedom for him as well as for his white comrades in arms.

Is this historically far-fetched? Well, actually, no. In a slave state like North Carolina in 1774 the punishment for killing a slave was a mere year's imprisonment and the value of the property that had been destroyed. But eight years later, after the Revolution had been won, the North Carolina legislature changed the law, saying the old law was "disgraceful to humanity and degrading in the highest degree to the laws and principles of a free, Christian, and enlightened country," because it drew a "distinction of criminality between the murder of a white person and of one who is equally an human creature, but merely of a different complexion." The new revolutionary law made the willful killing of a slave murder and punishable by death.

Ideas have powerful consequences, most of all in shaping the future. But so do bad ideas and false images. Ever since Communism's ignominious demise, the left has no longer bothered to defend its fantasy of the socialist future.[1] Its spirit is now consumed by nihilism; its message is entirely framed in an indictment of the American past, present and future.

Until recently, American public schools functioned as a crucible of citizenship. Immigrants who came to America seeking refuge and opportunity were educated in this social contract by their teachers. At the beginning of every school day, students would pledge allegiance to the flag of a multiethnic republic that was united into one indivisible nation by the commitment of all its citizens to a common national ideal. For these immigrants, public education was a process of assimilation into an American culture that had pledged itself to liberty and justice for all. But for decades now this contract has been under siege by radical multiculturalists who condemn America and its cultural heritage as bigoted and oppressive, and valorize instead the cultures—often authoritarian and misogynist—of peoples this nation is alleged to oppress. In this perverse but now academically orthodox view, the world is turned upside down. The nation conceived in liberty is reconceived as the tyrant that needs to be overthrown. A Zogby poll, taken in January, showed that nearly a third of America's college students declined to say that they are proud to be Americans.

This is a direct result of the fact that their left-wing teachers, as a matter of course, teach them to be ashamed of their national heritage. Recently, reading messages posted to a Sixties' list on the

---

[1]With the election in 2008 of Barack Obama, a radical from its ranks, even this was to change; media personalities (like actor Warren Beatty and MSNBC's Lawrence O'Donnell) and politicians who once hid behind the label "liberal" began to describe themselves openly as "socialists."

Internet, I came across a post that encapsulated this corrosive attitude. It was by Jeffrey Blankfort, a photographer who supplied *Ramparts* and other media with romantic images of the Black Panthers during the 60s. Blankfort is now a public school teacher and an unreconstructed missionary from the hate-America school of radical thought, the most enduring legacy of his radical generation to the nation.

This is what Blankfort wrote: "In the schools in which I have subbed and then taught, very few students stand for the pledge of allegiance unless coerced to do so by their teacher. Most of the students have either African, Latin American or Asian ancestry. When an occasional student does stand, I ask, in a friendly manner, if she or he can tell me of any moment in history where the inhabitants of this land actually enjoyed 'liberty and justice for all,' and beyond the words of the pledge, to show me any proof that such was ever intended." In other words, for Blankfort and his comrades, gone is the role of public education as an assimilator of immigrants and minorities into a liberating American culture; gone, too, is the task of integrating them into a system that offers them more opportunities than they would have in their countries of origin. Instead the task is to warn them against the society their parents have embraced.

Thirty years ago no teacher would have thought to abuse his or her authority over school children in this manner. But now educational institutions from kindergarten through college have been politicized by a radical left that respects no institutions and no standards, and for whom everything is political, including the lives of small children. This is an authentic movement of subversion, and it is new as well. My father was a Communist teacher during the 1930s and 1940s, unfairly purged in the McCarthy era from the New York City school system—but not for an act like this. He did not violate his classroom trust, nor did he intrude his

---

[2]I learned this from Arnold Beichman, a staunch anti-Communist who was one of his students in the 1930s.

political agendas into his lessons.[2] Even though my father belonged to a conspiratorial party that took its orders from a foreign power, it would have been unthinkable for him to attack America in its promise as today's leftists reflexively do.[3]

My father belonged to a party whose slogan was, "Communism is 20th-Century Americanism"— and he believed it. The socialism of which he and his comrades dreamed was incompatible, of course, with the American framework. But in their minds, however illogically, the future to which they aspired was going to be a completion, not a rejection, of the American idea. Accordingly, they named their organizations after American icons like Lincoln and Jefferson, men now routinely demonized by the left as "racists" and, in Jefferson's case, "rapists." Even though what Communists like my father really wanted was a "Soviet America," they would say when challenged (and I actually did say when I was young and among them): "We're the true patriots; we want America to live up to its ideals."

Some on the contemporary left have revived this line of self-exculpation, along with the political agendas of the "popular front" familiar from the 1930s. A Fourth of July weekend feature in *The New York Times* pitted *Nation* editor Victor Navasky as a proponent of this position against Norman Podhoretz, a former leftist turned neoconservative critic. According to Navasky, the current version of communism-is-really-Americanism line goes like this: "My definition of patriotism would involve fighting to make sure your country lives up to its highest ideals. And from that perspective, even those who burn the flag—not all of them but some of them—may have been as patriotic as those who wrapped themselves in the flag." In Navasky-speak, anti-American "progressives" are actually the true patriots. "[G]oing back to the beginning of our history ... those people who fought to achieve

---

[3]For a similar critique of the left by a leftist who grew up in the 30s, see Richard Rorty, *Achieving Our Country*, Harvard University Press, 1998.

the American dream of equal rights for all were scorned at the time as, in effect, unpatriotic and later on as Communists."

In a perverse way Navasky is right. Those Americans who fought for equal rights at the beginning of American history were unpatriotic—but they were unpatriotic to England, not America. Later on, during the McCarthy era, leftists did hypocritically invoke the First and Fifth Amendments to hide their anti-American agendas and loyalties from the American public. But these Communists were in fact loyal to the Soviet empire and they wanted to *overthrow* the American Constitution and its Bill of Rights. Podhoretz did not exactly let Navasky slip through this loophole: "One can be critical of the country while loving it," he agreed, but added: "I would submit that people who burned the flag during the Vietnam War or people who spelled the name of the country with a K to suggest an association with Nazi Germany or people who saw no difference between America and the Soviet Union during the Cold War, morally or politically, were not patriots."

By choosing not to make the issue personal, by not confronting Navasky with his own record in these matters, Podhoretz let him off a little lightly. Navasky was the editor of a magazine that supported every Communist dictator in his heyday—Stalin, Mao, Fidel, Ho, even Pol Pot—and in virtually every conflict between the United States and any of its sworn enemies during the Cold War and after. In their *Times* debate, Navasky was thus able to stand his ground: "Patriotism is best expressed in the struggle to make this a better place. And it is not best expressed in saluting the flag or in parades down Fifth Avenue, but in writing, in marching, in suing, in ... whatever it takes to fulfill the promise of the Bill of Rights."

It is the core alibi of the left and also a favorite defense of MIT professor Noam Chomsky, who invariably uses it to explain why he is able to muster such fervent hostility towards his homeland, as he did for example from the platform of a Marxist dictatorship in Nicaragua during the 1980s.[4] The hypocrisy here is easily

---

[4] Noam Chomsky, *On Power and Ideology: The Managua Lectures*, 1987

exposed. If it is a more authentic form of loyalty to attack the failings of one's own house, then why are leftists like Navasky and Chomsky so zealous in covering up the crimes of the left? *The Nation* was perhaps the last media institution in America to admit the guilt of the Rosenberg spies or the crimes of the Black Panthers, let alone of the monster Pol Pot. It has still not made its peace with the guilt of Alger Hiss. For decades *The Nation* writers made pariahs of the Trotskyist critics of the Stalin regime, while actively colluding in the cover-up of Communist atrocities throughout the Cold War. Moreover, they continue in the present to defame critics of the left, as (in the interests of full disclosure) they defamed me in a recent cover story.[5] The purpose of these defamations is always the same: to embargo an introspective look at themselves. It is hypocrisy of the very highest order to think of yourself as having a "social conscience" and as being a champion of dissent, while you shut off questioning in your own ranks and demonize those who persist.

"What of it?" someone might ask in Navasky's defense. "Victor Navasky is a genial man. The left has no gulags in America. The Soviet empire is dead. So what if Noam Chomsky is the most influential intellect on American campuses? So what if 60s leftovers like Jeffrey Blankfort are busily indoctrinating American youth in suspicions toward their own country? America can survive this." It is true that the Soviet empire is dead, and that the threat of treason, which the old Communist movement posed, is for the moment not a pressing concern.[6] Yet the left still poses a danger to America's future. America is a unique experiment—virtually the only successful, large-scale multiethnic democracy. It is towards the very construction of this multiethnic community that the contemporary left poses a threat, a task made possible by the growing ignorance of Americans about the country they live in. In a recent survey of seniors at 55 of the highest-rated American colleges and universities,

---

[5] Scott Sherman, "David Horowitz's Long March," *The Nation*, July 3, 2000

[6] This was to change dramatically after September 11, 2001.

including Harvard and Princeton, 80 percent of those questioned failed to get better than a D on a high-school-level history exam and could not identify Patrick Henry, for example, as the author of the phrase "Give me liberty or give me death," let alone provide its context. None of the 55 schools in the survey required a course in American history for graduation, and only 20 percent required their students to take any history classes at all.

Into this vacuum the left has marched with its corrosive ideology, utilizing literature courses and ethnic studies programs to indoctrinate students instead. Consider this anti-American, anti-white and astoundingly ignorant statement by leftist political scientist Philip A. Klinkner in the July 3 *Nation:* "Throughout American history, in nearly every instance in which they have been given a direct vote on the matter, the majority of white Americans have rejected any measure beneficial to the interests of blacks." Given the fact that whites have been the American majority throughout the nation's history, it would be interesting to hear leftists like Klinkner explain how blacks have made any progress at all, if they have not made it through the expressed will of the white majority: how the slave trade was ended; how the slaves gained their freedom; how the Constitution was amended not only to outlaw slavery but to guarantee equal rights; how segregation was ended; how civil rights were enforced; how voting rights were guaranteed; how anti-discrimination laws were passed; how affirmative action was launched; how the welfare system was funded; and how African-Americans became the freest, richest and most privileged community of blacks anywhere in the world.

Far from being eccentric, Klinkner's view of the American past is a cliché of the views held not only by white leftist academics but by their disciples in the leadership of what passes for the "civil rights" movement in the African-American community today. Klinkner is not merely a history professor, but a specialist in American race relations and civil rights—a fact that speaks volumes about the politicized state of American universities and the toxic messages they disseminate in the guise of "education."

12

Telling It Like It Wasn't

The year 1998 was a time for the nostalgia artists of the left to remember their glory days of thirty years before, and the magic of a moment that many of them have never left. It was a time in their imaginations of lost innocence, when impossible dreams were brutally cut off by assassination and repression. For them, it was a time of progressive possibility that has left them stranded on the shores of a conservative landscape ever since.

A summary expression of such utopian regrets is contained in Steve Talbot's PBS documentary *1968: The Year That Shaped a Generation*. Talbot's narrative is itself shaped by un-self-critical radicals of the era like Todd Gitlin and Tom Hayden, who are interviewed on camera. The choice of Gitlin and Hayden as the film's authorities is to be expected from someone like Talbot, himself the veteran of a movement that promotes itself as an avatar of "participatory democracy" but closes off debate within its ranks in a way worthy of the totalitarian regimes it once admired. Thus the *auteur* of *The Year That Shaped A Generation* excludes from this cinematic paean to his revolutionary youth any dissenters from the ranks of those who were there.

I am one of those veterans who does not share this enthusiasm for 1968, nor Talbot's view of it as a fable of innocents. One explanation

---

June 19, 2002, http://www.salon.com/1998/08/31/nc_31horo/; http://archive.frontpagemag.com/Printable.aspx?ArtId=24287; *Hating Whitey and Other Progressive Causes*, David Horowitz, Spence Publ., 1999, pp. 201–210

might be that I am ten years older than Talbot, and for that reason have a more adult view of us then. Yet Gitlin and Hayden are also pre-boomers. An age gap cannot really explain our different views of what took place. Naturally, I too would prefer to recall the glory days of my youth in a golden light. However, the era has been irreparably tarnished for me by actions and attitudes I vividly remember and they prefer to forget.

In Talbot's telling, the innocence of the decade is crystallized in President Lyndon Johnson's March 1968 announcement that he would not run for re-election. Talbot was nineteen years old and draft-eligible: "We were all like Yossarian in *Catch-22*," he recalls in an article written for *Salon* magazine about his documentary. "We took this very personally. 'They' were trying to kill 'us.' But now Johnson had abdicated. We were free. It felt, quite simply, like a miracle." The miracle, of course, was the democratic system, which the left had declared war on, but which had responded to the popular will all the same. In 1968, radicals like us were calling for a "liberation" that would put an end to the "System"—the American system—which for us was the enemy. But contrary to what Hayden, Gitlin, Talbot and all the rest of us were saying at the time, the democratic system actually worked. Looking back, we should all have defended it and worked within it, instead of what we did do, which was to try to tear it down. Gitlin and Hayden have elsewhere acknowledged this fact but without accepting its consequences and altering their judgments of what we did. Talbot fails to notice the difference. Nor does he reflect on the contradiction between what he and his comrades advocated then, and what everyone recognizes to be the case now.

The "they" Talbot refers to—meaning Johnson's democratically elected administration—were assuredly *not* "trying to kill us" in 1968. (Even in a retrospective mode the narcissism of the boomer generation is impressive.) The attentions of Lyndon Johnson and Richard Nixon were not on us but on the fate of Indochina and its people. They had committed American forces to prevent the Communist conquest of South Vietnam and Cambodia, and the bloodbath that we now know was in store for the Indochinese when the Communists won. As a result of the Communist victory and the left's efforts to make America lose, more people—more poor Indo-Chinese peasants—were killed by the victors in the first three years of the peace than had been killed on all sides in the thirteen years of the anti-Communist war. This is a fact that has caused some of us to reconsider our commitments and our innocence then. But not Talbot, or the other nostalgists he has invited to make his film. For them, the moral innocence of their comrades and themselves remains intact to this day.

According to Talbot and his enablers, their innocence was brutally crushed when forces inherent in the System they hated conspired to murder the agents of their hope: Martin Luther King and Bobby Kennedy. And it was only those 1968 murders that caused them to become radicals at war with America. "I experienced King's assassination as the murder of hope," writes Talbot in his *Salon* article, speaking for them all. In Talbot's film, Gitlin claims that this was his thought at the time: "America tried to redeem itself and now they've killed the man who was taking us to the mountaintop." But this is a false memory, and there is something extremely distasteful in the fact that it is proposed by a historic participant like Gitlin. For, as Gitlin well knows, in the year 1968 neither he nor Tom Hayden, nor the serious New Left radicals, thought of themselves as liberal reformers or followers of Martin Luther King.

For the New Left had turned its back on King two years earlier when King was toppled from the leadership of the civil rights movement by Stokely Carmichael and friends, and "black power" became the slogan of the hour, a slogan that King rejected. The New Left's abandonment of King's leadership and philosophy, and its embrace of a darker vision of America than his, is reflected in the fact that neither Gitlin nor Hayden nor any other white activist, nor antiwar spokesman, was in Memphis for the demonstrations King was organizing in 1968 at the time he was killed. In fact, no one in the New Left (at least no one who mattered) could still be called a serious supporter of King in the year prior to his assassination. The black heroes of the New Left now were prophets of separatism and violence—Stokely Carmichael, H. Rap Brown, Huey Newton, and the martyred Malcolm X. The agendas of the radicals who pushed King aside were black power and revolutionary violence, which supplanted King's pleas for non-violence and integration in the imaginations of the left.

Like other New Left leaders, Todd Gitlin was far from the idealistic liberal he impersonates in his book on the 60s or in Talbot's fanciful film.[1] Like practically everyone else in the New Left, Gitlin had stopped voting in national elections as early as 1964, by his own account, because, as the SDS slogan put it, "the revolution is in the streets."[2] To Gitlin and other New Leftists, the two main political parties were the Tweedledum and Tweedledee of the "corporate ruling class." Activists who saw themselves as revolutionaries against a "sham democracy," dominated by multinational corporations, were not going to invest hope in a leader like King whose political agenda was integration into the System, and who resisted joining their war on the Johnson administration, its imperialist adventures abroad and "tokenist" liberalism at home.

In Talbot's film, Hayden, too, embraces a doctrine of original innocence, but his disingenuous presentation of self involves fewer flat untruths than Gitlin's. Instead, he relies on subtle shadings and manipulations of the facts, a style of deception that was his political signature. "At that point," Hayden says of the King assassination, "I had been so knocked out of my middle-class assumptions that I didn't know what would happen. Perhaps the country could be reformed and Robert Kennedy elected president. Perhaps we would be plunged into a civil war and I'd be impris-

---

[1] Todd Gitlin, *The Sixties: Years of Hope, Days of Rage,* Bantam, 1987
[2] Even this slogan has been bowdlerized by New Left historians like James Miller, whose book *Democracy Is in the Streets* puts a far more innocent face on the movement than its activism merited.

oned or killed." The reality is that any middle-class assumptions held by Hayden or any prominent SDS activist had already been left by the wayside years before. Three out of four of the drafters of the famous 1962 "Port Huron Statement" were "red diaper babies" and Marxists. The fourth was Hayden, who by his own account in his autobiography, *Reunion*, learned his politics in Berkeley in 1960 at the feet of children of the Old Left. (Hayden names Michael Tigar and Richard Flacks, two red diaper babies in particular, as his mentors). By 1965, SDS president Carl Oglesby was proclaiming in a famous speech that it was time to "name the System" that we all wanted to destroy. The name he chose was "corporate capitalism," and it was accepted and analyzed by SDS leaders in pretty much the same terms as in the Party texts studied by the Communist cadres in Moscow, Havana, and Hanoi.

Hayden himself was already calling the Black Panthers "America's Vietcong" and planning the riot he was going to stage at the Democratic convention in Chicago that August. This pivotal event is described conveniently, but inaccurately as a "police riot" in Talbot's film, in Gitlin's book, and in Hayden's own memoir, which singularly fails to acknowledge his efforts to produce the clash that took place. Civil war in America was not something that was going to be imposed on the SDS revolutionaries from the outside or above, as Hayden disingenuously insinuates. Civil war was something that radicals, with Hayden foremost among them, were trying to launch themselves.

Talbot supports his mythologizing of the spring that led up to the Chicago confrontation by romanticizing the political ambitions of Bobby Kennedy and mis-remembering how the left reacted to them. "Out of the ashes of the riots in the wake of King's murder, new hope came in the form of Bobby Kennedy, who had undergone a profound transformation from Vietnam hawk and aide to Sen. Joe McCarthy to dove and spokesman for the dispossessed." It is true, of course, that Bobby Kennedy made a feint in the direction of the antiwar crowd and more than one gesture on behalf of Cesar Chavez's farm workers movement. It is also true that Hayden attended Kennedy's funeral and even wept a tear or two. But those tears had little to do with Hayden's political agendas at the time, which he summed up in the slogan "two, three many Vietnams," lifted from the Cuban Communist Che Guevara. Hayden's tears for Kennedy were personal, and he paid a huge political price for them among his revolutionary comrades who were not impressed by any Kennedy "transformation." After the funeral, SDS activists wondered out loud, and in print, whether Hayden had "sold out" by mourning a figure whom they saw not as the great white hope of the political struggle that consumed their lives, but as a Trojan horse for the other side.

With King dead in April and Kennedy in June, the stage was set for what Talbot calls "the inevitable showdown" in Chicago in August. Here he allows a glimmer of the truth to enter his narrative. "Both sides, rebels and rulers, were spoiling for a confrontation." But just as quickly he reverts to the mythology that Hayden and his cohorts first created and that progressive historians have since perpetuated: "Chicago's Mayor Richard Daley made it possible. He denied permits for protesters at the Democratic Convention." In short, the denied permits made confrontation inevitable. In fact, the famous epigram from 1968, "Demand the Impossible," which Talbot elsewhere cites, explains far more accurately why it was Hayden, not Daley, who set the agenda for Chicago, and why it was Hayden who was ultimately responsible for the riot that ensued. It is true that the police behaved badly in allowing themselves to be provoked (or welcoming the provocation); and they have been justly criticized for their reactions. But those reactions were entirely predictable. After all, it was Daley who only months before had ordered his police to "shoot looters on sight" during the riots after King's murder. In fact the predictable reaction of the Chicago police was an essential part of Hayden's calculation in making his plans for the convention.

It was also why many of us did not go to Chicago. In a year when any national "action" would attract 100,000 protestors, only about 10,000 (and probably closer to 3,000) actually showed up for the Chicago blood-fest. That was because most of us realized there was going to be violence and didn't want to be part of it. Our ideology argued otherwise as well. The two-party system was a sham; the revolution was in the streets. So why demonstrate at a political convention in an effort to influence elections? In retrospect, Hayden was more cynical and shrewder than we were. By destroying the presidential aspirations of Hubert Humphrey, he dealt a fatal blow to the anti-Communist liberals in the Democratic Party and paved the way for a takeover of its apparatus by the forces of the political left, a trauma from which the Party has yet to recover.

One reason the left has obscured these historical facts is that the nostalgists don't really want to take credit for electing Richard Nixon, which they surely did. As a matter of political discretion, they are also willing to let their greatest *coup*—the capture of the Democratic Party—go un-memorialized. Instead they prefer to ascribe the political realignment that followed to impersonal forces, which apparently had nothing to do with their own agendas and actions. In Talbot's summary: "While 'the whole world [was] watching,' [Daley's] police rioted, clubbing demonstrators, reporters, and bystanders indiscriminately. The Democratic Party self-destructed." Well, actually, it didn't self-destruct; it was destroyed by the left's riot in Chicago.

When the fires of Watergate consumed the Nixon presidency in 1974, the left's newly won control of the Democratic Party produced the exact result that Hayden and his comrades had worked so hard to achieve. In 1974, a new class of Democrats was elected to congress, which included antiwar activists like Ron Dellums, Pat Schroeder, David Bonior and Bella Abzug. Their politics were traditionally left as opposed to the anti-Communist liberalism of the Daleys and the Humphreys (Abzug had even been a Communist). Their first act was to cut off economic aid and military supplies to the regimes in Cambodia and South Vietnam, precipitating the bloodbath that followed. Though it is conveniently forgotten now, this cut-off occurred two years after the United States had signed a truce with Hanoi and American troops had been withdrawn

from Vietnam. "Bring The Troops Home" may have been the slogan of the so-called antiwar movement but was never its only goal.
The slogan was designed by its authors to bring about a "liberated"
Vietnam. If the troops came home, the Communists would win.
Within three months of the cut-off of military aid, the anti-Communist regimes in Saigon and Phnom Penh fell, and the genocide
began. The mass slaughters in Cambodia and South Vietnam from
1975 to 1978 were the real achievements of the New Left and
could not have taken place without Hayden's sabotage of the anti-
Communist Democrats led by Hubert Humphrey.

While Talbot forgets this denouement, he does get the signifi-
cance of the war right: "The war in Vietnam and the draft were
absolutely central. I remember a cover of *Ramparts* magazine that
captured how I felt: 'Alienation is when your country is at war and
you hope the other side wins.'" This is a softened version of what
we actually felt. As the author of that cover line, let me correct
Talbot's memory and add a detail. The *Ramparts* cover featured a
picture of a Huck Finn-like seven-year-old (it was our art director
Dugald Stermer's son) who was holding the Vietcong flag, the flag
of America's enemy in Vietnam. The cover line said: "Alienation
is when your country is at war and you *want* the other side to
win." This represented what we actually believed—Hayden,
Gitlin, Steve Talbot and myself. What lessons my former comrades draw from our service to the wrong side in the Cold War is
their business. I just wish they would remember the events the
way they happened. I also wish they would have the good grace
not to project onto themselves retrospective sympathies for the
struggle against Communism, a struggle they opposed and whose
true warriors and champions—however distasteful, embarrassing
and uncomfortable this must be for them—were Richard Nixon,
Ronald Reagan, and the political right they hated and despised.
Review the fifty years of the Cold War against the Soviet empire
and you will find that every political and military program to contain the spread of this cancer and ultimately to destroy it was

fiercely resisted by those who now invoke the anti-Communist "spirit of '68" in Eastern Europe as their own.

"Assassinations, repression, and exhaustion extinguished the spirit of '68," Talbot concludes his story. "But like a subterranean fire, it resurfaces at historic moments." Citing the socialist writer, Paul Berman, the originator of this myth, Talbot argues that "the members of '68 helped ignite the revolution of 1989 that brought liberal democracy to Eastern Europe and ended the Cold War." The distortion of this memory is one thing for Berman, who at some point joined a miniscule faction of the left that was indeed anti-Communist, while still hating American capitalism almost as much. (How much? In Berman's case, enough to support the Black Panthers in the 1970s as a political vanguard and to praise the secret police chief of the Sandinista dictatorship in the 1980s as a "quintessential New Leftist.") But this attempt to hijack the anti-Communist cause for a left that declared itself "anti-anti Communist" is particularly unappetizing, and doubly so in Talbot's case. Talbot, after all, made films into the 1980s celebrating Communist insurgents who were busily extending the Soviet sphere in Africa. America, bless its generous heart, has already forgiven Steve Talbot for his bad choices in the past. So why lie about them now?

Admittedly, New Leftists were critical of the policies of the Soviet Union (as at various times were Khrushchev, Castro and Ho Chi Minh). But their true, undying enemy was always democratic America, the hatred for which was never merely reactive (as they habitually claim) and never truly innocent. The world-view of this left was aptly summarized by the adoring biographer of the journalist I. F. Stone, who approvingly described Stone's belief that "in spite of the brutal collectivization campaign, the Nazi-Soviet Pact, the latest quashing of the Czech democracy and the Stalinist takeover of Eastern Europe ... communism was a progressive force, lined up on the correct side of historical events." Berman, Gitlin and now Talbot have mounted a preposterous last-ditch effort to save leftists from the embarrassments of their deeds by attempting to appropriate moral credit for helping to end the system the left aided and abetted throughout its career. It may be, as Berman and Talbot claim, that East European anti-Communists drew inspiration from anti-government protests in the West. But this was a reflection of their admiration for a democratic system that embraced dissent and promoted freedom, not for the anti-western agendas of the New Left demonstrators.

The unseemly attempt to retrieve an honorable past from such dishonorable commitments might be more convincing if any of these memorialists were able to remember a single demonstration against Communist oppression in Vietnam, or the genocide in Cambodia, or the rape of Afghanistan, or the dictatorships in Cuba and Nicaragua. Or if one veteran leader of the New Left had once publicly called on the Soviets to tear down the Berlin Wall, as Ronald Reagan actually did. Support for the anti-Communist freedom fighters in Afghanistan and Africa and Central America during the 1980s came largely from Goldwater and Reagan activists on the right, like Jeane Kirkpatrick, Grover Norquist, Elliott Abrams, Dana Rohrabacher and Oliver North, whom progressives, for this very reason, passionately despise.

It would have been encouraging if the thirtieth anniversary of the events of 1968 had been used to end the cold war over its memories and to start restoring a sense of the tragic to both sides. But, to do that, the nostalgists of the left would first have to be persuaded to give up their attempts to re-write what happened, and start telling it like it was.

13

The Leftist Media

[My Salon.com editor David Talbot wrote an article titled, "All Conservatives All The Time," which rehashed Eric Alterman's argument in What Liberal Media? *that American media are not dominated by the political left. This was my reply.]*

With a handful of exceptions, America's major metropolitan newspapers are firmly in the control of so-called "liberals" or, as I would prefer it, the political left. To name the most prominent: *USA Today, The New York Times*, the *Los Angeles Times, The Washington Post, The Boston Globe, The Philadelphia Inquirer*, the *Chicago Tribune*, the *Chicago Sun-Times*, the *St. Louis Post Dispatch*, the *San Francisco Chronicle*, the *Houston Chronicle, The Dallas Morning News*, the *Miami Herald, The Baltimore Sun, The Denver Post*, the *Minneapolis Star-Tribune, The Detroit News*, the *Detroit Free Press, The Oregonian*, the *Milwaukee Post Sentinel, The Seattle Times*, the *San Diego Union, The Sacramento Bee*, the *St. Petersburg Times*, the *Atlanta Journal-Constitution* and the *Pittsburgh Post-Gazette*. These papers regularly endorse Democratic candidates, their news features are designed to progressive tastes; they ritually celebrate liberal icons and just as regularly taint conservative leaders. Even *The Wall Street Journal*, whose two editorial pages are sometimes described as the party organ of the conservative movement,

March 11, 2003, http://archive.frontpagemag.com/Printable.aspx?ArtId= 19330

follows the pattern of media liberalism in its news and feature sections.

The same can be said for the major television networks and their hundreds of local affiliates—an even more important source of public information and political news. In summarizing Alterman's counter-claims, Talbot writes: "Talk radio is dominated by Rush Limbaugh and his imitators, the Web has fallen to Matt Drudge, and cable TV is ruled by Ailes and his wannabes at the rival channels." Of the three claims made in this statement, one is an absurdity and two are half-truths. The absurdity is Alterman's claim that Matt Drudge rules the Internet. No one rules the Internet. The idea is laughable on its face, even more so coming from a pundit whose employer, Microsoft, is the digital Standard Oil, with tentacles spreading liberal influence throughout the media universe. (For those who like hard statistics, MSNBC.com, where Alterman hangs out, is ranked 42 in volume of traffic among the million-plus sites on the worldwide web, while *Slate*—a Microsoft product—is ranked 2. The *Wall Street Journal*'s editorial page— opinionjournal.com—is rated 3,583.) Drudge does not editorialize on his site but posts other people's news—a point Alterman and Talbot seem to have missed. Moreover, Drudge's sensational news items often tan Republican hides.

It is true—but only half a truth—that Roger Ailes has recently challenged the liberal cable monopoly and is doing very well. The liberal *networks*, on the other hand, have ten times the cable audience, while CNN is a global media network that is far from dead. Cable also features a lot of Hollywood films that on balance reflect the prejudices of the political left. Alterman's final half-truth is that talk radio is a medium dominated by Rush Limbaugh conservatives. He forgets Howard Stern with 20 million listeners, and even more importantly he forgets public radio, a taxpayer-funded network hijacked by the left that has twelve million listeners and 600 stations which reach into every congressional district, and is far and away the most widely listened-to news source by legislators and opinion makers.

There are other forms of media that follow this pattern. The New York publishing industry is a liberal monopoly, and—with one exception that I am aware of—all the university presses and journals are run by the political left. The left-wing faculties of the university, moreover, are available to subsidize independent progressive magazines by providing their editors and writers with academic sinecures, while all the major journalism schools serve as training institutions for media liberals and leftists. Examples of the subsidies: *Nation* editor Victor Navasky is a professor at the Columbia School of Journalism; *Nation* columnist Robert Scheer is a professor at the Annenberg School of Communications at USC. I recently had lunch with the dean of the Annenberg School of Journalism at USC and he conceded that he could not identify a single member of his faculty who was not on the political left. My friend Christopher Hitchens, only recently departed from *The Nation*'s staff, is a professor at the New School and currently the I.F. Stone fellow at the Berkeley School of Journalism, whose dean is a well-known Berkeley leftist (and sometime *Nation* contributor), Orville Schell. Other *Nation* writers with faculty posts include Adolph Reed (New School), Patricia Williams (Columbia), Philip Klinkner (Hamilton), Jon Wiener (UC Irvine) Stephen Cohen (Princeton), Eric Foner (Columbia), Michael Klare (Professor of Peace Studies at the Five Colleges)—and that's just off the top of my head. I don't know of a single conservative magazine with a university-subsidized editorial board and staff.

Against this juggernaut, Talbot throws up the specter of right-wing money, vaguely identified of course and without the context of its counterparts on the left. To be fair, this is Alterman's problem rather than Talbot's (and in fact a common theme of left-wing complaints): "Alterman knows firsthand the way the right built a network of think tanks and publications to nurture young journalists, thanks to the fortunes of ardent conservatives like Richard Mellon Scaife. He started his own journalism career in Washington in the early 1980s, and it was grim enough to send a lesser man to business school. 'Between 1982 and 1984, I think I earned a grand total of about $500 working as a liberal journalist, for articles in *The Nation, In These Times,* the *Washington Monthly,* the Washington *City Paper,* and *Arms Control Today.* Meanwhile the bars and softball fields of the capital were filled with young right-wingers living on generous salaries and fellowships provided by the multi-million dollar institutions like the *Washington Times,* Heritage Foundation, and their various offshoots.... Many of the writers who worship at the shrine of the free market would be lost if any of them were ever forced to earn their living working for it.'"

This is pretty unkind coming from Alterman, who received a $180,000 subsidy from Bill Moyers's foundation to write his unread book on foreign policy. Alterman whines about a two-year unpaid apprenticeship in journalism twenty years ago and compares his lot with that of think-tank staffers, while ignoring the even higher salaries of his radical friends (not to mention himself) on university faculties. If one's expectations are elevated enough, and one's vision sufficiently narrow, I guess anything can seem a politically inflicted hardship. Bill Moyers's charitable cash cow is only one of more than 100 progressive foundations (I am taking this number from the progressive web) that have given tens of millions of dollars to such left-wing media institutions as *Indymedia.org, commondreams.org* and *TomPaine.com.* Moyers himself single-handedly transformed the feeble *American Prospect,* a little read bi-monthly, into a bi-*weekly* force in the Democratic Party with a $5 million grant. I won't go into all the money that *The Nation* has soaked up from the capitalist rich and their foundations; but all this left-wing largesse, as I have noted, is on top of the vast resources available to progressives from the university departments they dominate, while at the same time denied to conservatives.

To view the conservative think tanks rightly, one must see them as an alternative universe conservatives were forced to create because of their exclusion from universities as a result of the most sustained and successful blacklist in American history—a blacklist imposed and enforced by their leftist adversaries.[1] Even the endowment of the Heritage Foundation, the largest of the conservative think tanks, is a pittance compared to the resources of any university or its left-wing departments. As for the size of the casually overlooked left-wing foundations, MacArthur's assets alone are three times that of Scaife, Olin and Bradley *combined*.[2]

Alterman's suggestion that conservative intellectuals are a bunch of spoiled rich kids drowning in stipends while hard-working leftists have to live on scraps is typically 180 degrees from the facts. Senior editors at a major conservative opinion journal might make $40,000 a year. Contrast this to a progressive lightweight like Cornel West, another *Nation* contributor whose income is at least in the six-figure range and could exceed a million dollars a year. I am not privy to West's IRS returns, but as a star Ivy League professor he could make in excess of $200,000 for his salary alone. West has boasted that he gives 120 speeches a year. If he was paid for only half of them at his going rate of $10,000, that would be another $600,000. This is a privilege denied to most conservatives, since student activities funds are normally locked up by the left. Then there are additional revenues for the books West writes (or puts his name on) that are assigned as classroom texts by his progressive comrades.

Facts like these ought to close the book on the question of media dominance by the left. On the other hand, a lot of what David Talbot writes in his article in the way of advice to the left is quite good, and sounds like what I have been saying to conservatives for years: stop whining about the other guy's domination of the media and do something to compete. There remains one issue

---

[1] I am speaking of its effect—the indisputable exclusion of conservatives from universities. In practice it is more like a graylist whose workings I have described in the introduction and final two chapters of *The Professors*, Regnery 2006.

[2] In 2012 Jacob Laksin and I published a book documenting the more than ten-to-one advantage in assets of left-wing philanthropic funders: *The New Leviathan: How the Left-wing Money Machine Shapes American Politics and Threatens America's Future*.

between us, however, and by David's own account it is the main one. In an e-mail giving me the green light for this response, David had this to say: "I'd love to hear your response. But you're going to have to work hard to convince me and most of our readers that the major networks and newspapers and other such corporate, centrist institutions have a conscious strategy to advance a liberal agenda."

I understand why David and those who agree with him are not satisfied with a media establishment that is so obviously and overwhelmingly sympathetic to the left. Talk radio and cable TV are the arenas of direct political combat, and that's where they would like to be—on the terrain where conservatives seem to call the shots. But that is only because they ignore the billion-dollar public broadcasting networks—both TV and radio—that reflect progressive views. I certainly don't agree with David that the major networks and newspapers are corporate centrists, except in the sense that they are looking for large audiences and therefore don't want the appearance of narrow and bitter partisanship in their news and features. Think, on the other hand, of the advantages to the left that this attitude brings. Andrew Sullivan, Mickey Kaus and others have documented the way *The New York Times* has not only used its reporting to editorialize against the war in Iraq but has spun its entire news section to persuade its influential reader base that President Bush's policies are a bad idea.

To understand how fraternally the *Times* editors regard the hard left, consider the series of sympathetic articles they have run on Kathy Boudin, her family and her criminal cohorts. Boudin was convicted of participating in the robbery of a Brinks armored car with the intention of financing a revolution. With her direct assistance, three men, including the first black policeman on the Nyack force, were killed in the course of the robbery. Yet the *Times* has sympathetically followed her appeals and even given front-page coverage to her son's academic career.

Now imagine if *The Times* set about promoting a pro-life activist who had murdered an abortion doctor, presenting him as an idealist who had regrettably gone too far. Would leftists take the complacent view of *The Times'* "centrism" that they do now? Recently *The Times* did a major promotional piece on Leslie Cagan, the head of United for Peace and Justice, without mentioning the fact that she is a 60s Stalinist who remained a member of the Communist Party after the fall of the Berlin Wall. How many careers of left-wing writers and activists, movements and institutions have been launched and promoted by the neutral pose of *The New York Times* and how many conservative careers truncated or aborted by the same? The Black Panther murderers of my friend Betty Van Patter have been featured as 60s civil-rights activists by *The Times, The Washington Post* and other major media. The murderers tour college campuses drawing $10,000 fees and promoting more contemporary criminals like H. Rap Brown, whom they portray as a frame-up victim of Atlanta's legal and law enforcement establishments. Their speeches are even funded by Republican institutions like the Irvine Foundation, whose establishment boards are susceptible to persuasion by the authority of papers like *The Times*.

During the 2000 presidential campaign, a spurious left-wing academic study of death-penalty reversals was given front-page coverage by *The Times* and therefore by a large cohort of the nation's press (for whom *The Times* sets the standard) to the detriment of the Bush campaign. The tendentious nature of the study was evident when it suggested that two-thirds of California's death-penalty cases were reversed through legal incompetence, and concluded that the system was broken and Bush's support of the death penalty was therefore unreasonable. The report ignored the fact that the chief justice of the California Supreme Court, Rose Bird, had publicly declared that she would vote to reverse every death penalty on principle—which she did, all thirty-nine that came to her for review. California voters recalled Bird and her two cohorts on the bench for precisely this reason. But the report from Columbia University—which is in effect a left-wing think tank— ignored this and many other countervailing facts because its real purpose was to exert a negative impact on the Bush campaign.

To be able, like *The Times*, to pose an ideological agenda as information and advance it behind a façade of objectivity is a far more effective weapon than, say, having an angry scowler like *Salon* writer Joe Conason, or a sanctimonious pontificator like Mario Cuomo, square off against a personable opponent like Sean Hannity. But is it the case that NPR, ABC, CBS, NBC, Time-Warner, *Newsweek* and the metropolitan press advance no overt agenda? That they don't for example, editorialize on pivotal issues like race preferences, abortion and the Bush tax refund, which goes to the heart of the political debate? If you are against the Bush tax refund, you believe that government should take legally earned money from one class of citizens and put it in the pockets of another class. That's a socialist agenda and pretty basic to what makes the left the left. Does anyone seriously think the media establishment is neutral on these issues, or that it doesn't place its weight heavily on one side of the scale?

It feels a little odd to be comforting leftists. It must be the *Salon* syndrome or something. (I have always enjoyed my relationship with this magazine.) The fact is that conservatives like me welcome the competition of ideas. Unlike the left, we are not afraid of an argument, because we can be confident that we are right.

14

Harvard Lies

The number one book on this week's *New York Times* best-seller list is *Lies and the Lying Liars Who Tell Them*, written by comedian Al Franken. It's actually not a funny book—unless you happen to be an exceptionally mean-spirited and ill-informed liberal who thinks all Republicans are racists, and that President Clinton was a pro-military foreign policy hawk who devoted more time to tracking down Osama bin Laden than he did to the Monica Lewinsky mess. Franken's book is so gratuitous in dispensing its partisan venom that one of its hapless targets is the civilized and articulate progressive Alan Colmes, who is unfairly damned for failing to mount a Franken-style attack as a co-anchor on Fox's "Hannity & Colmes." Franken prints Colmes's name in small type throughout the book to imply that Colmes is a mouse or, in Franken's words, a "zeta male" to Hannity's alpha. Such is the humor of this meretricious screed.

Yet there's no denying that the book is a commercial success. A prime reason for this is the publicity boost provided by a misguided (and subsequently aborted) lawsuit that Fox News filed against Franken in an attempt to stop his use of their logo "Fair and Balanced" in his subtitle. (What *could* Fox have been thinking?). But there is another reason as well. For while it pretends to be a funny book the real purpose of this nearly 400-page tome is quite serious. It's designed as a kind of a campaign manual for the

September 12, 2003, http://archive.frontpagemag.com/Printable.aspx?ArtId=16399

next presidential election, touching every major point of partisan dispute: Who tanked the economy? Who created the mean-spirited political tone? Who "stole" the 2000 election? Who is stronger on defense? Who has the support of biased media? Who is more anti-terrorist? No surprise that its answers line up relentlessly in the Democrats' favor. They come backed by facts and figures and cita-tions from so many sources it would take a team to produce them.

Which raises an interesting question. How did a comedian assemble such a team? The answer is Harvard. According to Franken himself, the Kennedy School of Government called him up and offered him a "fellowship." Harvard told him, "you can run a study group on a topic of your choosing," and, yes, the study group can be about how Republicans are racists and liars and you can use fourteen of our graduate students to provide you with your research and write as much of your book as you care to let them. And at our expense.

By disclosing these facts with the breathless candor of a kid who has stumbled into a candy store with free merchandise, Franken has exposed, for all who care to look, a national educa-tional disgrace. While liberals like Franken regularly complain about the unfair advantage "big right-wing thanks" provide to the Republican cause, Harvard and in fact the entire Ivy League pro-vide infinitely larger left-wing think tanks to serve the Democratic cause.

Ann Coulter has written a parallel bestseller (but under her own steam) that attacks liberals and Democrats like Al Franken. Can anyone imagine Harvard soliciting Coulter to lead a graduate study group whose students would research and write her book, leaving her to put in the jokes? When I looked at the faculty roster of Harvard's Kennedy School of Government, I was able to identify only 5 Republicans out of 155 faculty members—and one them was the political switcher David Gergen. A just-released study conducted by my Center for the Study of Popular Culture, and based on primary voter registration lists, shows that among 32 elite colleges and universities including the entire Ivy League, registered faculty Democrats outnumbered Republicans 10–1. At schools like Brown, Wellesley and Wesleyan the figure exceeded 25–1. A parallel study conducted by the Center showed that, over a ten-year period, the commencement speakers at the same 32 schools were biased in favor of Democrats and liberals by a factor of 15–1. At twenty-two of those schools, not a single Republican or conservative had been invited to speak at a commencement in 10 years.[1]

Two years ago I placed a full-page ad in *The Harvard Crimson* headlined: "Harvard U: No Republicans or Conservatives, and Few White Christians Need Apply." (Harvard's student body is 18 percent white Christian, whereas in the nation at large the figure is 73 percent.) The administration and faculty of Harvard—and of American universities generally—don't seem to care about *this* kind of academic bias. "Diversity" is the buzzword in the world of higher education but "intellectual diversity"—the diversity that really matters to a good education and a healthy democracy—is not on their radar screens.

---

[1]For more on these matters see Volume 7 in this series, *The Left in the University*.

15

The Progressive Myth Machine

David Brock has written a new book called *The Republican Noise Machine: Right-Wing Media and How It Corrupts Democracy*, in which he purports to expose the vast right-wing media conspiracy, a menace Brock claims to know first-hand as someone who was once a cog in its malignant machine.[1] First-hand knowledge is an important claim for Brock because, as a famous self-confessed liar, he is aware that he stands on shaky ground as he attempts to extend the successful career he has made out of his political about-face. A similar dilemma haunts the second acts of other reborn dissemblers like Stephen Glass and Jayson Blair.[2] Brock's advantage over these fabricators in his quest to find a readership willing to suspend their disbelief is that he is selling a message his new political audiences are eager to hear.

I have the dubious distinction of appearing as one of the villains in Brock's profile of what he claims is a vast right-wing media conspiracy. In a dozen pages of *The Republican Noise Machine*, Brock offers readers an account of my career as a right-wing conspirator and polluter of the nation's journalistic airwaves. I do not intend to examine the general thesis of Brock's book other than to

June 25, 2004, http://archive.frontpagemag.com/Printable.aspx?ArtId=12503
[1] http://www.amazon.com/The-Republican-Noise-Machine-Right-Wing/dp/BoooFVQV16/ref=sr_1_fkmro_1?ie=UTF8&qid=1373937200&sr=8-1-fkmro&keywords=The+Republican+Noise+Machine%3A+How+It+Corrupts+Our+Democracy
[2] These are journalists who were fired from the *The New Republic* and *The New York Times* respectively for making up the stories they "reported."

observe that it is preposterous. According to Brock, unscrupulous, partisan conservatives have invaded arenas previously governed by impeccable standards of fairness and objectivity, corrupting American journalism and politics in the process. Only the ideologically blinded will be persuaded by special pleadings like this. What I propose instead is to use Brock's account of my alleged role in this effort to assess his reliability as a reporter of facts. Brock's methods unfortunately are typical of those employed by progressives to describe those who disagree with them, as several decades of my own experience at their hands will attest.

I am a revealing subject for such an inquiry because I have published a lengthy autobiography and left a clearly defined trail of the details of my career in many books and articles readily available on the Web. If David Brock wanted to get the bare facts of what I have done and what I have said by checking the sources, he could easily have done so. He would not have had to track them down or conduct interviews with people who knew me, or with myself. A comparison of Brock's version to this published record offers a fairly precise way for readers to gauge his accuracy as a reporter and his reliability as a guide to evidence, quite apart from any political conclusions he draws from it. In order to be fair to Brock, without unnecessarily boring the reader, I will attempt to cover every factual statement about me that is made in his book.

Brock begins inauspiciously. "In the 1960s, Horowitz had been an editor of *Ramparts*, one of the most violently radical organs of the New Left."[3] While *Ramparts* was indeed a radical organ, it was hardly one of the most violent. Among these one might include *Prairie Fire* (the publication of the terrorist Weather Underground), *The Black Panther*, the *Revolutionary Worker*, the *Berkeley Barb* and other vanguard publications of movements actively organizing for terrorist and revolutionary agendas. By contrast, movement activists generally regarded *Ramparts* as a "sellout" publication

---

[3]*The Republican Noise Machine*, David Brock, Crown Publishers, 2004, p. 100.

because the magazine was published in a slick four-color format for newsstands as opposed to the underground style of most movement magazines. Moreover, its staff members were conspicuously not activists themselves. During the 1968 riots at the Democratic Party convention in Chicago, for example, *Ramparts'* staff was roundly criticized for setting up headquarters in the "Pump Room" of the Hilton instead of joining other radicals in the dangerous streets. In 1971, *Ramparts* published an article condemning the violent tactics of the Weather Underground and in 1974 an editorial appeared in the magazine condemning the violence of the Symbionese Liberation Army. I wrote both pieces myself. All these facts are reported in my autobiography, *Radical Son*, which was a text readily available to Brock, and if he doubted my account he could have checked the articles himself.

Brock continues: "Horowitz was the author of a book, *The Free World Colossus*, an influential New Left text indicting U.S. foreign policy. His thinking was shaped by his friend and mentor Isaac Deutscher, a Marxist historian and a biographer of Leon Trotsky."[4] Isaac Deutscher was indeed my friend and mentor but, as I explained in my autobiography, our personal relationship had no influence on *The Free World Colossus*, in part because I hadn't even met him at the time, since I wrote the book in Sweden in 1962-3 and didn't meet Deutscher until the winter of 1964-65 after I moved to London. Time factors aside, the account of our meeting in *Radical Son* explicitly refutes Brock's claim that my thinking in the book was shaped by Deutscher. In *Radical Son* I describe our first encounter in the living room of Ralph Miliband, where I eagerly presented Deutscher with one of the theses I had advanced (and was most proud of) in *The Free World Colossus*. This was the notion that Russia's possession of nuclear weapons was a principal cause of the Sino-Soviet split. Deutscher was so contemptuous of my idea that he rudely turned his back on me and continued to

---

[4]Ibid.

refuse to speak to me for the rest of our meeting.[5] Once again in the face of clearly available evidence, Brock prefers to make up a version which serves his political purposes.

Brock then devotes several sentences to my involvement with the Black Panther Party, adhering reasonably to the facts as he recounts how I raised money for a school for Panther children and recruited Betty Van Patter (whom the Panthers subsequently murdered) to keep its books. But these facts are only a setup for the sentences that follow, which purport to explain (and denigrate) my political transformation: "Hugh Pearson, author of a history of Huey P. Newton and the Black Panther movement, believed this emotional trauma caused Horowitz to go 'berserk with regard to the left-liberal community.' A few years later, Horowitz re-emerged on the public stage, launching a bitter attack on his former friends and colleagues on the Left and announcing with much fanfare, that he had voted for Ronald Reagan."[6]

This is a falsification on several levels. Hugh Pearson was a left-wing writer for the *San Francisco Weekly*, whom I had met only once for a two-hour interview for his book on the Panthers, and whom I never spoke to again. Pearson is entitled to his off-the-cuff opinion about my psychological state. But the claim that I went "berserk" and launched a "bitter attack" on my former friends is a lie. Betty Van Patter's body was discovered in February 1975. Far from turning in bitterness on my friends (as Brock himself did), I made no political statements at all—let alone statements that could be regarded as attacks on my former friends and allies—for *ten years* after Betty's death, by which time they had pretty well cut me off because of my political second thoughts.[7] The article in which I revealed that I had voted for Ronald Reagan, and to which Brock refers, didn't appear in the *Washington Post*

---

[5] *Radical Son*, David Horowitz, Touchstone, 1998, p 142
[6] David Brock, op. cit., p. 101
[7] An article I wrote about my political doubts was published four years after Betty's death in *The Nation*. The article, "Left Illusions," is reprinted in *My Life and Times*, Volume 1 in this series.

until March 17, 1985 and did not refer to any individual by name. This was the first time I had expressed any conservative thoughts in print since Betty's murder.[8]

The *Post* article, "Lefties for Reagan," was a purely political statement and—unlike Brock's announcement of his own transformation—did not name a single former friend or colleague in its indictment of radical posturing in behalf of Third World revolutionaries and Communists. It could hardly be said to be an expression of personal bitterness, since it was co-authored with another writer, Peter Collier, who had experienced a similar bout of second thoughts. During the ten-year political silence I observed between Betty's murder and the article in the *Post,* I wrote only two political articles, and both were written from a leftist point of view. They appeared in *The Nation* in 1979 and in *Mother Jones* in 1981 because as late as that—six years after Betty's murder—I still wanted to believe that I was part of this "liberal community," which according to Brock I had turned on in sheer derangement. All these facts would have been available to Brock in my autobiography *Radical Son,* but he either didn't bother to check them or didn't care.

"He then wrote a book, *Destructive Generation: Second Thoughts About the Sixties,* which sought to blame contemporary social ills on the 1960s."[9] In fact the book was not about "social ills" but about the Sixties movements themselves, and it was not written by me alone but was co-authored with Peter Collier. We devoted a chapter to the Weather Underground, a chapter to the solidarity movements, a chapter to radical activities in Berkeley, and three chapters to memoirs by Peter and myself about our political transformations. The *gravamen* of our indictment was that our generation of leftists had refused to make an accounting

---

[8]The article, "Goodbye To All That," was co-authored with Peter Collier and is included in *My Life and Times,* Volume 1 in this series.
[9]David Brock, op. cit., p. 101

of what they had done or to concede that they had been wrong. They just moved from one cause to the next without ever looking back.

"In 1987, Horowitz was recruited to do work for the Reagan Administration...."[10] Not exactly. The facts are that Peter and I were asked by the State Department to go on a three-day trip to Nicaragua to share our political views and experiences, as American citizens, with the democratic opposition to the Sandinista dictatorship. This invitation and these experiences are described in *Destructive Generation.* "And he wrote speeches for Bob Dole in the 1988 presidential campaign. So began Horowitz's incendiary second career as a highly paid shock trooper for the Republican Right that would lead to accusations from *Time* columnist Jack E. White that he was a 'real live bigot,' and that would bring him, by 2000, into the circle of Bush advisor Karl Rove."[11]

Where to begin with these smears and misleading snippets of facts? Collier and I did write two or three speeches for Dole, but we weren't paid for them, handsomely or otherwise. I wasn't paid by the Republican Right as a "shock trooper" or anything else. In 1988 I created a 501(c)3 I called "The Center for the Study of Popular Culture," which is now supported by over 30,000 donors, all but a handful of which are individuals. I began receiving a salary from the Center in the early nineties. It is true that Jack White, a racially hostile columnist for *Time,* slandered me *a dozen years later* as a "bigot" for questioning the political efforts of the NAACP to sue gun manufacturers for the homicides committed against young black males (details Brock deliberately omits).[12] But it is also the case that *Time's* editor-in-chief, Walter Isaacson, personally apologized to me for White's unjustified attack and that *Time* subsequently ran a very positive review of my book *Hating*

---

[10]Ibid.
[11]Ibid.
[12]An account of this episode can be found in Volume 6 of this series, *Progressive Racism.*

Whitey & Other Progressive Causes The book contained the *Salon* article that had offended White, which was called, "Guns Don't Kill Blacks, Other Black People Do."[13] *Time*'s reviewer, Lance Morrow, praised *Hating Whitey* as "indignant sanity" and indicated that I would eventually be proved right on the issues and my critics wrong. There is no excuse for Brock's misrepresentation of this incident, since I have described everything that happened in regard to Jack White in detail on the Drudge Report, in *Frontpagemag.com* and in my book *The Art of Political War*. Brock simply ignored these sources because they inconveniently contradicted what he wrote. Finally, I have never for one second been in Karl Rove's "circle" or worked for him in any capacity.

Brock then describes me as "another mouthpiece for the same band of conservative funders—Scaife and Bradley among others—who supported an array of his political projects, mostly under the umbrella of the Los Angeles-based Center for the Study of Popular Culture...."[14] I have received no funding from Scaife and Bradley for "political projects." The laws governing 501(c)3 foundations do not permit funds to be used for partisan political purposes. I did conduct one such project during the 2000 presidential campaign, which I funded entirely through individual donations unconnected to the Center or to Bradley and Scaife. I created a 527(c) "political committee" called PoliticalWar.com (now defunct) to print and distribute two political pamphlets I wrote called *The Art of Political War* and *How to Beat the Democrats*. I received no Bradley or Scaife money for this project. As for my tax-exempt Center, Bradley and Scaife account for less than 10 percent of its budget. The individual donors to the Center disagree among themselves and with me on a host of issues—abortion, gay marriage, free trade and the war in Iraq, to name a few. To say that I am a "mouth-

---

[13]*Hating Whitey and Other Progressive Causes*, David Horowitz, Spence, 1999. The article is included in Volume 6 of this series, *Progressive Racism*.

[14]David Brock, op. cit., pp. 101–102

piece" for Scaife and Bradley is like saying *The Nation* is a mouth-piece for Paul Newman because he contributes money to the magazine, or that Noam Chomsky is a mouthpiece for the Ford Foundation because he spoke at the World Social Forum, which Ford funded. There is no left-wing writer—no political writer generally—whose career is not somewhere or in some way underwritten by other people's money. But facts like these are no obstacle to David Brock's determination to turn me into a hired gun.

Brock's slanders continue: "[Horowitz's] handling of racial issues is more controversial still. Horowitz's book *Hating Whitey*, in which he made controversial claims about the incidence of rape of white women by black men, was rejected by his publisher, the conservative Free Press."[15] This is a nice string of incriminating clauses, all false. In the 290 pages of *Hating Whitey* there is only one sentence about rape of white women by black men. It was inserted to refute an absurd comment by the author bell hooks to the effect that, while whites committed harmful acts against blacks, there was no parallel evidence of black aggression against whites.[16] Rape seemed to me an indisputable act of aggression, which is why I referred to the statistic. The sentence about rape was challenged (on the Internet) by one leftist, and that reference has been indiscriminately used by other leftists against me (which is how it came to be in Brock's account). When I checked my original reference, which was to Dinesh D'Souza's *The End of Racism*, his text did not actually source the statement. So I did some research and produced a second statistic comparable in every way to the first but sourced from U.S. government statistics. I published this on *Frontpagemag.com* as a rejoinder to the critic. In other words, the claim itself is not controversial, as Brock reports, but incontrovertible.

That is only the first misrepresentation in this Brock sentence designed to tar me as a racist even by conservative standards. Mis-

---

[15]David Brock, op. cit., p. 102
[16]*A Killing Rage*, bell hooks, Owl Books, 1995

representation number two is that *Hating Whitey* was rejected by a *"conservative* publisher," namely The Free Press. The Free Press is a subsidiary of Simon & Schuster, hardly a conservative institution. It is true that the Free Press once had a reputation for being a conservative imprint, but this was when it was a division of Macmillan and run by the late Erwin Glikes. By the time I got around to proposing *Hating Whitey* as a project, Macmillan and the Free Press had long since been bought by Viacom, the parent company of Simon & Schuster. At the time *Hating Whitey* was rejected by my editor, Chad Conway—a friend of Brock's and no conservative—the publishing head of the Free Press was a woman who had previously run the very liberal University of California Press (Berkeley).

Finally, the rejection of *Hating Whitey* had absolutely nothing to do with its contents as Brock's sentence is constructed to imply. At the time *Hating Whitey* was rejected, the book had not even been written. The proposal for *Hating Whitey* was rejected because of the *title* I wanted, which was *Hating White People Is a Politically Correct Idea.* "The Free Press will never publish a book with that title," are the exact words Chad Conway used. The book was finally accepted by Tom Spence, the owner of a small conservative press in Dallas, where the title was changed to *Hating Whitey.* In other words, Brock managed to pack three false statements into one sentence in order to create the impression once more that I was a racist.

Brock's contempt for the facts goes well beyond racial issues. "In addition to his role as aging campus agitator and inflamer of racial tensions, Horowitz is a sometime Republican Party strategist...."[17] I am not now and have never been a Republican Party strategist. As a self-employed writer, I did publish the two pamphlets already mentioned, which later became books published by Regnery, along with a newsletter called I called *The War Room,*

---

[17]David Brock, op. cit., p. 103

which offered advice to any Republican who cared to take it. But this is hardly what Brock is claiming in an authoritative declaration: "Along with Myron Magnet of the Manhattan Institute and Newt Gingrich protégé Marvin Olasky, Horowitz became part of a triumvirate of thinkers advising the Bush campaign, and Bush himself, behind the scenes."[18] The facts? I wrote as an outlier about political tactics in exactly two election cycles—the presidential campaign of 2000 and the congressional campaign of 2002—but my advice was never solicited by any candidate, nor was I ever hired as a consultant. I was never an adviser to the Bush campaign; I never participated in a Bush strategy session, and I never spoke to the presidential candidate himself except in reception lines, as an interviewer for *Salon*, and at one private lunch in the governor's mansion before his campaign began. I never gave him advice (except at the lunch) other than was printed in my public newsletters, pamphlets and books (which he most likely never read). I never talked to Olasky or Gingrich about the campaign.

Despite the non-existence of any role as a Republican or Bush adviser, Brock presents me as having orchestrated the Bush campaign: "Everything from the symbolic presence of blacks at the 2000 convention to Bush's claim to be a new kind of conservative seemed to come straight from Horowitz's playbook."[19]

Note the inconsistency of Brock's inventions. It is true that, in my political writings, I urged the Republican Party to be inclusive and to take up the cause of African-Americans who had been left behind, but how does this square with Brock's attempt a few sentences earlier to tar me with the brush of racism? David Brock could care less about being logical or consistent or factually accurate; his agenda is to make me, and conservative intellectuals like me, look toxic. In explaining my support for "compassionate conservatism," for example, Brock says this: "Americans, Horowitz wrote, side with the underdog; so in order to win Republicans

---

[18]Ibid.
[19]Ibid.

were going to have to make it look as though they did, too." I never advised Republicans to *pretend* to care. I proposed that Republicans sponsor a $100 billion voucher program for all the kids in Title I failing schools. I argued at length in my pamphlets that Republican policies are, in fact, better than the policies of the Democrats for minorities, the poor and powerless. The problem was that Republicans identify Democrats, who control every significant inner city in America, as the oppressors of minorities and the poor that they actually are.[20]

"To this end, [Horowitz] suggested the term 'compassionate conservative' as a new branding slogan for the Republican Right." Yet another falsehood. When I first wrote about "compassionate conservatism," it had already been adopted as the slogan of the Bush camp and I took the phrase from them, not the other way around. "But Horowitz himself was not so compassionate, agreeing with Vladimir Lenin's tenet 'not to refute your opponent's argument, but to wipe him from the face of the earth.'"[21] The phrase is taken from *The Art of Political War.* But here are the words that follow it (and Brock omits them): "We do not go as far as Lenin, but destroying an opponent's effectiveness is a fairly common Democratic practice. Personal smears accomplish this, and Democrats are very good at them."[22] Obviously the statement had nothing to do with my compassion or lack thereof, and obviously I was not proposing myself as a re-born Leninist. I was warning Republicans that this is what Democrats do, and that they needed to be prepared for it.

Since Brock's book is about media, he devotes considerable attention to my brief role as a critic of public broadcasting. "Long before he played media strategist to the Bush campaign, Horowitz teamed up with Senator Dole as the architect of an attack on the

---

[20]*How To Beat the Democrats,* David Horowitz, Spence Publ., 2003, pp. 79–86
[21]David Brock, op. cit., p. 103
[22]*The Art of Political War,* David Horowitz, Spence, 2000, p. 24
[23]David Brock, op. cit., p. 103

Public Broadcasting System."[23] What I actually did was to launch a campaign—not an "attack"—to pressure PBS to be more inclusive and fair, and in particular to include some conservative programming as required under the terms of the Public Broadcasting Act of 1967. In particular, I did not call for the defunding of public broadcasting as many conservatives did. I only asked that the system observe the fairness provisions of the Act that created it, and I did this well in advance of any discussions that I had with Senator Dole or his staff about Public Broadcasting. It is a misrepresentation to call these discussions coordinating with the Senator. As majority leader, Dole had agendas with the Senate Democrats, which involved putting holds on their bills in retaliation for the holds they put on his. The authorization bill for public broadcasting was one that he chose for such a hold. My staff provided him with information and the arguments that we had developed for our agendas, which he then used to justify his own. These had little to do with public broadcasting as such. When the procedural battle with the Democrats was over, Dole lifted his hold on the public broadcasting authorization bill without regard for our goals or demands, which had not been met. That is the long and short of it.

By employing reckless innuendo to create a chain of guilt-by-association, Brock makes my very public, modest and moderate campaign sound like a racist Republican cabal: "In 1970, Dole had become a Nixon favorite after telling the President that his nominee for the Supreme Court, G. Harrold Carswell, who was rejected by the Senate because of his history as a racist, instead had been done in by the 'liberal media.' Horowitz, too, received praise from Nixon in the form of a fan letter he displayed on the office wall of the Center for the Study of Popular Culture."[24] The fan letter from Nixon had nothing to do with public broadcasting but was written after the appearance of the *Washington Post* article Peter Collier and I wrote in 1985, years before I embarked on my PBS campaign.

---

[24]David Brock, op. cit., p. 104

It was one of many that Nixon wrote to his former critics after his resignation, and had nothing to do with his appointment of Carswell, which took place when I was still on the left.

Brock's conspiracy saga continues: "In 1988, while advising the contras at the behest of Reagan State Department official and future Iran-*Contra* scandal figure, Elliott Abrams, Horowitz founded the Committee on Media Integrity (*COMINT*) to monitor PBS programming...."[25] Brock is here referring to a three-day trip Peter Collier and I made to Nicaragua at the request of the State Department to meet a broad spectrum of Nicaraguan political figures, including a socialist leader who supported the Sandinistas. The one group Collier and I *never* met with in our three days in Nicaragua or at any other time was the *contras*. But Brock's tale requires this fantasy in order to forge a sinister link in its conspiracy chain: "One of the first subjects *COMINT* tackled was a PBS *Frontline* episode on the Iran-*Contra* affair that Horowitz found displeasing. After Horowitz made a stink, PBS aired a pro-*contra* broadcast "Nicaragua Was Our Home," funded by a Moonie group called CAUSA, which raised money for the *contras* after Congress terminated funding."[26]

The program I responded to on the Iran-*Contra* affair was a *Frontline* segment by Bill Moyers and was called "High Crimes and Misdemeanors," basically accusing Reagan of treason. PBS actually ran two Moyers specials on Iran-*Contra* and no defense of Reagan, which was the basis of my complaint. The Public Broadcasting Act of 1967, under which PBS operates, requires that all current affairs programming must be "fair, objective and strictly balanced." My campaign consisted of suggesting that PBS should honor that clause of its authorizing legislation by creating an alternative series to the *Frontline* shows that might provide, for example, a case for the other side. I had nothing to do with the PBS decision to run the CAUSA program, never pushed it, never talked

---

[25]Ibid.
[26]Ibid.

to its sponsors, was not aware of it in advance of its airing and never saw the program itself. So much, once again, for Brock's respect for the facts.

But the plot continues to thicken: "In a microcosm of the over-all right-wing media strategy, the same group of conservative funders now underwrote a two-track strategy to move PBS to the right: threatening PBS funding and seeking to stigmatize as biased and censor programming it did not approve of.... The coordinated campaign against PBS drew together all four right-wing media monitoring groups—[Reed] Irvine, the Lichters, [Brent] Bozell and Horowitz...."[27] This is more Brock fantasy. I never had any conversations with Bozell or the Lichters or Reed Irvine about any strategy involving PBS. Moreover, I never called for the censoring or removal of *any* PBS program. In fact, the only group I actually joined forces with in my PBS battles was a coalition of left-wing filmmakers seeking to get their documentary series on the air. I presented their case in a meeting I had with Jennifer Lawson, then President of PBS. I even publicly supported their demand for a program hosted by Noam Chomsky. I did this in an effort to demonstrate my commitment to fairness and intellectual diversity on public television, which is the very opposite of what Brock describes me as doing. My entire effort was to promote inclusion by PBS, not to remove left-wing programming, however offensive to conservative sensibilities. None of this is a secret. In addition to publishing a quarterly magazine about PBS for four years, my Center has published an entire book of writings by myself and my associates, called *Public Broadcasting and the Public Trust*. The articles in this book make crystal clear that it was never my agenda to "move PBS to the right" by de-funding and privatizing it, but merely to make its programming inclusive of other views, as its public mandate required. For two years, I even hosted a show called "Second Thoughts" on public radio station KCRW in Los Angeles and went on air to raise money to support the station.

---

[27]Ibid.

Although a glance at my writings—not to mention my public broadcasting history—would show my support for the public broadcasting medium and its continued government funding, Brock exhibits no awareness of these facts, which are all part of the public record. Instead, he describes me as the architect of a coordinated right-wing plan to take PBS away from the public and put it under right-wing corporate control. "Instigated by Horowitz, congressional hearings on 'balance' at PBS were convened. Big Bird from "Sesame Street" came under attack; and funding was cut, although the bid to privatize PBS foundered."[28] These are more Brock fantasies. I instigated no hearings. There were indeed hearings, but I had nothing to do with them. They were held not because of the lack of programming diversity or balance at PBS, but because there was a budget crunch and shows like "Barney" and "Sesame Street" had become billion-dollar businesses which were not returning money to the system that had made their investors rich. The "bid to privatize PBS" came from Speaker Newt Gingrich. I was frankly disturbed by his proposal because I knew it would fail and in doing so derail my agendas. When it did fail, I closed up my shop and terminated the publication of my magazine about public broadcasting.

Brock's reckless disregard for the facts, which usually serves his ideological agendas, has also led him to understate my role in a project to provide an alternative to *Frontline*. "Another series, originally called 'Reverse Angle' was a heavily subsidized collaboration between two conservative columnists, Fred Barnes and Mort Kondracke, and Lionel Chetwynd, a conservative Hollywood producer and co-founder of the Wednesday Morning Group. Horowitz was hired as a consultant."[29] In fact, the Reverse Angle series was not "heavily subsidized" but entirely funded by the Corporation for Public Broadcasting. It was also entirely my idea, although the name itself was Chetwynd's suggestion. The idea for

---

[28]David Brock, op. cit., p. 104
[29]Ibid.

the Reverse Angle series was a natural outgrowth of my campaign to promote diversity in public television and I approached Chetwynd to help me realize it, introducing him to Barnes and Kondracke, whom I already knew. Since "Reverse Angle" was funded through the Center for the Study of Popular Culture of which I was president, it is hard to see how Chetwynd, Barnes and Kondracke could "hire" me. Nor did I ever receive a dime for my efforts. "The Wednesday Morning Group" to which Brock refers is actually the Wednesday Morning Club; and while Chetwynd contributed the name, it is a program of my Center, which funds it and runs its programs. Chetwynd has never had a position or played a role in the Center.

Brock describes one of the hosts of the series (which was later called "National Desk") as "a right-wing African-American radio talk show host who almost lost his show owing to charges of racism until Horowitz raised $500,000 for a campaign to keep him on the air."[30] These claims, as usual, are grossly inaccurate. The talk show host, Larry Elder, was a libertarian opposed to welfare dependency and to racial preferences. He was the target of a boycott by black extremists, who didn't like the fact that as a black man he wasn't a leftist, and who regarded opposition to welfare dependency and race preference as—racist. The president of KABC didn't like Larry, apart from the boycott which played into her hands; she cut his on air hours in half and told him his days were numbered. I raised $300,000 to put a series of ads on local television to promote his show and to defend him as an important on-air voice. The campaign was successful, raising his ratings 30 percent; Larry's hours were restored and Disney fired the president who had been gunning for him.[31]

On another front, Brock writes: "Leaders of right-wing organizations appear to buy their own books in bulk and give them away. For example, in December 2003, David Horowitz's Scaife-funded

---

[30]David Brock, op. cit., p. 108
[31]His popular show is still on the air nearly fifteen years later.

Center for the Study of Popular Culture was offering free copies of his book *Left Illusions* for those who contributed $50 to his Frontpagemag.com."[32] My Center is not a Scaife operation; a book is not exactly given away if you get $50 in return; and as the author of the donated book I was making a contribution of my royalty to the Center in the process.

The foregoing reviews almost every specific statement Brock made about me in *The Republican Noise Machine*. On the evidence presented above, probably 95 percent of what Brock said about me is false; either cynically misrepresented, or so sloppily reported as to give an entirely erroneous impression, or simply made up. Nor is there anything unique in Brock's distortion of my career as opposed to the distortions in his accounts of other conservatives and conservative institutions. It is just the Brock method at work.

I have gone through this somewhat tedious point-by-point account because David Brock has become a major player in Democratic Party circles as the head of a website called Media Matters for America, which describes itself as a "progressive research and information center dedicated to comprehensively monitoring, analyzing, and correcting conservative misinformation in the U.S. media."[33] In fact Media Matters is a left-wing attack site dedicated to smearing conservatives using the same methods on display in Brock's attack on me. The initial budget for Brock's site was $8.5 million (several million dollars larger than mine, for example, after 16 years). The money was raised with the help of billionaire George Soros, the Clintons and other Democratic Party heavyweights. Its product is exactly what one would expect from a compulsive liar who has made a career out of sleaze, the betrayal of friends, an alarming lack of scruples and a generally contemptuous attitude towards the truth.

---

[32]David Brock, op. cit., p. 359
[33]http://mediamatters.org/about

PART III

Sexual Politics

Origins of a Political Epidemic
(co-authored with Peter Collier)

[This article appeared just as the AIDS epidemic was about to break out of the three gay communities –San Francisco, Los Angeles, and New York—in which it had taken root. HIV had not yet been isolated and identified as a cause, and there were 3,000 confirmed AIDS cases nationwide compared to a cumulative total of over 1.8 million today. What are now irrefutable facts regarding the spread of AIDS were condemned by gay activists as homophobic prejudice at the time, and to a large extent still are. California Magazine *was picketed by gay activists when it published this article.]*

Liberty Baths may have the look of a sexual YMCA—showers and a sauna, hair dryers, Coke machines, and gay men cruising the halls with towels wrapped around their waists—but it is actually part of a medical and political controversy over a sexually transmitted disease that is tearing San Francisco apart. In the basement are scores of private rooms with muffled sounds of ecstasy coming from behind closed doors. One door is open, and an unclothed man lies face down on a cot

---

This article first appeared in *California Magazine,* July 1983, under the title "Whitewash," and was reprinted in Peter Collier and David Horowitz, *Deconstructing the Left* (1995). It is based on personal interviews with the people involved. We were alerted to the story and guided to sources like Catherine Cusic by Randy Shilts, who alerted us to this story while explaining he could not do it himself because his sources would be cut off. Four years later, Randy completed and published *And the Band Played On,* a definitive history of the epidemic. He died of AIDS on February 17, 1994.

presenting himself seductively to anyone who might happen by. On the top floor is a carpeted viewing room where naked men watch gay porn on a movie screen while idly fondling each other. Down the hall a middle-aged man stands at one of the stalls that have "glory holes" cut in at waist level while a faceless stranger on the other side of the partition performs *fellatio* on him.

The only place where there seems to be conversation is at the lunch counter, where two naked men are munching on hamburgers and talking about the AIDS epidemic that has begun to terrify the city. "I could get back into the closet right now," says one of the men, "and still get it in a year or so. So what would I have achieved? Celibacy?" The other nods enthusiastically. "I know," he says. "We're just little time bombs, aren't we?" Then he stands, stretches, and wipes his mouth with a napkin. "Well, I don't know about you, but I'm going to have some fun while I tick." After they have gone, the short-order cook shakes his head. "Did you hear that? It's like some straight joke about queers."

The humor has gotten grimmer in San Francisco. ("How does Anita Bryant spell relief?" goes one of the sicker jokes. "A-I-D-S.") And beneath this brittle bravado, the city exhibits the signs of profound anxiety and turmoil. Police requisition latex masks and surgical gloves when they have to deal with gays; gay landlords evict tenants who show the telltale purple lesions of Kaposi's Sarcoma, a rare skin cancer associated with AIDS; patrons worry about frequenting the city's restaurants, where many of the service workers are gay; health workers who do not hesitate to deal with most grotesque street maladies treat hospitalized AIDS patients like lepers, shunting them off in remote rooms and sometimes allowing call buttons to go unanswered.

It might be expected that the very organized and most powerful gay political machine in the country would have been able to deal with this situation. And in a limited way it has. Led by San Francisco's only gay supervisor, Harry Britt, and supported by Mayor Dianne Feinstein, the San Francisco Board of Supervisors appropriated $4 million for the present fiscal year to combat AIDS, and the congressional offices of the late Phillip Burton (Democrat, San Francisco) and Barbara Boxer (Democrat, Marin County) have rigorously lobbied Washington for more money. But, for the most part, gay leaders have resolutely, and astonishingly, refused to speak out on the basic issue of AIDS, specifically the medical consensus that it is contracted and spread through sexual contact, and they have failed to demand the prophylactic measures that could help contain the disease.

Recognizing this as an issue that could derail the gays' political momentum and prevent their taking control of the board of supervisors within the next decade, gay leaders have made the matter of AIDS transmission into a dirty little secret. As a result of their influence, until May of this year there was not a single piece of health-department literature in the city's health clinics to inform their high-risk clientele of the fact that AIDS is transmitted through blood and semen. Public health officials have suppressed information about the extent of the epidemic. Attempts to close places such as the gay baths, where the anonymous public sex implicated in the spread of the disease takes place, have been preemptively crushed. And those gay public figures who have tried to provoke a discussion of the issue have often felt pressure and intimidation.

Catherine Cusic is a lesbian who heads the Gay/Lesbian Health Services Committee of the Harvey Milk Gay Democratic Club's AIDS Task Force. She is outraged by the dereliction of the gay leadership. "It is a pattern that goes back to the first appearance of AIDS," she says. "There are leaders in this community who don't want people to know the truth. Their attitude is that it is bad for business, bad for the gay image. Hundreds, perhaps thousands, are going to die because of this attitude. The whole thing borders on the homicidal."

As the medical community has worked to isolate and identify the virus it now feels certain is the cause of AIDS, there has been a parallel struggle to define the disease socially. Some of the most violent talk has come from Christian fundamentalists, who compare

AIDS to a biblical plague, and from secular moralists, who use the ready-made metaphor of Mother Nature finally striking back at transgressors against her laws. Gays, too, have been guilty of rhetorical excess. This may be understandable, given the history of discrimination and oppression from which they have so recently emerged. Carelessly using terms such as "genocide" and "holocaust," they view the slow progress of medical research as evidence of homophobia and compare it with the quick response to Legionnaires' disease and toxic shock syndrome. The AIDS virus just happens to have struck the gay community first, they say, and could just as easily have had its malignant genesis in the heterosexual world.

In fact, the federal health bureaucracy has reacted forthrightly, if not especially swiftly, as AIDS has attained the critical mass necessary to make it a significant national health issue. Dr. Edward Brandt, assistant secretary of the U.S. Health and Human Services Department, has identified the disease as the "number-one priority" for the U.S. Public Health Service. In May, Congress moved to appropriate $12 million to fight the epidemic, which would bring the total federal expenditures to $26 million—considerably more than was spent battling either Legionnaires' disease or toxic shock syndrome over a longer period of time.

Gay leaders have reacted by charging that this money represents the tardy cynicism of a society worried that AIDS will jump the boundaries of the gay world and become a general menace. In fact, the disease has affected three narrowly defined high-risk groups in addition to bisexuals and gays with multiple partners: drug addicts, hemophiliacs, and Haitians. Moreover, while heterosexuals have been affected, there has often been a link to homosexuality: Drug users sometimes share needles with gays; hemophiliacs receive blood from gay donors; and, according to Haitian officials, more than 30 percent of the victims in that country are homosexuals. In California, particularly, the epidemic has imploded on gays, who constitute at least 90 percent of AIDS victims. Because the disease is communicable, spreading as a result of sexual contact, the only way in which the analogy with Legionnaires' disease or toxic shock syndrome would hold is if the Legionnaires had insisted on returning to the hotel where they contracted their malady, or if women had continued to use the dangerous tampons.

Columnist Herb Caen was one of the first to alert San Francisco to the confusion and schisms within the gay community. In late May he reported in the *San Francisco Chronicle* that a gay doctor had run into three of his AIDS patients in one of the baths and ordered them out, only to have them refuse to leave and threaten to sue him for breach of confidentiality. But the gay community's ambivalence in facing up to the disease is nothing new. Several months ago, Catherine Cusic asked the city's public health department to put up posters about AIDS on buses and in other public places. The suggestion was presented to Pat Norman, a lesbian who coordinates the city's lesbian/gay health services, but no action was taken. Since then, while more and more gays have contracted AIDS, the department has maintained a curiously uninvolved stance. Most public health experts, including gays, have come to the conclusion that the disease is sexually transmitted and that unprotected anal intercourse significantly increases the risk. "The agent is probably a blood-borne virus in many ways similar to hepatitis B, which can be transmitted by direct inoculation of blood and through intimate sexual contact . . . where bleeding takes place," said Dr. Marcus Conant, who works with the gay-run Kaposi's Sarcoma/AIDS Foundation, at a recent city sponsored AIDS symposium. However, in a pamphlet prepared by the foundation and distributed by the city, references to anal sex or any sex connected with trauma were omitted.

Cusic and other members of her committee have come to regard all this as a "conspiracy of silence," although at times it seems more to resemble a campaign of disinformation with clear political overtones. They point out that Pat Norman, and the gay health activists who support her in the moderate Alice B. Toklas Memorial Democratic Club, have ties to the mayor's office and to political patronage. And the Toklas club apparently fears that taking a stand on the issue of the transmission of AIDS will cause a backlash against the city's institutionalized gay lifestyle and against gay businesses, which have become an important aspect of San Francisco's economy. When the Harvey Milk Club recently joined a recall campaign against Mayor Feinstein, the Toklas Club backed the mayor (who herself worried that the AIDS scare might keep the city from becoming a site for the 1984 Democratic Convention).

The politics involved in AIDS are not only intramural and civic but sexual as well. The philosophy of the Stonewall Gay Democratic Club is "Sex doesn't cause AIDS, a virus does." This has become the rallying cry of gays who fear the hidden message inherent in acknowledging that the disease is sexually transmitted: Physician, heal thyself. In the words of one gay leader, "[People] worried that if they admitted the disease was spread sexually, everything that had been said about their lifestyle would seem true. They just wouldn't admit it, whatever the evidence."

The extent of this willingness to suppress information became clear earlier this year. Andrew Moss and Michael Gorman, two researchers at UC San Francisco Medical Center, completed a study showing that 1 of every 333 single men in the Castro area (including Noe Valley and the Haight) had already been diagnosed as having AIDS. On January 16 and on several occasions over the following weeks, Moss and Gorman met with gay health activists from the Kaposi Sarcoma/AIDS Foundation, the Bay Area Physicians for Human Rights, the three gay Democratic clubs, and public health officials to discuss their findings. Despite some dissent, however, the consensus at these meetings was against making the Moss-Gorman figures public, lest they be "misinterpreted."

At a meeting in early March to draft a statement on AIDS for the Lesbian/Gay Freedom Day Parade, Bill Kraus, an aide to the late Congressman Phil Burton, and Dana Van Gorder of Supervisor Britt's office, strongly urged inclusion of the Moss-Gorman findings. Their proposal was defeated by Pat Norman and the other committee members, and the report languished until later that month, when it was leaked to Randy Shilts, a reporter on the *Chronicle*'s gay beat. Public health director Mervyn Silverman now says, "It didn't tell us anything we didn't already know." But he admits that he never saw the study, which was held back by health department officials. "There was never a decision that it should not be put out," Norman says, "but a question as to what context it should be put out in." Dr. Selma Dritz, assistant director of the health department's communicable disease division and a collaborator on the report, did not push the study either. She says the decision of whether or not to publish was up to Moss and Gorman.

Explaining his decision to publish the report, Shilts, who is gay, says, "The people in the Castro had a right to know this. If they're tricking in the bars, they've got a real good chance of tricking with somebody who has the disease. I got a call from Gorman, telling me not to print the information. Gay political leaders called, including Randy Stallings [president of the Toklas club and co-chair with Norman of the Coalition for Human Rights, the umbrella organization for all the gay groups in San Francisco]. In eight years as a journalist, I've never been under such pressure to suppress a story. People kept telling me it would hurt business in the Castro, hurt the gay rights bill in Sacramento. My feeling is, what the hell, if you're dead, what does the rest of it matter?"

Other gay leaders, who had been pushing to get the conclusions of the Moss-Gorman study publicized and acted upon, also found themselves under pressure. One of them was Kraus. "I kept saying that people have a right to know this," he observes. "Those who wanted to keep the report under wraps said that if it got out, people would be afraid to come to the Castro, that AIDS patients would be thrown out of restaurants and all that. I went through an agonizing period saying to myself, 'What the hell is going on here? How can these people do this? How can they try to suppress this data?' It's still not entirely clear to me why they did it, but I do know how. They intimidate people into silence by saying that they're homophobic, anti-sex, and all kinds of other things people don't want to be called." [Kraus was diagnosed with AIDs a little over a year after this article appeared. He died a year and a half later.]

Ironically, during the time that this debate was going on, 68 new cases of AIDS were reported. The connection between promiscuous sex and AIDS was by now so obvious to some gays that they had started masturbation clubs, were seeking more stable relationships, and had begun to criticize those who were spreading the disease. "We Know Who We Are," an article by Michael Callen and Richard Berkowitz, two gays who have AIDS, was circulating in something like *samizdat* form before finally being printed by the Sacramento gay newspaper *Mom ... Guess What!* They cited medical evidence that gays are particularly susceptible to the disease because of repeated shocks to their immune systems caused by treatment for other sexually transmitted diseases and concluded that gays must take personal responsibility for their condition. "The present epidemic of AIDS among promiscuous urban gay males is occurring because of the unprecedented promiscuity of the last ten to fifteen years," they wrote. "The commercialization of promiscuity and the explosion of establishments such as bathhouses, bookstores, and back rooms is unique in Western history. It has been mass participation in this lifestyle that has led to the creation of an increasingly disease-polluted pool of sexual partners."

Yet, while there were individual efforts to try to control the disease, there was not enough support to make it a majority movement. In a study conducted early this year, three gay psychotherapists, Leon McKusick, William Horstman, and Arthur Carfagni, compiled questionnaire responses from 600 gay men and concluded that, while fears about AIDS were increasing and some modification of sexual activity had occurred, an alarming number of men were still engaging in high-risk behavior. An article about this study in the *Bay Area Reporter*, a leading gay paper, said that a large proportion of those interviewed were "continuing to engage in behavior that could transmit an AIDS infective agent and at the same frequency as before they found out about AIDS." Perhaps most devastating of all was the finding that "the gay men surveyed are still poorly informed about the disease transmission or are unwilling or unable to change sexual patterns."

The Lesbian/Gay Freedom Day march, scheduled for June 26, presented an opportunity for some remedial education, but also for disaster. An estimated 300,000 gays from all over the United States would be coming to San Francisco and could spread the disease to uninfected gay communities throughout the country, especially if they patronized the city's bathhouses, which feature precisely the kind of sex most likely to spread AIDS. On May 24, the Harvey Milk Club met and finally voted 80-1 to put out a pamphlet warning of the sexual transmission of the disease. Members of the club, among them congressional aide Bill Kraus, also joined with other concerned gay leaders to try to persuade bathhouse owners to dispense condoms and post warnings that oral and anal sex greatly increase the chances of contracting the disease. Kraus recalls that "not only were the bathhouse owners totally incensed that we'd suggest that they do something, but the Toklas Club made a statement saying that what we were proposing did not represent their policy. We wound up on the defensive, spending our time explaining how 'we weren't really breaking ranks, et cetera, et cetera.'"

In desperation, Kraus joined with Cleve Jones, a gay aide to San Francisco assemblyman Art Agnos, and with Ron Huberman of the Harvey Milk club, and wrote a manifesto that was printed (after editor Paul Lorch had sat on it for six weeks) in the *Bay Area Reporter.* "What a peculiar perversion it is of gay liberation to ignore the overwhelming scientific evidence, to keep quiet, to deny the obvious when the lives of gay men are at stake," they wrote. "What a strange concept of our gay movement it is to care more about what they may do to us than about the need to spread the news about this disease to our people so that we can protect each other." The letter convinced Supervisor Harry Britt to take a stand on the bathhouse issue. "I didn't think he'd have the guts to do it," says Randy Shilts. "But after Kraus, Jones and Huberman published their letter, he finally saw that this was the side to be on and said in effect that we can't keep on humping like bunnies."

Others, however, saw the letter as treason to the gay cause. With the sophistry that was coming to dominate the debate, Toklas Club president Randy Stallings wrote in a letter in the *Bay Area Reporter:* "No one knows what causes AIDS or how it is transmitted, but one thing is certain. If this illness is sexually transmitted, it can be transmitted from someone met in church as easily as someone met at a bathhouse. To single out one type of gay business as somehow 'responsible' for the epidemic is to begin the process of destroying our community.... Labeling San Francisco as unsafe for our people is inaccurate and a direct attack on the social and economic viability of our community." [Randy Stallings died of AIDS in 1991.]

But others tried to get Health Director Mervyn Silverman to close the bathhouses for the parade weekend. The public-health director's response was: "It is not the bathhouses that are the problem, it's sex. People who want to have sex will find a way to have it." Shilts points out the consequences of such logic: "If one guy has sex with ten guys in a night—and some do—the risk becomes 1 in 33 for this guy. And he can take his dormant case of AIDS back to Iowa or wherever and start it going there." And Shilts sees an ultimate irony in all this: "People organizing the march want large numbers so they can have a show of force to press the federal government on AIDS research."

Shilts got so upset by the posturing and procrastination that he spent a day lobbying the board of supervisors and the mayor, eventually securing a commitment that literature specifying the risks of bathhouse sex would be distributed to patrons. At first Silverman denied that he had the authority to enforce such a request. However, Mayor Feinstein (who was on the verge of signing sweeping legislation regulating smoking in the workplace) quoted to him the article of the city code giving him the power to act. Finally Silverman met with bathhouse owners in a new mood of realism. "Their businesses are likely to be affected if people keep dying from this damned thing," he said. "It is in everybody's interest—through altruism and humanitarianism, but also capitalism—to get this thing taken care of."

Privately, many gay spokesmen claim that they would like to see the bathhouses closed altogether. They worry about the conclusion that can be drawn from the spread of AIDS—that homosexuality can be hazardous to one's health. But some activists insist that the bathhouses must be defended precisely because they are the center of the most extreme form of public gay sexual behavior. And so the bathhouses have become a perverse and inchoate symbol of gay liberation itself.

Lesbian/Gay Freedom Parade co-chairman Konstantin Berlandt is a former editor of UC Berkeley's *Daily Californian* and antiwar activist. He sees the proposals to close the bathhouses as "genocidal" and compares them to the order requiring homosexuals to wear triangular pink shirt patches in Nazi Germany. Berlandt wrote a *Bay Area Reporter* account of the first closed meeting of concerned gays and bathhouse owners, which was widely credited with torpedoing the effort to get them to inform patrons that they were at risk. "We fought Anita Bryant and John Briggs [anti-homosexual crusaders], and we'll fight against AIDS. Every time the community has been attacked the parades have been larger," he says, defending his opposition to the warning. "You have a situation where institutions that have fought against sexual repression for years are being attacked under the guise of medical strategy." Despite mounting medical evidence, Berlandt believes that transmission of the disease via bodily fluids is nothing more than a "theory" being used to attack the gay lifestyle. "I haven't stopped having sex," he says. "I feel that what we're being advised to do involves all the things I became gay to get away from—wear a condom, that sort of thing. So we have a disease for which supposedly the cure is to go back to all the styles that were preached at us in the first place. It will take a lot more evidence before I'm about to do that." [Konstantin Berlandt died of AIDS in 1991.]

For gays who have worked hard and, so far, unsuccessfully to get the community to face up to the consequences of AIDS, to its symbolism and its reality, such a statement represents denial at an elemental level. It is an inability to admit the magnitude of what is unfolding and an inability to accept responsibility for the role that personal excess has played in this health crisis. It also represents a mentality that insists on making a political and ideological argument out of what remains, above all, a personal tragedy.

Catherine Cusic, in addition to working with the Harvey Milk Club's health services committee, is a respiratory therapist at San Francisco General Hospital. What she sees there in the intensive-care unit gives her a perspective that gay politicians and ideologues do not have. "It's my job to take care of patients unable to breathe on their own, without the help of a machine, in other words, the dying AIDS patients," she says. "You see these young people come in and die so quickly and in such agony. Their family comes in and watches. It's terrible when parents outlive their children. In some sense what I witness is political for me. I say to myself, 'We're queers. They don't care about us. They're glad we're dying.' But it's also personal. I watch these young men die. Their mothers start to cry. Their lovers have been sitting in the room, smiling and smiling, and then I see them at the elevator just standing and sobbing. It's horrible. And it's a horrible death. The patients waste away until they look like Dachau victims in the end. I see all this happen, and I have to admit that some of those responsible are gay leaders. In my mind they're criminally negligent. They've betrayed their own community."

2

Homo-McCarthyism

You've got to be careful what you say in Hollywood these days. In fact, you don't even have to say it in Hollywood to get into trouble. Mel Gibson recently gave an interview to the Spanish newspaper *El País* and by the time it was over there was an asterisk after his name. "He was asked about his apparent concern when he was first becoming an actor that people might think he was gay," says Richard Jennings, board member and spokesman of the Los Angeles chapter of the Gay and Lesbian Alliance Against Defamation (GLAAD). "And he pointed to his rear end and said, 'This is only for sh—ing. How could people think I'm gay? I don't talk that way. I don't look that way.'" To top it off, Gibson said he didn't think women had a right to an abortion; then, when gays protested his "ignorance and homophobia," instead of apologizing, he complained on *Good Morning America* that the protestors "were interfering with his right to hold an opinion."

Prior to Gibson's comments, says Jennings, the star had been popular in the gay community, but all that is in doubt now, especially since Gibson has not yet signed on with "Hollywood Supports," the anti-homophobia and anti-AIDS discrimination movie industry organization which was founded and funded last September

First published in the April 1992 issue of *Heterodoxy Magazine,* this article is based on interviews with Richard Jennings, Chris Fowler and others. http://www.discoverthenetworks.org/Articles/1992%20April%20Vol%2 01,%20No.pdf

by Fox chairman Barry Diller and MCA president Sid Sheinberg, and which Jennings now heads. When one considers that the organization is backed by the heads of all the major studios, the networks, the Motion Picture Association and such heavyweights as Norman Lear, Barbra Streisand, Billy Crystal, Kevin Costner, Sylvester Stallone, Goldie Hawn, David Geffen, Peter Guber, Spike Lee, Jack Nicholson, Brandon Tartikoff and Michael Ovitz, it is no wonder that Richard Jennings comments ominously: "I think Mel Gibson is going to find himself fairly isolated in Hollywood if he continues to espouse anti-gay views."

If this were an isolated incident, it would be no more than a gossip-column item. But it is not. Mel Gibson isn't the only one to have crossed the invisible, but clearly perilous, line which GLAAD has drawn in its increasingly effective attempt to censor what it regards as unacceptable viewpoints. Other recent offenders include:

- Joseph Epstein, editor of *The American Scholar,* for using the word "homosexual" instead of "lesbian" or "gay" which, in GLAAD's view, is a continuing "affront" to the homosexual community.
- *Silence of the Lambs* for featuring a killer who owns a white poodle, speaks in an affected voice, wears women's clothing and sports a nipple ring.
- Norman Lear (the epitome of otherwise politically correct views) for trying to "de-lesbianize" the two young heroines of *Fried Green Tomatoes.* After complaints from GLAAD, the heroines were re-lesbianized and the film was given GLAAD's Media Award for Outstanding Depiction of Lesbians.
- Pat Buchanan, who ridiculed New York mayor David Dinkins for "prancing with sodomites" in the St Patrick's Day parade.
- Paul Verhoeven for his upcoming psycho-thriller *Basic Instinct,* a film about three murderous man-hating women, one of whom is bisexual and the other two lesbian. "That is what is so appalling," says GLAAD acting director Christopher Fowler.

"There is one lesbian serial killer known to exist in all of crime reporting in the United States and there are three of them in this film."

- PBS executives for previewing and then withdrawing an anti-Catholic film called *Stop the Church*, which featured ACT UP activists invading a worship at St. Patrick's Cathedral, desecrating the Host and denouncing Cardinal John J. O'Connor as a murderer. GLAAD turned out its troops in defense of the film.
- Oliver Stone for portraying New Orleans businessman Clay Shaw as a swishy, decadent masochist in *JFK*. (This portrayal, as one critic has noted, "is one of the few truthful things in the film.")

GLAAD's newsletter complains, "Not only is every gay male portrayed as the requisite sadist, child molester and/or transvestite, but in this film gays also got credit for murdering President Kennedy." GLAAD, which acquired a shooting script, met with Stone during the early stages of *JFK*. According to Jennings, Stone had originally planned to include a "seamy," "gratuitous" public toilet scene showing an attempted frame-up of Jim Garrison for allegedly soliciting sex, but Stone voluntarily cut that scene before meeting with GLAAD representatives and shortened the sado-masochistic sex scenes with Clay Shaw to brief flashes. He also assured Jennings that he understood GLAAD's concerns and joined Hollywood Supports. Even so, the leading gay paper, *The Advocate*, tore into *JFK*, calling it "the most homophobic movie in the history of Hollywood."

Although GLAAD has not yet put together an apparatus like that of the Hollywood McCarthyites in their heyday 45 years ago, it has been able to make its presence felt because its seven thousand supporters help monitor radio, television and print, and because of tips it receives from friends inside the film industry, many of whom are well-placed and well-informed. Thus the organization runs special programs, with its $230,000 operating budget, to "sensitize" the creative staffs at key media and entertainment organizations. In its media work, GLAAD concentrates as much on correct language as on what it considers incorrect portrayals. When writing about gays, Richard Jennings suggests that reporters use "'sexual orientation' instead of 'sexual preference,' as used by the far right to suggest that homosexuality is just a whim, whereas most of us feel we never had a choice." Yet some leftists beg to differ. According to Michigan law professor Catharine MacKinnon, a champion of political correctness, "sexual preference" is the favored term of radical lesbians because it is "a positive affirmation of women's choice to love women."

According to GLAAD's guidelines, reporters should avoid the phrase "innocent victim" in stories regarding AIDS (as for instance regarding a child that contracted the virus through transfusions). Such usage implies that there are such things as "guilty victims," says Fowler, and places what GLAAD calls an unacceptable "value judgment on sexual behavior." By the same token, there is also no such thing as an "avowed homosexual," says Jennings. "We don't take vows." The preferred usage is simply to note that the person is "openly gay or lesbian." When writing obituaries, the GLAAD media guide suggests, reporters should be sure to include the name of a gay man's lover and to avoid the use of the phrase "gay lifestyle," a term invented by the gay liberation movement in the early 70s to defuse the stigma of homosexuality, but now no longer politically correct. Being gay, the guide asserts, is not a lifestyle—it is a sexual orientation. Reporters should also avoid referring to men who have sexual intercourse with boys as homosexuals; they are pedophiles. Finally, reporters should understand that, while sexual relations between adults and children are universally condemned, sexual relations between adult males and boys over 14, are considered in many societies to fall into "a grayer zone."

As a way of spreading its message, GLAAD gives awards to reporters who take an especially correct approach, and meets with editors and station managers to complain about reporters who do not. It has a quick-reaction phone tree to deluge stations, studios or papers that commit what the organization regards as a particularly egregious offense. "It is very effective when hundreds of calls are received quickly," the GLAAD newsletter says. To reach young reporters early in their careers, every year GLAAD speaks to journalism classes at around 25 local colleges and universities, and additionally schedules outreach programs for high schools. "We call it Homosexuality 101," says Fowler. The hope is that the media will so internalize GLAAD's concerns that, when an issue involving homosexuals arises, reporters will either immediately ask for input from the homosexuals on their own staff or simply contact GLAAD for guidance. About a dozen times a day, irate gay and lesbian callers phone GLAAD's media-monitor hotline to complain about something they have just seen, heard, or read. At this point GLAAD springs into action, demanding meetings with writers, directors, producers, editors, reporters and station managers, staging letter-writing campaigns, holding sensitivity training sessions with staffs, and, if all this doesn't work, alerting the activist groups who specialize in public harassments of political enemies: Queer Nation and ACT UP. There are also persistent rumors that GLAAD has on occasion threatened to "out" studio executives who are not proving cooperative. In a recent issue, the GLAAD newsletter quoted Alex Cockburn's recommendation that the test of outing should be whether "the person benefitted from being in the closet in careerist terms."

These tactics have worked. During the past year, GLAAD has solidified its position as a significant player in Hollywood. Sympathetic insiders now anonymously send GLAAD copies of scripts they consider offensive and tell of meetings about projects touching on homosexuality. In other cases, people with potentially sensitive projects are practicing self-censorship by voluntarily coming to GLAAD for a script review that they hope will gain an imprimatur marking their project as accurately reflecting the organization's view of what is good for the gay and lesbian community. Warner Brothers, for example, had a film in development called *Sessions*, which was about a lesbian psychiatrist who hunted down anyone interested in the younger woman for whom she served as mentor. "Some people in Warner Brothers had a problem with the script," says Richard Jennings. "We joined our voices with theirs ... and Warner Brothers ended up dumping the script. Our understanding is the writer, who ended up shopping the script to another studio, changed the therapist to a man."

When subtle pressures fail, GLAAD is ready to play hardball with protests and other forms of direct action. On one occasion, GLAAD packed the audience of a Rush Limbaugh TV taping in order to "deaden" the audience response and to sabotage the show with hostile interruptions. The outbursts of GLAAD's hecklers eventually became so raucous that the network had to clear the set. In another case, after Dutch director Paul Verhoeven had refused to soften the homosexual sub-themes in *Basic Instinct,* GLAAD contacted its allies, Queer Nation and ACT UP. Protesters carrying "Ass Ugly Douglas" signs, referring to its star Michael Douglas, disrupted filming until the producers got a court order forcing them to stop. In Jennings's view, Verhoeven had no business trying to shoot a film like *Basic Instinct* in San Francisco. "It is somewhat akin to Nazis going to Skokie to march."

Undaunted by its inability to stop *Basic Instinct,* GLAAD has since been trying to get the distributor, CAROLCO, to put together a public service announcement to coincide with the opening which would condemn anti-homosexual violence, and thus implicate films like *Basic Instinct* in the spread of that violence—a constant GLAAD theme. "It has become a cause célèbre," says Jennings, "a *Cruising* for the nineties," referring to an Al Pacino film with homosexual themes. If GLAAD does not receive cooperation from CAROLCO, he warns, there could be demonstrations around the country when *Basic Instinct* opens. According to press reports, GLAAD is threatening to rent public billboards to reveal the film's surprise ending and thus kill its box-office appeal.

As Jennings and Fowler tell it, GLAAD's sole purpose is to fight for "accurate depictions of gays and lesbians" to balance the continual wave of negative gay images which wash over audiences from print, radio, film and TV. But even they acknowledge that the notion of media hostile to the concerns of the homosexual community is political hyperbole. "I was joking [yesterday] and told my office manager it was Gay Day in the *Times*," he says, referring to Los Angeles' largest paper. "There were at least four articles that dealt with gay or AIDS issues and at least two of them were astounding stories. It is comforting to look through the paper and see three or four stories like that which related to my life." Because people move around so much at the *Times*, working with the paper has been both a "great and horrible experience," says Fowler. Just as soon as you get someone "up to speed" about what is and is not acceptable, "she's gone and you have to start all over with someone new." But even the *Times*, in Fowler's perspective, can be guilty of tremendous acts of insensitivity. On "National Coming Out Day," he notes, instead of running an op-ed piece by a gay editor or reporter talking about his or her own coming out, the *Times* ran a piece by a member of the Mattachine Society—one of the oldest homosexual organizations—stating that the people marching in the streets were not representative of homosexual opinion and that activist organizations like GLAAD spoke only for those who have "the compulsion to flaunt their sexual preference." Complains Fowler: "To come out with that article on the one day that celebrated National Coming-Out Day was horribly irresponsible. I was on the phone [with *Times* editors and reporters] for four hours that day."

The effort to intimidate *Times* staff over an article by a politically incorrect homosexual may explain the growing (if still covert) opposition to GLAAD in Hollywood. Among GLAAD's opponents are people who are socially liberal but strongly resist the notion that an organization with a political agenda should have the censorship power this organization has accumulated. GLAAD just isn't your typical activist organization, says one veteran writer-director who is worried enough about the group to ask not to be named: "If you want to put a Jew or a Catholic into a project, you are not expected to go to a board for a pre-clearance. Not even the Reverend Donald Wildmon, a man for whom I have utter contempt, expects to be entitled to prior restraint. GLAAD is the only group which has the nerve and the clout to do that." The same director, who is Jewish, denies that homosexuals are somehow singled out by the media. "There is nothing in *JFK* or *Silence of the Lambs* that is as objectionable as what Spike Lee did in *Mo Better Blues* to the American Jewish community and no one attempted to stop his film. And what about Italian-Americans? They are the most demeaned, defamed group around. They are either shown as marginally functional human beings like John Travolta in *Saturday Night Fever* or violent criminals in *Goodfellas*. Yet I don't hear the Italian community clamoring for prior restraint."

Randy Shilts, who covers the gay community for the *San Francisco Chronicle*, believes that the tendency of activist groups to demand that homosexuals be portrayed only in a positive light is counter-productive. As Shilts observes, it is one thing to speak up for homosexual interests but quite another to demand veto power over who is to be considered an authentic homosexual, who is to be allowed to portray homosexuals, and what is to be defined as homosexual reality. It is a problem Shilts has faced first-hand. When word got out that Oliver Stone was going to make a feature film out of *The Mayor of Castro Street*, his biography of the murdered San Francisco Supervisor Harvey Milk, some gay activist groups took the position that Robin Williams shouldn't be allowed to play Milk because he wasn't homosexual. This is sheer bigotry, comments Shilts, adding that the very same groups would "go crazy if someone said that a gay actor couldn't play a straight male. They're acting like Brownshirts. It's not up to the gay community to decide who does a movie about them..." If this sort of thing continues, warns Shilts, no Hollywood producer or director will want to take on any project with a homosexual theme, no matter how positive the story is. If the GLAAD criticism of *JFK* succeeds in making Stone drop *The Mayor of Castro Street*, that will be the end of it, laments Shilts, "because no one else is going to touch this story."[1]

GLAAD's inquisitional strategy is fast producing exactly the situation the organization wants to avoid. Because of the threat of intimidation or reprisal, many producers are now beginning to resist tackling subjects that will attract GLAAD's attention. In a financially risky business, the prospect of being told to surrender artistic control or suffer political guerrilla warfare is one that no producer wants to face. Rather than deal with such a possibility, writes John Voland in the February issue of the Screenwriter's Guild *Journal*, "some writers and producers—even those who belong to ethnic or cultural minorities—are censoring themselves, either by altering characters to suit the requirements of the activists, or by devoting themselves to mainstream projects that couldn't possibly invoke their ire."

GLAAD, of course, vehemently denies that its activities amount to censorship, claiming that it is not asking for laws to ensure compliance with its concerns. But what Joseph McCarthy did in the 1950s wasn't inscribed in law either.

---

[1]Shilts was only partially right. Stone did drop the film project, and Randy never lived to see it made. But in 2009, fifteen years after Randy's death from AIDS, the story appeared on film under the title *Milk*, with heterosexual Sean Penn playing the lead.

3

A Radical Catastrophe

T o the rest of humanity, the institutional forms of capitalist democracies appear as liberating environments that enable individuals to breathe free and pursue their desires, without descending into anarchy and chaos. It is the Hobbesian dilemma resolved: liberty ordered by the rule of law and by market constraints. But to the alienated radical democracy is a particularly diabolical form of tyranny because it only appears to be free and is not. Liberal capitalism, in the celebrated words of Herbert Marcuse, is a system of "repressive tolerance." To the post-modern left, America's ordered liberty is not "a reflection on human nature" and an appreciation of its limits, as the authors of the *Federalist* maintained, but an instrument of race/class/gender oppression that they are obliged to destroy. In this malevolent confrontation, it is the principle of tolerance for those who differ from them that queer revolutionaries and radicals most reject, and it is this rejection that defines them as radicals. For them, tolerance is repressive because it denies their most cherished illusion—that *they* are the authentic voice of humanity, and theirs the universal political solution.

Radicals do not want integration into a democratic system or equal status in a democratic state. Nothing could be more self-defeating for their "transformative" schemes than to be counted one among many. For radicals, accepting the idea of a democratic

Adapted from "A Radical Holocaust," *The Politics of Bad Faith*, Free Press, 1998

norm is merely to collude in one's own oppression, to embrace "false consciousness" in place of a revolutionary vision. At the recent 10th anniversary conference of the National Council for Research on Women, its feminist president cited the term "unwed mother" as an example of "androcentric" bias because "it presupposes that the norm is to be a *wed* mother." Yale professor Michael Warner, the author of a seminal tract called "Fear of a Queer Planet," writes: "Formally, the state is male, in that objectivity is its norm." In this revolutionary vision the goal is a "queer" society where norms no longer exist. Hetero-normative, androcentric, Euro-centric: for radicals, the very idea of the normal community—the non-queer—is a mark of oppression.

It is in this sense that the idea of the queer or, what is the same thing, the deconstruction of the normal can be seen as the core inspiration for all those experiments that produced this century's political nightmares. To the revolutionaries, in the famous phrase from Marx's *Eighteenth Brumaire*, "all that exists deserves to perish." In the last decade, the deconstruction of the normal has proceeded so rapidly that even the nature of the family has been put into question. What is a family? Are there consequences for not caring about the answers to such questions? For not having a sense of what is normal?

Normality can be either descriptive or prescriptive, or both. A "normal procedure" in medicine or in public health is a procedure that is *usually* prescribed. It is usually prescribed because it has been previously tried and proven successful. It is by trial that we arrive at procedures, institutions and laws that bring our efforts into conformity or coherence with the orders of our nature. When gays object to the prescriptive use of the word "abnormal," they claim it means that homosexuality is unnatural and should be illegal. But abnormal is also a descriptive term. Homosexuality can be both a fact of nature and abnormal. According to the best statistics available, between two and five percent of a population will be homosexual in any given society, whether that society is tolerant or intolerant of homosexual behavior. Studies of identical twins indicate that upbringing has little bearing on homosexual development. The conservative conclusion will be that homosexuality is normal in that it is rooted in nature, but that socially it is abnormal in that the vast majority of people are not and will never be homosexually inclined.

The description of homosexuality as socially abnormal does not lead to any conclusion as to whether it is immoral or not. Some communities and religions do view homosexuality as immoral. These attitudes may be "oppressive" to homosexuals, but no more so than are some religious attitudes towards Jews as souls condemned to eternal damnation. Jews can live with this attitude in a society that protects their rights as citizens and invokes tolerance of differences as its central virtue. The demand that homosexuality should be made illegal, on the other hand, is a demand that violates the social contract and its pluralist imperative, and undermines the very idea of America: *e pluribus unum.* The ideal of American pluralism is the embrace of diverse communities. America's pluralistic norm *requires* that the deviant community and the abnormal citizen (black, homosexual, immigrant, Jew) be equal before the law and enjoy the same inalienable rights as everyone else. To violate *this* norm is to break America's social contract and invite terrible consequences, as the bloodiest and most shameful pages of America's history attest. But it is precisely integration into America's civic community that radicals, who are at war with America and its social contract, reject. In doing do, they have created their own social Frankenstein in the contemporary epidemic of AIDS.

Who would *not* have understood in 1969, the year of "Gay Liberation," that promiscuous anal sex was unsanitary for individuals and a danger to public health? Yet gay liberation was defined by its advocates as just that: promiscuous anal sex, a challenge to the repressive "sex-negative" culture of what queer theorists now call "heteronormativity"—the heterosexual and monogamous norms, the first descriptive and the second prescriptive. In the radical view, existing sexual prohibitions reflected nothing about humanity's biological experience, but were merely a social construction to preserve the privileges of a dominant group.

Gay liberation was identified with a sexual agenda that did not seek civic tolerance, respect, and integration into the public order of bourgeois life. It was defined instead as a defiant promiscuity, the overthrow of bourgeois morals and sexual restraints and, consequently, of bourgeois standards of public hygiene. No natural or moral barriers were to stand in the way of the radical project. In 1969 the Gay Liberation Front issued a manifesto that proclaimed: "We are a revolutionary homosexual group of men and women formed with the realization that complete liberation of all people cannot come about unless existing social institutions are abolished. We reject society's attempt to impose sexual roles and definitions of our nature."[1]

The effect of this radical agenda was immediate and chilling. At the height of the 60s, which coincided with the flowering of the sexual revolution, the incidence of amoebiasis, a parasitic sexually transmitted disease, increased *fifty* times in San Francisco because of promiscuous oral-anal sex among gays. Despite the consequences, a Toronto leftist paper defended the practice in an article titled "Rimming as a Revolutionary Act."[2] During the next decade, the tolerant American civil order made way for the sexual revolutionaries. Public officials licensed sexual gymnasiums called "bathhouses" and turned a blind eye towards homosexual activity with strangers in bookstore backrooms, bars and "glory hole" establishments, until a $100 million public sex industry flourished by decade's end, in what activists described as a homosexual "liberated zone." Simultaneously, nature began to assert itself with ever more devastating results.

As opportunistic but still treatable infections flourished in the petri dish of the liberated culture, gay radicals increased their defiant

---

[1]"Gay Revolution Comes Out," *New York Rat Magazine,* August 12–26, 1969
[2]Randy Shilts, *And the Band Played On,* St. Martin's Press, 1987, p. 19

acts. Even the overloaded venereal disease clinics became trysting places in the liberated culture. In his authoritative history of the AIDS epidemic, author Randy Shilts describes the atmosphere in the liberated zones on the eve of its outbreak: "Gay men were being washed by tide after tide of increasingly serious infections. First it was syphilis and gonorrhea. Gay men made up about 80% of the 70,000 annual patient visits to [San Francisco's] VD clinics. Easy treatment had imbued them with such a cavalier attitude toward venereal diseases that many gay men saved their waiting-line numbers, like little tokens of desirability, and the clinic was considered an easy place to pick up both a shot and a date."[3]

Far from causing radical activists to re-think their agenda, the burgeoning epidemics prompted them to escalate their assault. When Dr. Dan William, a gay specialist, warned of the danger of continued promiscuity, he was publicly denounced as a "monogamist" in the gay press. When playwright Larry Kramer issued a similar warning, he was accused in the *New York Native* of "gay homophobia and anti-eroticism." At a public meeting in the year preceding the first AIDS cases, Edmund White, co-author of *The Joy of Gay Sex*, proposed that "gay men should wear their sexually transmitted diseases like red badges of courage in a war against a sex-negative society." Michael Callen, a gay youth present at the meeting, had already had 3,000 sexual partners and was shortly to come down with AIDS. When he heard White's triumphant defiance of nature's law, he remembers thinking: "Every time I get the clap I'm striking a blow for the sexual revolution."[4]

The first clusters of AIDS victims were formed not by monogamous civil reformers who had come out of the closet to demand tolerance and respect, but by sexual revolutionaries who pushed their bodies' immune envelopes to advance the new liberated order. Callen, who later founded People With AIDS, wrote one of the rare candid reflections on this revolutionary path to come out

---

[3]Randy Shilts, *And the Band Played On*, op. cit., p. 39
[4]Michael Callen, *Surviving Aids*, Harper Collins, 1990

of the gay community: "Unfortunately, as a function of a microbiological ... certainty, this level of sexual activity resulted in concurrent epidemics of syphilis, gonorrhea, hepatitis, amoebiasis, venereal warts and, we discovered too late, other pathogens. Unwittingly, and with the best of revolutionary intentions, a small subset of gay men managed to create disease settings equivalent to those of poor third-world nations in one of the richest nations on earth."[5]

The diseases were being transformed as well. As Shilts explains, the enteric diseases—amoebiasis, Gay Bowel Syndrome, giardiasis and shigellosis—were followed by an epidemic of hepatitis B—"a disease that had transformed itself, via the popularity of anal intercourse, from a blood-borne scourge into a venereal disease."[6]

Where were public-health officials as these epidemics took their toll? Why didn't they intervene, close the bathhouses and undertake vigorous education campaigns among gays to warn potential victims of the danger? The reason was the revolution itself. So successful was the radicals' protest campaign that it made the enforcement of traditional public-health practices politically impossible. Even when officials attempted to close the sexual bathhouses, which were the epidemic's breeding grounds, their efforts were successfully opposed by gay political leaders who defended the disease sites as "symbols of gay liberation."[7] Don Francis, the Centers for Disease Control official in charge of fighting the hepatitis B epidemic, explained: "We didn't intervene because we felt that it would be interfering with an alternative lifestyle."[8]

In the early 80s, the AIDS epidemic was still confined to three cities with large homosexual communities (San Francisco, Los

---

[5]Michael Callen, op. cit.
[6]Randy Shilts, op. cit. p. 39
[7]My interview with Konstantin Berlandt
[8]My interview with Don Francis

Angeles and New York). At the time, the numbers were small enough that aggressive public-health methods might have prevented the epidemic's outward spread. But every effort to take normal precautionary measures was thwarted in turn by the political juggernaut the gay liberation movement had managed to create. Under intense pressure from gay activists, for example, the director of public health of the City of San Francisco refused to close the bathhouses, maintaining that they were valuable centers of "education" about AIDS, even though their only purpose was to facilitate anonymous, promiscuous sex.[9]

Not only were measures to prevent the geographical spread of AIDS in gay communities thwarted by radical politics, but measures to prevent its spread into other communities were obstructed as well. Thus, when officials tried to institute screening procedures for the nation's blood banks and asked the gay community not to make donations while the epidemic persisted, gay political leaders opposed the procedures as infringing the "right" of homosexuals to give blood. The San Francisco Coordinating Committee of Gay and Lesbian Services, chaired by Pat Norman, a city official, issued a policy paper asserting that donor screening was "reminiscent of miscegenation blood laws that divided black blood from white" and "similar in concept to the World War II rounding up of Japanese-Americans in the western half of the country to minimize the possibility of espionage."

The result of these revolutionary attitudes was to spread AIDS among hemophiliacs and drug-using heterosexuals. Similar campaigns against testing and contact-tracing—standard procedures in campaigns against other sexually transmitted diseases—insured the metastasis of AIDS into the black and Hispanic communities, which eventually accounted for more than 50 percent of the known cases.

The war against civilization and nature, which is at the heart of the radical enterprise, inevitably produces monsters like AIDS.

---

[9]My interview with Dr. Mervyn Silverman

The epidemic has now taken a toll of 300,000 Americans, with a million more infected. The implementation of real public health methods is nowhere in sight. Even as the ashes of the Communist empire grow cold, the lessons of the disaster have not been learned. The nihilism that rejects nature and the idea of the normal, as it sets out to create a radical new world, is as blindly destructive as its consequences are predictable.

4

The Epidemic Is Just Beginning

Fourteen years and more than 300,000 deaths ago, Peter Collier and I wrote a story for *California* magazine about the AIDS epidemic in San Francisco.[1] At the time the virus had not yet been isolated and there had been only 3,000 cases nationally. But it was already clear to the medical community that the culprit was a retrovirus for which there might never be a cure, and that AIDS cases among gays were doubling every six months. If the behavioral patterns of gays and drug users did not change, there would be more than 300,000 people dead by 1997, which is what has happened.

In normal circumstances, the minimal public-health response to an impending epidemic would have been to identify the carriers of the disease by mandatory testing of at-risk communities, close off "hot zones" of the epidemic such as gay bathhouses and drug "shooting galleries," and conduct "contact-tracing" of those who had been in touch with the already sick. In addition, there would have been honest public education about the dangers of promiscuous anal sex among gays and needle-sharing among drug addicts. But as Collier and I found when we did our investigation in 1983 at the beginning of the epidemic, not one of these measures was acceptable to a powerful lobby of gay activists. They were all labeled "discriminatory" and "homophobic," and gay leaders

April 14, 1997, http://www.salon.com/1997/04/14/horowitz970414/;
http://archive.frontpagemag.com/Printable.aspx?ArtId=24406
[1]See "Origins of a Political Epidemic," above.

made clear to public-health officials who advocated them that they would be doing so at the risk of their careers.

As a result, none of the standard public-health measures were consistently deployed against the contagion. Instead, a series of politically correct ideas and "community-approved" policies became the only measures acceptable for political leaders to advocate, for the media to promote, and for public health agencies to pursue. The acceptable measures included a number of emotionally comfortable but medically misleading myths: that AIDS was an "equal opportunity" virus as threatening to heterosexuals as homosexuals; that government skinflints and homophobes weren't devoting enough money to medical research and were thus impeding the containment of the epidemic; and that the promotion of "safe sex" practices—using condoms and taking advantage of government-promoted "needle-exchanges" for drug users—were adequate preventive measures.

These myths were eagerly spread by an irresponsible press that failed to scrutinize the politically restricted campaigns which falsely reported "explosions" of the virus in the heterosexual community, among teenagers and women. Such reports were based on statistics deceptively interpreted by the Centers for Disease Control and Prevention in Atlanta, whose public health mission had been subverted early on by the progressive AIDS lobby. It is true, for example, that from time to time the percentage of heterosexuals and/or women contracting the virus has increased. But this is because the gay population has been so saturated with the disease that the percentage of new cases among gays relative to the total of new cases has declined. Moreover, the heterosexuals who are infected are mostly the wives and girlfriends (mostly black, Hispanic and poor) of drug users.

A new book written by gay journalist and activist Gabriel Rotello, *Sexual Ecology: AIDS and the Destiny of Gay Men*, confirms the grim epidemiological knowledge acquired over the past two decades. As Rotello's reporting makes clear, the authorized approach to AIDS was misguided to the point that it exacerbated the problem. There is no heterosexual AIDS epidemic, nor is there any likelihood of one developing, while the "safe sex" campaign among gays has not only failed to stem the tide of infection, but has encouraged a complacency that is resulting in a "second wave" of the epidemic among the younger gay population—a generation fully aware of the epidemic's threat to its health and survival.

An equally disturbing conclusion from the data compiled by Rotello is that the epidemic will not be ended by new "drug cocktails" and other anti-viral medical fixes. This is not only because of the nature of the AIDS retrovirus, which has a greater power to mutate than any previously known microbe, but also because of the historical failure of drugs to wipe out sexually transmitted diseases. The discovery of penicillin was once thought to herald the eradication of syphilis. But because it created a false sense of invulnerability, and its repeated use led to the emergence of drug-resistant strains, there are more deaths worldwide from syphilis today than when no medical remedy existed. While some drugs, or combination of them, appear to have had some success in slowing down the virus in some American victims of the disease, there is little prospect of a medical cure in the near future. At the same time, more powerful strains of the HIV virus have already been identified in Thailand, raising the specter of an even more virulent phase of the epidemic to come.

In these circumstances, the only way to arrest the AIDS epidemic is the remedy that has traditionally been thwarted by leaders of the gay community: Change the behaviors that feed it, in particular promiscuous sex. Epidemiological studies show that "core groups" of aggressively promiscuous gays have been the key to the epidemic's progress in the United States. But these core groups and their institutional support system—public bathhouses and sex clubs—have been fiercely defended from the start of the epidemic by gay activists and their political allies as a "civil right;" efforts to close them have been successfully opposed as an assault on gay liberation. As one gay activist, quoted by Rotello, wrote: "Gay liberation means sexual freedom. And sexual freedom means more sex, better sex, sex in the bushes, in the toilets, in the baths, sex without love, sex without harassment, sex at home and sex in the streets." It also can mean death.

To help contain the AIDS epidemic, all gay bathhouses should be closed immediately; so should gay sex clubs with names like "Blow Buddies." Public health officials also need to institute mandatory testing and contact tracing targeted at communities at greatest risk, and they need to issue clear warnings about the dangers of promiscuous anal sex. Those officials who fail to carry out these duties are guilty of criminal neglect, and should be sued.

5

Respect, Yes; Equivalence, No

I am a heterosexual man who believes that most gays are homosexual by nature. Therefore, I believe that gays should be accorded the same rights and moral approbation as everyone else. But I am also persuaded that the campaign for same-sex marriage is politically misguided, socially destructive and bound to fail.[1]

The campaign for same-sex marriage is rooted in the same elitist principles that have already created powerful backlashes on issues like abortion and prayer in the schools. With same-sex marriage, gay activists are trying to force an issue that is radical, deeply personal and profoundly divisive through the most arbitrary and undemocratic avenue of government available: the liberal courts. Knowing that today they would lose this battle in the legislative arena—the popular assemblies where the electorate can voice its opinion—gays decided to use the judiciary to ram through their proposed change to an institution that is not only thousands of years old, but regarded by many as the cornerstone of civil society.

Had they succeeded in their legal push, one case decided by courts in Hawaii (itself an overwhelmingly liberal state) would automatically have become law throughout the entire United

June 9, 1997, http://archive.frontpagemag.com/Printable.aspx?ArtId= 22670; http://www.salon.com/1997/06/09/horowitz970609/
[1]Obviously I was wrong about its failing. But the legal strategy did delay these rights for gay couples for the next 16 years, and longer.

States—not only in other liberal enclaves like Minnesota and Massachusetts but in conservative strongholds like Utah, Wyoming and the Bible Belt South. A rebuff was inevitable, and gays got one, when Clinton—their erstwhile friend in the White House—signed the "defense of marriage" act empowering states to ban same-sex marriage.

It's not that their cause is without merit. Andrew Sullivan, the gay former editor of *The New Republic*, wrote a most intelligent argument for it in his book *Virtually Normal*. In the preface to his newly published reader *Same-Sex Marriage: Pro and Con*, Sullivan appeals to conservatives to endorse gay marriage. His reasoning: it will strengthen the values of commitment and family in the gay community, which is surely a good thing for society as a whole. I think many conservative Americans would agree with Andrew that society has an interest in promoting stability and monogamy in gay households, particularly in the age of AIDS.[2] I also think most Americans would like to see gays enjoy some of the partnership rights that go with marriage. One that has often been cited is visitation rights for loved ones in hospitals. But these benefits could be achieved by something other than gay marriage. There is even a legal term for it: "domestic partnership" or "registered partnership," which grants state or local recognition of committed gay relationships but stops short of transferring, in one sudden, unreflective act, all the entitlements of marriage which have evolved over hundreds of years with heterosexual and child-rearing couples in mind.

Why is this not enough for Sullivan and other gay activists?[3] Because not only should marriage, like voting, be a basic civil right open to all, but same-sex marriage would signal a complete acceptance of homosexuality by American society. "No other measure would signal approval in such a stark and unambiguous way," he writes. "[Heterosexuals] are prepared to tolerate, yes, even, in

[2]http://www.salon.com/1997/05/02/gay_4/
[3]http://www.salon.com/1997/05/02/gay_4/

some ways, approve. But they are not yet ready to say that their heterosexual relationships are equivalent to homosexual ones."

But that is the reality, Andrew. Homosexual relationships are not "equivalent" to heterosexual ones, any more than men are equivalent to women. At bottom, what gays like Sullivan seem to desire is that they be regarded as "normal" by the majority that defines what normal is. But how can that be when being "gay and proud" and a heightened, testosterone-driven sexuality are the defining traits of gay life? Even within its own natural family, the gay child is destined to be different. The heterosexual parent of a gay child can surely love that child equally with its heterosexual siblings; but can that parent really regard this child as *equivalent* to, not different from, a child created in its own heterosexual image?

Perhaps the gay community can learn something from the Jews. Try as some of them might, Jews will never be regarded as entirely normal in a predominantly Christian society. That doesn't seem to have stopped their progress. Being different, not "normal," within the culture of the majority—be it Christian, heterosexual or ethnically European—is not such a terrible thing. In fact, it's the American way.

6

The Boys in the Bathhouses

S ix months ago I wrote in *Salon* that the AIDS crisis was "just beginning." Despite, or even *because* of the development of anti-viral drug "cocktails" and a modestly declining death rate, the sexual promiscuity among gay males that fueled the epidemic was even likely to increase. Now there is evidence suggesting just that. According to a newly released report from the Centers for Disease Control and Prevention, studies at 26 VD clinics across the nation show a dramatic rise in gonorrhea among gay males, traditionally a marker for rising HIV infection rates. The cause? According to the *Los Angeles Times* account, "Experts suggest that the increasing success of HIV treatment with triple-drug therapies has lulled gay men into a false sense of security that may lead to a disastrous recurrence of the AIDS increase observed in the early 1980s."

Of course, neither the *Times* nor any other mainstream medium reporting these statistics has focused on the real source of the problem: the re-emergence of a bathhouse-sex club culture that fosters large cohorts of promiscuous strangers spreading the infection in urban gay centers. San Francisco, the most developed of these subcultures, currently has the highest gonorrhea infection rates by a wide margin. Cowed by the politically correct activists who have crippled the battle against AIDS, the media have turned

November 3, 1997, http://archive.frontpagemag.com/Printable.aspx? ArtId=24384; http://www.salon.com/1997/11/03/nc_03horo/

a blind eye to the rash of new sex clubs and refuse to make the connection that AIDS is as much a behavioral as a clinical disease.

About the time my *Salon* article appeared, a group of left-wing academics known as "queer theorists" met at the Lesbian and Gay Community Services Center at New York's City Hall. Among those present were professors Michael Warner of NYU and Kendall Thomas of Columbia University, living examples of how the universities routinely provide a platform for political extremists.[1] The group gathered to found an organization called Sex Panic, whose agenda was twofold: first, to oppose any attempts by health authorities to curtail or restrict public anonymous sex and the institutions that support it; and second, to destroy the reputations of the handful of courageous gay activists—Gabriel Rotello, Michelangelo Signorile, Larry Kramer and Andrew Sullivan among them—who have become fed up with the homicidal strategies of the gay left and had the guts to say so publicly.

Warner is Sex Panic's best-known theorist. He declares himself (and all queer theorists) a militant opponent of "the regime of the normal," including standard public-health methods for fighting epidemics. Here is Warner defending the death camps of the current contagion: "The phenomenology of a sex club encounter is an experience of world making. It's an experience of being connected not just to this person but to potentially limitless numbers of people, and that is why it's important that it be with a stranger. Sex with a stranger is like a metonym." (Warner is a professor of English literature.)

The October *Lingua Franca* describes a recent public meeting of Sex Panic at which the assembled treated with respectful silence a convicted child molester and his declaration that he was one of them. Another gay man, who said that he felt the gay community's celebration of promiscuity made it more difficult for him to maintain a monogamous relationship, was heckled. The flyer

---

[1]Warner is now a professor at Yale.

announcing the event was headlined "DANGER! ASSAULT! TURDZ!" The "turdz" in question were Rotello, Signorile, Kramer and Sullivan. The author of the *Lingua Franca* article, a gay graduate student at Columbia University, could not find one queer theorist who defended the infamous four, or who believed that shutting down sex clubs or avoiding promiscuous anonymous sex had anything to do with battling AIDS. Instead, Warner and his fellow queer theorists proudly declare that they are opponents of "not just the normal behavior of the social, but the idea of normal behavior."

They couldn't have it any other way. Any acknowledgment of "normality" would suggest that the promotion of promiscuous sex in the midst of the AIDS epidemic is perverse at best and accessory to murder at worst. If heterosexuals were defending gay sex clubs in the face of the AIDS epidemic, their motives would be properly suspect. Still, their silence, whether in the groves of academe or the pages of the liberal mainstream press, lends a quiet support to this intellectual fascism and sexual fanaticism that diminishes the prospects of survival for so many of America's gay men.

7

Homosexuality and Sin

The flap over Sen. Trent Lott's remarks about homosexuality illustrates the way people on both sides of the political debate have come to talk about this issue—and shouldn't. For those who missed it, Lott was asked on a radio talk show whether he thought homosexuality was a sin. Instead of passing the question to the theologians whose opinion would be more appropriate, Lott answered that he did. His answer was gobbled up by the carnivorous media and spat in the direction of House Majority Leader Dick Armey. Instead of recusing himself for a similar lack of professional competence, Armey pulled out a Bible to "prove" that it was. He quickly added that, as a Christian, he was instructed to love the sinner and hate the sin, as though that made everything all right. Eager to exploit a political opportunity, the Clinton White House joined the fray. Lumping all Republican legislators with the two culprits, press secretary Mike McCurry said: "The president thinks the American people understand how difficult it is to get business done in Washington sometimes when you're dealing with people who are so backward in their thinking."

In almost the same breath with which he had called forth the lightning, Lott made an attempt to show that he was actually progressive in his thinking. Genuflecting to the therapeutic standard that liberals and progressives have created, and under whose rubric

June 29, 1998, http://archive.frontpagemag.com/Printable.aspx?ArtId=24311; http://www.salon.com/1998/06/29/nc_29horo_2/

everything from alcoholism and cigarette addiction to gang activity and gun violence is officially construed as a public health problem, Lott backed away from the stern authority of the Biblical text to explain that homosexuality was a kind of disease and that its victims should be helped "just like alcohol or sex addiction or kleptomaniacs." This genuflection proved even more damaging than the original comment. "It's an indication of how the extreme rightwing has a stranglehold on the leadership [of Congress]," cried Winnie Stachelberg, political director of the Human Rights Campaign, a 250,000-member gay and lesbian political organization. Her comment was immediately seconded by other gay leaders. Lost in the outcry were Lott's efforts to show that he was tolerant towards homosexuals, while establishing that theirs was a "lifestyle" he does not approve.

The things that are wrong with this picture are the result of formulations that have been introduced into our public discourse by both left and right in recent decades. The idea of homosexuality as a "lifestyle" originated with the left and is still maintained by many specifically "queer theorists" in the academy. If homosexuality is a life-style—a political and moral choice—then it is perfectly appropriate for some to regard it as an immoral choice and to reject it on those grounds. Furthermore, if homosexuality is a lifestyle (and therefore a choice), it might even be appropriate for politicians like Armey and Lott to make such comments when they are responsible for billion-dollar AIDS programs made necessary by the sexual practices of gay males.

But what if this is not the case? If homosexuality—as most centrist gays now maintain (and as I personally believe)—is nature, if it is a genetic given that cannot be altered by the assertion of individual will, then the moral and therapeutic posturing of both conservative politicians and queer theorists is inappropriate and offensive.

The Biblical injunction against homosexuality is real and cannot be argued away (though many have tried). What, then, is the appropriate way for a democracy like ours to deal with this problem? We are a pluralistic society. We do not have an established state religion. We are in fact composed of ethnic and religious communities so diverse that, in other parts of the world, war is the normal condition of their relations. Serbs and Croats, Arabs and Jews, Christians and Muslims co-exist in America but elsewhere are at each other's throats. How did we Americans achieve this? By requiring our political institutions to treat everyone equally, and by a single standard.

It is perfectly appropriate for Dick Armey, as a religious believer, to regard homosexuality as a sin, just as it would be appropriate for any Christian to believe that Jews are damned as unbelievers. Muslims regard both Christians and Jews as infidels, and therefore damned. Provided Jews, Christians and Muslims respect America's constitutional framework, which regards us as children of a single creator and instructs secular authorities to treat us equally, there should be no problem. One nation under one God. Atheists are given the option of observing the form of this miraculous arrangement without acknowledging the substance. It works just as effectively. But as soon as people forget the limits of the political sphere and confuse it with the realm of the religious, they are asking for trouble. Senator Lott and Congressman Armey should not have blurred this distinction. What their private conscience tells them is one thing; what they comment on as legislators is quite another. ("Render unto Caesar that which is Caesar's and unto God that which is God's.")

It seems clear that neither Lott nor Armey actually intended their religious comments as political statements or policy agendas. For that reason, it was no service for the presidential press secretary or gay leaders to escalate the confusion that had already been sown. There is no resolving religious differences except by religious warfare. That is why the conflict in the Middle East is so intractable, and why our constitutional framework allows the same groups to coexist here in peace. Therefore, it is advisable for all parties in our political debate to back off from such fundamental confrontations and seek out a common ground.

8

The Plague-Abettors

As countless news stories, articles and editorials have reminded us, this is the 20th anniversary of the onset of the AIDS epidemic in America. It is a grim anniversary. More than 450,000 Americans, mostly young, are dead. After years of so-called public education efforts, and billions of dollars in AIDS-related government programs, the infection rates for new HIV cases are rising back to their peak 1980s levels. The new infection rates are highest among blacks and Hispanics, who now make up more than half the dead but who were hardly affected in the first years of the epidemic. In those years, when the number of infections was small, and effective public-health methods might have contained their spread, more than 90 percent of those affected were white homosexuals living in New York, Los Angeles and San Francisco, intravenous drug users in the same locations and a tiny cohort of hemophiliacs and immigrants from Haiti.

On this anniversary, you will read many stories about the medical research on AIDS which, however remarkable in itself, has failed to produce an effective vaccine, let alone a cure for the disease. This failure was predicted at the very outset of the epidemic, a fact I wrote about at the time. The leading experts on the AIDS virus warned then that the only way to stem the tide of the epidemic was through proven public health methods. You will read many stories about the heroic efforts of activists in the gay community to lobby the

June 11, 2001, http://www.salon.com/2001/06/11/aids_9/; http://www.salon.com/news/col/horo/2001/06/11/aids/index.html

government for more AIDS money, and to care for the sick and dying.[1] None of these efforts should be confused with public-health methods, which were the only means of containing the epidemic.

What you will *not* read is a single story about those methods, or how epidemics were combated—often successfully—for a hundred years before gay activists inserted their views into public health policy. What you will not read is how the proven public-health methods were opposed by AIDS activists, and how public health officials surrendered to the activists' demands for veto control over what methods were acceptable and what were not; in other words, how they colluded in subverting the system that had proved so successful in combating public health threats in the past.

What you will not read is any evaluation of the government-financed AIDS campaigns—mainly in public "education"—that the activists demanded in place of the proven methods. Yet the harrowing figures released on this anniversary show these politically correct billion-dollar education campaigns have failed to contain the epidemic or to prevent it from spreading into other communities, particularly the African-American and Hispanic communities.

As a result of the obstruction of testing, reporting, contact tracing and infection-site closing by gay leaders and their allies in the Democratic Party that controlled the major urban centers, public health officials were unable to warn the specifically gay communities in the path of the epidemic. In fact, because there were politically inspired bans on testing, reporting and contact tracing, they were not able to find out what that path was. As a result, while by the end of the first decade of AIDS Hispanics were 14 percent of those infected and blacks 26 percent, a decade later Hispanics were 19 percent of those infected and blacks an astounding 45 percent.

What you will not read in the 20th-anniversary coverage of the epidemic is any story pointing out that today—as we move into

---

[1] http://www.salon.com/2001/05/01/aids_8/

the third decade of the epidemic with infection rates rising and the death toll climbing—the subverted public-health system still does not require reporting of individual cases, testing of at-risk communities, contact tracing to warn individuals of possible infection or the closing of sex clubs and other potential sites of infection.

Thus, in addition to being a grim anniversary from the vantage of the dead and those who loved them, this is a disheartening occasion for those of us who have watched in disbelief the criminally ineffectual efforts that have been deployed in the name of political correctness, and have tried in vain to draw attention to a dereliction that has caused so many needless deaths. This anniversary also makes it clear that, as a nation, we have learned nothing from the follies of the past, and are headed into the next decade still prisoners of orchestrated ignorance and still relying on the remedies that failed.

Typical of the media reports on this anniversary is the lead story in the health section of the *Los Angeles Times*, written by "health writer" Linda Marsa, which rehashes the party line on AIDS and thus conveys information that is brazenly ignorant and entirely false. In perfect self-parody, the article is titled "A Legacy of Change":

> It was a sheer accident that AIDS first struck a relatively cohesive group: young homosexuals in cities such as New York, Los Angeles and San Francisco, many of whom had honed their organizational and political skills during the gay rights movements of the 1970s. This was extraordinary: Terminal illnesses don't discriminate, hitting rich and poor alike without regard to ethnicity, geography or sexual orientation.

In fact, the AIDS epidemic is more accurately described as a *product* of the gay rights movement of the 1970s, inevitably concentrated in the very centers of gay life in America—San Francisco, New York and Los Angeles—and impossible to conceive without the presence and agitations of the radical gay movements that directly preceded it. It was the gay left that defined promiscuous anal sex with strangers in public environments—the primary cause of the AIDS epidemic—as "gay liberation."

It was the gay liberation movement that thought nothing of the massive epidemics of amoebiasis, rectal gonorrhea, syphilis and hepatitis B that swept through gay communities in the decades preceding AIDS, producing astronomical infection rates and depleted immune systems in the process. It was the gay movement that regarded any intrusion by public health authorities to close the public sexual gymnasia called "bathhouses" as a threat to gay liberation, both before *and* after the onset of AIDS. It was the gay left that successfully prevented the reporting, testing, contact tracing and other public health methods that had been proven effective in combating epidemic diseases in the past. It was the gay left that blocked government prevention programs from targeting at-risk communities, using the same lie as the *Times* writer, that "AIDS is an equal opportunity disease;" and it was the gay left that persuaded government officials instead to put all the anti-AIDS eggs in the basket of incredibly expensive and—as everyone can now see—completely ineffective "education" campaigns. These campaigns were ineffective because, out of considerations of political correctness, they did not specify anal sex as the primary sexual transmission route and were addressed not to those who were specifically at risk, but to "everyone," and thus in effect to no one.

The late Michael Callen, creator of the organization People With AIDS and a pioneer of candor in the midst of these lies, described how he had come to New York as a young man from the sticks and heard gay radicals like the writer Edmund White address audiences in the gay community on the subject of sexual liberation. White told one such audience including Callen that "gay men should wear their sexually transmitted diseases like red badges of courage in a war against a sex-negative society."[2] The

---

[2] Charles Silverstein and Edmund White, *The Joy of Gay Sex*, Outlet Books, 1977

ever-courageous Camille Paglia pointed out some years ago the obvious truth: "Everyone who preached free love in the Sixties is responsible for AIDS. This idea that it was somehow an accident, a microbe that sort of fell from heaven—absurd. We must face what we did."

Callen explained exactly what that meant. "Some of us believed we could change the world through sexual liberation and that we were taking part in a noble experiment. Unfortunately, as a function of a microbiological ... certainty, this level of sexual activity resulted in concurrent epidemics of syphilis, gonorrhea, hepatitis, amoebiasis, venereal warts and, we discovered too late, other pathogens. Unwittingly, and with the best of revolutionary intentions, a small subset of gay men managed to create disease settings equivalent to those of poor Third World nations in one of the richest nations on earth."

It was a tragedy that those who pioneered the cause of gay rights should have been swept up in a radical illusion that they could also change the world, including the laws of nature. But that is what happened. This left successfully demanded political control of the battle against AIDS, which sabotaged it from the start, and has been directly responsible for the killing fields left in its wake. This includes especially the spread of AIDS into the black and Hispanic communities, which could have been prevented if traditional public health methods had been aggressively deployed. The Hispanic and black communities are for the most part separated from the gay communities where the epidemic first took hold. If there had been testing and tracing of those infected, and focused warnings to those in their path, who knows how many lives could have been saved?

I offer these observations with no hope that they will have an effect. I have written about this radical holocaust for nearly the entire duration of the epidemic. Many others have since raised their voices as well. Michael Fumento's *The Myth of Heterosexual AIDS*, and Gabriel Rotello's *Sexual Ecology* are two of the books that have made the case for ending the political obstruction of the war against AIDS and for a more scientifically sound approach. Early ACT-UP radicals like Larry Kramer, Michelangelo Signorile and Rotello have had second thoughts about their former attitudes, faced what they did, and tried to turn the tide. But to no avail.

The chief obstacle to any change in this tragic story lies with the media. AIDS is without question the worst-reported story in the history of American journalism. From the press coverage of this anniversary, no one can take any hope that the next 10 years will show any improvement in the mortality statistics, unless there is a medical breakthrough. Without accurate information about this politically induced nightmare, there is no chance that the American public will wake up and finally decide that enough is enough.

9

Issues That Dare Not Speak Their Name

A sure sign of political correctness is when the other side of a controversial subject is identified as forbidden territory. To cross the invisible boundary renders one's motives immediately suspect, while opposition marks one as indecent, a bad person, a relic of the reactionary past, and an obstacle on the path to human progress. This was the case when I opposed reparations for slavery—an injury committed so long ago that there are no slaves and probably no children of slaves still alive—and further observed that to make those reparations payable on the basis of skin color instead of injury was "a bad idea and racist too."[1] For the heresy of opposing the left on this issue I was tarred and feathered as a bonehead "racist." Not only was I a target of these vicious attacks; so were the journalistic institutions that printed my ad in the interests of free speech. The attacks were accurately described by my *Salon* colleague Joan Walsh as "political correctness run amok," for which I thank her. Yet they were also lent credence and support by commentators who are generally regarded as reasonable, such as Jonathan Alter, Clarence Page, and Richard Cohen of *The Washington Post*.

An interesting case of the vitality of political correctness was provided recently by Andrew Sullivan, in a column that appeared

---

June 25, 2001, http://archive.frontpagemag.com/Printable.aspx?ArtId=24433; http://www.salon.com/2001/06/25/gays_9/
[1]An account of my campaign is the subject of *Uncivil Wars: The Controversy Over Reparations For Slavery*, Encounter Books, 2001

in *The New York Times Sunday Magazine*. In it, Andrew addressed the subject of gays in the military in a way that I found morally persuasive and poignant on the one hand but politically correct and, practically speaking, obtuse on the other. His column, called "They Also Served," asked for "some ... recognition in today's war nostalgia of the role that gay men have played in the past in defending their country." In the film *Pearl Harbor*, for example, "Cuba Gooding, Jr. played the brave segregated Negro, fighting back for his country." In *Saving Private Ryan*, "the sensibilities of the 90s were projected backward. We didn't see just soldiers; we saw a Jewish-American soldier, an Italian, a WASP and so on." Actually Andrew is wrong here. This wasn't the sensibility of the 90s. It was the same sensibility I saw as a kid in the 1940s, when World War II films invariably featured the identical rainbow and, in features like *Home of the Brave*, included Negro soldiers too.

This is the part of Andrew's argument I can wholeheartedly embrace—and I believe a majority of Americans can, too. When a socially conservative president appoints an openly gay man to an administration post, as happened recently, it is a sign that things have really changed. But the recognition of gays who served their country is not the main agenda of Andrew's column. Establishing the point that we should acknowledge the service gay men have performed is only as a wedge for the argument that the armed services should abandon its "Don't Ask, Don't Tell" policy and embrace a gay presence in its ranks. Andrew calls this goal a "diverse military" and wonders why "we seem to be going in reverse."

It is at this point that Andrew's argument abruptly incorporates the telltale syntax of political correctness. His opponents are reactionaries, driven by prejudice against "diversity" and gays. The assumption is that no serious concern other than lingering social prejudice exists for current military policy. Opposing it requires no military argument.

The indictment, however, is counter-intuitive. Of all social institutions, the military is the most pragmatic. Its task, brutal in its simplicity, is to develop the most efficient killing machine that money can buy and intelligence devise. This singularity of purpose creates a paradoxical result. The military can indeed be seen as retrograde in some of its aspects. It is not a democracy, for example. On the other hand, it is more progressive in other aspects. Precisely because the military's overriding purpose is to win wars, free black fighting units were incorporated into its ranks more than 100 years ago, at a time when slavery was still legal. Less well known is the fact that free black troops and military support units were part of the Confederate war effort as well. For most of those hundred years, black soldiers were still segregated and confined to subordinate roles. But in 1947 the military was integrated. That was seven years before the Supreme Court decision integrating the nation's schools, and eighteen years before segregation was ended in the South. The racial progress in the military was made notwithstanding the fact that the military culture is largely a southern culture. In short, because of its pragmatic focus, the military has shown itself to be historically more flexible, progressive, and ready to adapt in this crucial terrain of social conflict than the democratic political process itself.

What then is the military's problem with including gays, other than prejudice? It is a sign of the power of political correctness in our culture that there is probably not one among a hundred readers of these words who could answer the question. Because of the embargo that political correctness puts on even considering the other side of this issue, the conventional "wisdom" is that an institution that pioneered racial integration is run by individuals, many themselves minorities, who are more prejudiced against gays than they were against blacks. Is this an argument that makes sense? Yet it is precisely an argument that all supporters of gays in the military currently make. For all such advocates, including my friend Andrew, the "Don't Ask, Don't Tell," policy is just a hypocritical attempt to appease lingering social prejudice.

In fact, there *is* a military argument against the inclusion of gays in combat, which has nothing to do with social prejudice. It may or may not be a sound argument. I am not a military expert and any position I take is necessarily based on intuition rather than experience. I certainly am open to counter- arguments. It is just that nobody on outside the military culture is offering any.

Andrew's argument in *The Times* is more interesting than most, in that it credits the Army with having important agendas that are worthy of respect. Andrew observes that current policy of "Don't Ask, Don't Tell" creates a standing loophole for anyone who wants to leave the service. This is bad for the military, and an argument for changing the policy. Well and good, but hardly persuasive for a service that relies on volunteers. To make a credible argument for changing the policy, Andrew and others would have to address the military rationale for the policy, which is this: "Don't Ask, Don't Tell" is a way of containing the destructive force of sex on a combat capability called "unit cohesion." To create the perfect killing machine, the military works hard to drain recruits of their individuality and their self-interested desires in order to make them think like cogs in a machine. An essential part of the military mind is that the members of a fighting unit don't think for themselves but do as they are told. They work as a unit in which each performs an appointed task. The mission objective—not personal consideration—guides their actions. Suppose a commander were faced with the choice of risking his unit or risking the life of his own son, for example. Suppose the life of his son were threatened, but to save him would risk the military objective his superiors had set. Suppose he let human feeling override the imperatives of the military machine. He would be doing what was natural, but the military objective he sacrificed might cost the lives of hundreds or thousands.

To avoid such breaches of discipline, military policy does not allow family members to fight in the same unit. The same principle underlies its policy towards gays. Sacrifice of unit cohesion and military order is the threat that sexual attraction between soldiers poses for any combat force. The open inclusion of gays in the military is regarded by military men who oppose it as a threat to the effectiveness of the military as a fighting force. This is an issue almost completely absent from the current public debate.

The military argument has nothing to do with the individual fighting capability of gay males. It is about unit cohesion. It is about making every soldier a cog in a machine whose larger purpose he cannot understand but is bound to serve. Suppose two men in a five-man unit are sexual partners. What will that do to the cohesiveness and effectiveness of the fighting unit? What impact will it have on its ability to carry out its mission? These are the questions that gave rise to the ban on gays in the military and then to the policy of "Don't Ask, Don't Tell." Because once a soldier is able to tell, and remain in the military, there is no containing the problems that sexual attractions create.

As a comeback, some may be tempted to ask: What about the fact that women now serve in combat units? Far from taking care of the problem, this comparison only underscores the dangers in letting politicians treat the military as a social experiment. In one sense, of course, we don't really know the magnitude of the problems this situation creates, since we haven't been in a ground war since women were allowed combat roles, and in any case we can't presume information about these problems is going to be readily available. But we do know that every military that has attempted to place women in combat positions—the Israeli, the German and the Russian are three—has abandoned the practice because of its negative impact on unit cohesion. We do know that, since women have been included in these roles, requirements and standards have been dramatically lowered, and along with them morale, a crucial if unmeasurable element of military success.

Moreover, we know that once the politically correct foot is in the door, the possibility of reasserting pragmatic controls becomes ever more remote. The same "progressive" intolerance that forced the original issue will prevent any rational assessment of the result. The admission of women into the American military was not a military decision but a political act. The Presidential Commission on the Assignment of Women in the Armed Forces, which was created during the first Bush administration, recommended *against* putting women in combat positions. The Clinton administration ignored the recommendation and slipped the new policy into place without a public discussion and with no congressional debate. During the Gulf War, women in the armed services failed to report to combat duty at rates many times that of men. When you don't show up for your combat assignment, you are effectively sabotaging existing battle plans. On one ship, the Aurora, ten percent of the women en route to the war zone in the Gulf managed to get themselves pregnant before they got there. The military looked the other way. No one was court-martialed for cowardice or dereliction of duty. In other words, under the force of political correctness, the military has already surrendered to the fact that it will be a less effective fighting machine.

The integration of women in the military and in combat forces is a politically created blow that has already weakened America's defenses. The open inclusion of gays in the military could have an even more damaging effect, with unknown consequences for untold lives. If proponents of gay inclusion want to make their case persuasively, they need to make it not on the battlefields of political correctness but here.

10

Unnecessary Deaths

A new report from the Centers for Disease Control and Prevention reveals that 40 percent of people infected with the AIDS virus didn't realize they had the virus for ten years after being infected. They only became aware of their condition through the appearance of full-blown AIDS. The same government agency estimates that roughly 800,000 Americans are infected with the virus.[1]

There are two grim and unarguable consequences of these statistics. First, those who carry the virus undetected deprive themselves of the enhanced possibilities of survival through early treatment by drugs. By the time AIDS becomes full-blown, the body's immune system has already been severely damaged and the patient is subject to life-threatening infections and cancers. But, from an epidemiological view, this isn't even the worst news. The presence of the virus in the blood and sperm of those infected means that, if they are sexually active or sharing drug needles, they are unknowingly infecting others. According to the government's own estimates, this means that roughly 320,000 Americans are infecting unsuspecting others all the time.

This march of illness and death is made possible by the surrender of public health authorities to the pressures of political groups

---

August 21, 2001, http://archive.frontpagemag.com/Printable.aspx?ArtId= 24441; http://archive.frontpagemag.com/readArticle.aspx?ARTID=24441; http://www.salon.com/2001/08/21/aids_13/
[1]http://www.cdc.gov/hiv/resources/reports/pdf/hiv_prev_us.pdf

opposed to what once had been the standard procedure for fighting epidemic diseases like AIDS: testing. Without testing of at-risk individuals and groups, there is no way to insure that individuals will know their lives are in danger, or that they are endangering the lives of others. Yet irresponsible zealots have successfully removed testing from the public health system's arsenal of weapons available in the battle against AIDS. They have even managed to pass laws against testing, in states like California and New York, which have by far the largest concentration of AIDS cases, HIV carriers and people at risk.

As I have previously observed, AIDS is the worst-reported story in the history of American journalism. Although the media dutifully reported these new statistics about silent AIDS carriers, there was not a single press query about the government's lackadaisical attitude towards testing, even though the statistics show that we are in the midst of a monstrous pandemic. Despite the efficacy of new drugs, 40,000 young Americans are still dying every year. Yet the press has raised no questions about the need for mandatory tests, made no comments about the political obstruction of public health methods like contact tracing and reporting, and had no observations about the feckless surrender of public health officials to the prejudices and paranoia of gay activists. What a contrast to its attitude towards the problems caused by cigarette smoking or guns.

For more than a decade now, the word "prevention," as used by the chief government agency for combating epidemic diseases, has been a cruel Orwellian deception. By "prevention" public health officials mean only voluntary, mainly educational, measures. But the experience of the last two decades has clearly shown that such measures are inadequate to the task of actually containing the epidemic. In this situation, with hundreds of thousands of individuals unknowingly carrying the virus and infecting healthy people, prevention is officially confined to voluntary measures that mainly involve education and counseling. In other words, if you are willing, you can get tested. If you are willing, you can get information. If you are willing, you can wear a condom and not use someone else's needle. But we know that not enough people are willing. There is no community that has been bombarded with more general information about AIDS than the gay community, and yet AIDS is on the rise in the gay community, which accounts for 60 percent of new infections.

As for voluntary counseling, a frightening study of Seattle men, reported by David Brown in *The Washington Post*, found that among gay men who contracted a venereal disease only 50 percent got any counseling about safe sex for AIDS. In other words, half the gay men who were treated by doctors for venereal disease were not warned that they could get AIDS if they continued practicing sex without condoms. If, after the expenditure of billions of dollars on AIDS education and prevention programs, *this* group did not get counseling, one can hardly expect the necessary information to reach groups that do not have venereal diseases, are symptom free, and may be having sex with individuals who are completely unaware that they are carrying the virus. Yet no one in the AIDS public health community is even discussing the need for mandatory testing, let alone sanctions against reckless behavior endangering the lives of others. The only possible conclusion is that 40,000 deaths a year from an entirely preventable disease is perfectly acceptable to the American government because it is perfectly acceptable to the political groups that make up the AIDS lobby.

Last week the Centers for Disease Control and Prevention held a gathering in Atlanta, nobly titled the "Second National HIV Prevention Conference." But ninety-seven pages of conference agenda, listing more than two hundred conference panels, failed to turn up a single one devoted to the question of whether there should be mandatory testing of any at-risk group whatsoever, whether drug-addicted pregnant women, visitors to VD clinics, or residents of neighborhoods with a high incidence of the disease.[2] Not one. Instead there were panels like "HIV Prevention Programs

---

[2]http://www.thebodypro.com/content/art30538.html

for Women," which discussed topics like "Women of Color: Doing It for Ourselves" and "Brushing Up on HIV Prevention at the Beauty Parlor." The only panel devoted to testing-policy issues that came even close to raising the question about the efficacy of testing asked: "Does the Availability of Anonymous Testing Really Affect HIV Testing Rates?" It was a question that seemed to answer itself, a sure sign of enforced conformity. How about, for example, "Does the fact that testing is *anonymous* hinder our ability to combat this epidemic?"

I asked Jessica Frickey of the Centers for Disease Control and Prevention about mandatory testing, and she confirmed that there was "no discussion of mandatory testing at the conference." She then added, "the CDCP doesn't recommend mandatory testing," and explained that "people are scared of getting HIV tested because they might not get insurance." Well, there are obvious answers to this objection. First, insurance companies will test for AIDS anyway, and second, if this were the case, why not press for a law that insurance can't be denied for such reasons, or have the government *provide* an insurance program for those who test positive for AIDS? Another obstruction to sound prevention methods is the argument of AIDS activists that, if testing is made mandatory, those at risk will avoid both tests and treatments. But it is this very argument, by people who claim to be leaders of the battle *against* the disease, that helps to create the resistance.

I asked David Brown, the *Washington Post* staff writer who reported the widespread ignorance of AIDS carriers about their condition, why the press was not asking about the need for mandatory testing. He replied: "The media profession has accepted the fact that mandatory testing is off the agenda. Mandatory testing even for pregnant women has been rejected." This is true, but it is like saying that bans on abortion have been rejected. No reporter in his right mind would ignore the fact that a lot of people remain on the other side of the issue. Are there no doctors, no epidemiologists, no scientists involved with AIDS who think that the failure of existing measures calls for stronger ones? Of course there are.

But in an atmosphere where advocating testing is not politically correct, reporters are not going to seek them out.

When I pressed Brown further, he said that mandatory measures were off the table because there was "no precedent for coerced medical treatment of adults in the United States." Which is simply false. Every couple applying for a marriage license thirty years ago was required to get a test for syphilis. This was a measure designed to control an epidemic that was no longer even lethal. Individuals who are recognized to be a medical threat, such as tuberculosis carriers, can still be legally forced to take a full course of drugs in order to prevent contagion. Yet getting tested for AIDS is hardly as invasive as being coerced into taking a dose of medicine. Why not test if it means saving hundreds or thousands (or even tens of thousands) of lives?

Of course, testing is just the tip of the iceberg when it comes to the current political obstruction of proven public health measures. Real prevention of new AIDS infections would also involve reporting and contact tracing, and the closing of infection sites like public sex clubs. All these methods were proven indispensable in fighting contagious diseases before AIDS. Yet all the political battles over whether to deploy these weapons against AIDS were successfully resisted by the political leadership of the gay community more than a decade ago. Not coincidentally, this lobby is funded by the epidemic it fuels. One of the facts most studiously ignored by pliant media is that AIDS activist organizations have grown rich off the mounting toll of the dead. A whole industry has been created out of the successive failures of current public health policies. The bigger the epidemic resulting from these failures, the more government money is available to "AIDS providers." This is not to suggest that AIDS providers want people to die. Obviously they don't, and a lot of their effort is the work of very dedicated and idealistic people who have extended themselves to help others. The same, however, could be said for defense workers in the famous military-industrial complex. The problem is that, in both cases, the symbiosis of service and profit has negative side-effects.

Many people in the AIDS battle who know better, doctors and scientists for example, are constrained from advocating changes in failed AIDS policies because they are afraid of being cut off from the community on which their work depends. An epidemiologist researching AIDS who strenuously advocates testing and draws attention to the flaws in current policy may find the grants on which his work depends cut off. Explaining why misguided policies go unchallenged, Gabriel Rotello writes, "gay leaders frequently made it plain to researchers that anyone who raised questions about gay sexual freedom for any reason, whether ethical or biological, would be equally accused of anti-gay bias. Few researchers were willing to venture into such a political and social hot zone, and the few who did found that they consequently lost influence within the gay male community, a bad position to be in if your research required a high level of cooperation from gay men."[3]

Only an aroused public can break this vicious cycle, which has had a crippling effect on the war against AIDS. The idea that heterosexual couples can be forced to take tests for syphilis, which is curable, but gay couples and IV drug users can't be tested for AIDS, which is not, is absurd. Yet this absurdity is killing nearly a thousand young people in this country every week of every year.

---

[3]Gabriel Rotello, *Sexual Ecology*, Dutton Adult Books, 1997

11

Fatal Ignorance

*"The vast majority of young gay and bisexual men in the
United States who were found to have the AIDS virus
in a new study were unaware of their infection,
according to findings reported as the 14th International
AIDS Conference opened here today."*
—THE NEW YORK TIMES, BARCELONA, SPAIN, JULY 7, 2002

These coolly phrased words, written by reporter Lawrence
K. Altman, conceal what is without question the greatest
scandal in American history and one of the worst atrocities ever to take place on American soil. Approximately 800,000
Americans are already infected with AIDS and roughly 500,000 are
dead.[1] But the fact is that most of these infections and deaths
could have been prevented by the employment of standard public
health practices in place for more than half a century up to the
inception of this epidemic. These practices include testing, contact tracing, reporting and closing of infection sites. They were all
abandoned under intense and unrelenting political pressure from
gay activists, the AIDS lobby and the Democratic Party.

The statistics released at the Barcelona AIDS conference are
chilling. Ninety percent of gay black men aged 15–29 who have
the virus and were surveyed in the study did not know they had it
until the researchers informed them. This means that, without the

July 8, 2002, http://archive.frontpagemag.com/Printable.aspx?ArtId= 23784
[1]http://www.amfar.org/thirty-years-of-hiv/aids-snapshots-of-an-epidemic/

intervention of the AIDS researchers, they would not be getting treatment for their illnesses and would be infecting other young men as well. In the Hispanic gay community, the figure is 70 percent infected by AIDS and ignorant of their condition; and in the white gay community it is 60 percent.

Does any reasonable person believe that, if testing for AIDS were mandatory for every gay male and every individual in a risk group for AIDS, the infection rates among gays would be as high as they are now? Or that there would be 10,000 new AIDS cases in America every month? Yet this is the situation that public health authorities and the politically correct have conspired to perpetuate for the entire 20 years of the AIDS epidemic.

12

Pride Before a Fall

In four Gospels, including the Sermon on the Mount, Jesus neglected to mention the subject of homosexuality. But that hasn't stopped a handful of self-appointed leaders of the so-called religious right from deciding that it is an issue worth the presidency of the United States. In what *The Washington Times* described as a "stormy session" last week, the Rev. Lou Sheldon, Paul Weyrich, Gary Bauer and eight other religious conservatives read the riot act to Republican National Committee chairman Marc Racicot. They reproved him for daring to meet with the Human Rights Campaign, a group promoting legal protections for homosexuals. Racicot's indiscretion, they said, "could put Bush's entire re-election campaign in jeopardy."

According to *The Times'* report by Ralph Hallow, the RNC chairman defended himself by saying, "You people don't want me to meet with other folks, but I meet with anybody and everybody." To this Gary Bauer retorted: "That can't be true because you surely would not meet with the leaders of the Ku Klux Klan." Nice analogy, Gary. Way to love thy neighbor.

This demand to quarantine a political enemy might have had more credibility if the target, the Campaign for Human Rights, were busily burning crosses on social conservatives' lawns. But they aren't. Moreover, the fact that the Ku Klux Klan burns *crosses* might suggest a little more humility on the part of Christians

May 20, 2003, http://archive.frontpagemag.com/Printable.aspx?ArtId=18134

addressing these issues. Just before the launching of the 2000 presidential campaign, George Bush was asked about similarly mean-spirited Republican attacks. His response was that politicians like him weren't elected to pontificate about other people's morals, and that his own faith admonished him to take the beam out of his own eye before obsessing over the mote in someone else's.

The real issue here is not religious. It is tolerance for differences in a pluralistic society. Marc Racicot is chairman of a political party, not a religious order. Tolerance is different from approval, but it is also different from stigmatizing and shunning those with whom we disagree. I say this as someone who is well aware that Christians are themselves a persecuted community in liberal America, and as one who has stood up for the rights of Christians like Paul Weyrich and Gary Bauer to have *their* views, even when I have not agreed with some of their agendas. Not long ago, I went out on a public limb to defend Weyrich when he was under attack by *The Washington Post* and other predictable sources for a remark he had made that was (reasonably) construed as anti-Semitic. I defended Weyrich because I have known him to be a decent man without manifest malice towards Jews, and I did not want to see him condemned for a careless remark. I defended him in order to protest the way in which we have become a less tolerant and more mean-spirited culture than we were.

I have this to say to Paul and his colleagues: A demand on the chairman of the RNC that he have no dialogue with the members of an organization for human rights is itself intolerant, and serves neither your ends nor ours. You told Racicot: "If the perception is out there that the party has accepted the homosexual agenda, the leaders of the pro-family community will be unable to help turn out the pro-family voters. It won't matter what we say; people will leave in droves."

This is disingenuous, since you are community leaders and share the attitude you describe. In other words, what you are really saying is that if the Republican Party is merely *perceived* to have accepted the "homosexual agenda," you will tell your followers to defect, with the disastrous electoral consequences that may follow. As a fellow conservative, I do not understand how in good conscience you can do this. Are you prepared to have President Howard Dean or President John Kerry preside over our nation's security? Do you think a liberal in the White House is going to advance the agendas of social conservatives? What *can* you be thinking?

In the second place, the very term "homosexual agenda" is an expression of intolerance as well. Since when do all homosexuals think alike? In fact, thirty percent of the gay population voted Republican in the last presidential election. This is a greater percentage than blacks, Hispanics or Jews. Were these homosexuals simply deluded into thinking that George Bush shared their agendas? Or do they perhaps have agendas that are as complex, diverse and separable from their sexuality as do women, gun owners or Christians?

In your confusion on these matters, you have fallen into the trap set for you by your enemies on the left. It is the left that insists its radical agendas are the agendas of blacks and women and gays. Are you ready to concede that the left speaks for these groups, for minorities and in general for "the oppressed?" isn't it the heart of the conservative argument that liberalism (or, as I would call it, leftism) is bad doctrine for all humanity, not just for white Christian males?

If the president's party, or conservatism itself, is to prevail in the political wars, it must address the concerns of all Americans and seek to win their hearts and minds. It is conservative values that forge our community and create our coalition, and neither you nor anyone else has, or should have, a monopoly in determining what those values are.

13

Render Unto Caesar

Of all tyrannies, a tyranny exercised for the good
of its victims may be the most oppressive. It may be
better to live under robber barons than under omnipotent
moral busybodies. The robber baron's cruelty may
sometimes sleep, his cupidity may at some point be
satiated; but those who torment us for our own good
will torment us without end, for they do so with
the approval of their consciences.

—C. S. Lewis

In a previous article, I took several Christian conservative leaders to task for protesting RNC Chairman Marc Racicot's appearance at a meeting of the Human Rights Campaign, which is the largest group of gay-rights activists. The Christian leaders complained about the very fact that Racicot, who is the head of one of America's two largest political parties, had met with the group. In explaining their position, one of the conservatives invoked the Ku Klux Klan, which Racicot wouldn't think of addressing; another implied that Christian conservatives might withhold their votes in the next presidential election over the gay issue; while a third demanded that the RNC chairman declare homosexuality "immoral." I called this behavior intolerant and politically self-destructive. I pointed out that I was a defender of Christian conservatives against the vicious slanders of

---

May 27, 2003, http://archive.frontpagemag.com/Printable.aspx?ArtId=
18015

the left. I could have added that I have sponsored amicus briefs opposing the left's attacks on the Boy Scouts, that I have decried the intrusion of the gay left's sexual agendas into the public schools, and that I have written the harshest critiques of its promotion of organized promiscuity and its subversion of the public health system. Yet the response to my article was anything but tolerant. One of those present, Robert Knight, responded with an article that appeared on the website of Concerned Women for America, titled "David Horowitz Owes Christians an Apology."

Robert Knight is the director of the Culture and Family Institute, an affiliate of Concerned Women for America, one of the groups that met with Racicot, and which I criticized. I share its concerns about the left's assault on American values and on the American family in particular. I have appeared on radio and TV shows sponsored by Concerned Women for America and would do so again. I consider the partisans of the Christian right generally to be important elements of the conservative coalition who made significant contributions to the conservative cause. Through moral persuasion, they have succeeded in dramatically reducing the number of abortions, helped to strengthen the American family, and been on the frontlines opposing the left's malicious assault on America's culture and institutions.

In short, I am a supporter of Christian conservatives, even though we disagree on the matter at hand and perhaps on the larger issue that underlies it. That issue, politically expressed, is the issue of tolerance. Theologically, it involves the distinction between the sacred and the profane, between this world and the next. Why do I owe Christians an apology, since I have not attacked Christians? To accuse a Jew of attacking Christians is a serious matter and goes to the heart of the political problem that religious conservatives often create for themselves when they intrude religion into the political sphere. Why is religion even an issue in a *political* discussion?

Perhaps what triggered this response was the way I began my article—by pointing out that homosexuality did not seem to be high on the scale of Jesus's priorities, since Jesus never mentioned it. Knight and others who responded to my piece have lectured me on the moral views of the Old and New Testaments, as though I were trying to dissuade conservative Christians from their moral views. "With all due respect, Mr. Horowitz owes Christians an apology for his crude distortion of Jesus' teachings, and for his implied charge of bigotry," wrote one respondent. But I did not charge *Christians* with anything. Nor did I make pronouncements on the subject of Jesus's moral teachings. Perhaps this is too fine a point. I did not say that Jesus approved homosexuality, but only contrasted the degree to which Jesus considered it important to the salvation of one's soul and the way some conservative Christian leaders consider it important to the coming election of an American president. I have publicly defended Christians' rights to their moral views, specifically on their views of homosexuality, though I do not share them. I have publicly condemned spokesmen of the gay left for their attacks on Christians who voice their views. I have criticized gay activists as often "anti-Christian" and "intolerant." The essence of tolerance in a political democracy is that individuals who hate, despise and condemn each other privately should live side by side in the same political community in relative tranquility. Respect for differences is not the same as endorsing what is different.

Jesus's views on homosexuality, if he had any, are irrelevant to the question of whether the chairman of the Republican National Committee, who is a *political* leader, should make moral pronouncements on the issue, as Knight and the others demanded. Is homosexuality a threat to civic order? Should it be a crime? Should there be legislation to regulate it or make it a crime? These are the kinds of questions that politicians and legislators need to confront; these are the questions appropriate for a *political* movement as opposed to a religious faith. My point was actually a famous admonition attributed to Jesus: *Render unto Caesar the things that are Caesar's and unto God the things that are God's.*

Conservatives who believe in limited government should be the first to embrace this principle, Christian conservatives more than others. The Christian right was born as a reaction to the government assault by secular liberals on religious communities in the 1970s. We do not want government intruding on the voluntary associations we make as citizens, or dictating to us our moral and spiritual choices. Robert Knight, and others who have objected to my article, do not seem to grasp that it is important to separate the political from the religious; or that the realm of government should be limited in this regard. In my original article I made a point of objecting to the term "homosexual agenda," saying that one has to distinguish between those homosexuals who are politically left and support radical agendas, and those homosexuals who are conservatives. I observed that a higher percentage of homosexuals voted Republican than did blacks, Jews or Hispanics. Here is Knight's response: "Mr. Horowitz's assertion that 'the very term homosexual agenda is an expression of intolerance' is unfathomable. Christian conservatives have an agenda. Environmentalists have an agenda. Homosexual activists have an agenda."

Christian *conservatives* refers to a political group, as opposed to "Christians" which does not. There many liberal and even radical Christians whose agendas are indistinguishable from the agendas of Communists whom Robert Knight and I both oppose. "Homosexual activists" refers to what? Is there a political agenda that is homosexual? If so, how is it that 30 percent of homosexuals vote Republican and regard themselves as conservatives? "Mr. Horowitz's agenda here seems to be to accuse Christian conservatives of bigotry, pure and simple, as if they could have no valid reasons for opposing the political agenda of homosexual activists." What I said was that the validity of a *political* opposition to any group of activists should depend on whether the *political* agenda of those activists is conservative or radical. It is bigoted to fail to make the distinction. The Human Rights Campaign—which is the homosexual group in question—is a radical group. So are the NAACP and the ACLU, and there has been no Christian conservative démarche over an RNC chairman who met with those groups. But Knight will have none of this. "The idea that there is a 'respectable' gay movement that will go only so far and that will help the GOP win elections is a dangerous fiction. As a veteran of leftist revolutions, Mr. Horowitz should know better."

As veteran of leftist movements, I know the difference between a gay leftist and a Log Cabin Republican, and so should Robert Knight. It is not a fiction that homosexuals, as politically active citizens, can help Republicans win elections. It is a fact.

Knight's final comment and self-revelation is this: "Our agenda ... is to dissuade people from becoming trapped in homosexuality." In my view, this statement is a prejudice dressed up as a moral position. It presumes that homosexuality is a choice, while all evidence points to the contrary. The conversion movements have been miserable failures. They have recruited a highly motivated and extreme minority among homosexuals—people so unhappy with their condition that they are desperate to change it—and the results are pathetic. Only a tiny minority of what is itself a tiny minority achieves a heterosexual result.

Even if Knight were correct in thinking that homosexuality is a moral choice, and that Christians and Jews have a moral obligation to oppose it, this would not alter the fact that it is inappropriate and self-defeating for conservatives to make this their political agenda. A mission to rescue homosexuals is a religious mission; it is not an appropriate political cause. Would Robert Knight like the government to investigate all Americans to determine whether they are homosexual or not, and then compel those who are to undergo conversion therapy or else? This is a prescription for a totalitarian state. No conservative should want any part of it. But this is how Robert Knight sums up the political agenda of religious conservatives. Those who agree with him should think again.

14

Silent Slaughter

Since 1981 more Americans have died from AIDS than died in the Second World War, roughly 500,000. About 40,000 new AIDS cases are reported in the United States every year. About half of the victims are under 25 years of age.

Back in the 1980s, when most of the dead (about 350,000 of them) were still alive, I interviewed Don Francis, an immunologist and epidemiologist for the Centers for Disease Control, who was a generally recognized hero of the battle against AIDS. Francis had been the CDC official in charge of the fighting the hepatitis B epidemic in the 1970s. I asked him how epidemics are fought. He said that there was really only one way to fight an epidemic, which was to identify the carriers of the infection and to separate them from those in their path. How to manage this separation, he said—whether by quarantine, education or other methods—was a political question.

I then asked him whether testing was important in this process. He said it depended on whether the symptoms manifested themselves immediately on the body's surface, particularly on the face of the victim, or whether they were latent and difficult to detect when the infection was present. With the HIV virus a person can be a carrier for a decade without symptoms. It seemed obvious that mandatory testing would be a crucial factor in any

June 10, 2003, http://archive.frontpagemag.com/Printable.aspx?ArtId= 17796 effort to contain the AIDS epidemic; yet at the time there was no testing, while the opposition to it was fierce.

Opponents of testing, including the entire leadership of the gay community and the Democratic Party, maintained that tests could not be kept confidential and that AIDS carriers would thus become the targets of persecution. I asked Francis if this were a reasonable fear. He said, "We have been studying gay diseases since before Stonewall [the 1969 demonstration that launched the gay liberation movement] and I don't know of a single case of breach of confidentiality."

I asked him when there would be mandatory testing in the United States. He answered: "When enough people are dead."[1]

Apparently, half a million dead are not enough.

There are still no federal laws requiring testing for the AIDS virus or reporting of AIDS infections. There is no move to close public infection sites like bathhouses and sex clubs. The state of California, which has the second most cumulative AIDS infections in the country (124,000), publishes a "Brief Guide to California's HIV/AIDS Laws, 2002," which is posted on the Internet.[2] The very first section of the guide is titled, "Voluntary HIV Testing." It begins: "For most individuals outside the criminal justice system, the decision to test for HIV is a voluntary one." The very next section is titled "Prohibitions Against Mandatory Testing," and informs citizens that the "Health and Safety Code Section 120980 prohibits HIV testing to determine suitability for employment ... and ... insurance." State laws also prevent doctors and medical workers who perform the voluntary tests from reporting the names of tested individuals to public health authorities. There is thus no contact tracing to inform sexual partners of the person infected that they may have contracted the virus as well. In other

---

[1]David Horowitz, "A Radical Holocaust," in *The Politics of Bad Faith*, Free Press, 1998, p. 199n

[2]http://www.dhs.cahwnet.gov/ps/ooa/Reports/aidslaws/pdf/AIDSLaws20 02.pdf

words, the AIDS virus is protected by law so that it can pursue its silent course through the body of the nation, affecting tens of thousands of individuals who do not know they have it (by some estimates half of those infected) and who are putting others in danger through contact.

On June 4, *The Seattle Times* reported that new AIDS cases had nearly doubled in the last year and are expected to increase by another 60 percent this year. "It's the most dramatic increase since the beginning of the epidemic," said Dr. Bob Wood, director of AIDS control for Seattle's King County, as quoted in *The Times*. "One of the most important things you can do in HIV prevention is make sure people know if they are positive or negative," Wood said. "Studies show that people make major changes in behavior when they learn their status." Well, yes.

How did this state of affairs come to pass? How have roughly half a million young Americans been allowed to die without being protected by public health authorities? Without the government intervening to deploy the most basic measure that could save them? How have both political parties remained silent or collusive in this dereliction of their responsibilities as guardians of the public trust? How can the media have ignored, as they have, decisions that have meant serious illness and death for so many Americans? How can reporters have ignored a story about the needless suffering and deaths of people whom proven health methods might have saved? Why has there been no interrogation of the interests responsible for derailing the health system, specifically AIDS groups who have benefited by receiving most of the government AIDS funds, billions upon billions of dollars allocated to fight the epidemic but instead consumed in ministering to its hapless victims?

The answers lie in way Democratic officials in the three urban centers of the epidemic were unable to withstand the pressures of the gay left, whose self-destructive political correctness prevailed. It was convenient for the Democrats not to insist on hard choices for the stricken community but instead to allow AIDS activists to blame Ronald Reagan and Republican "homophobia." It was good politics to ignore the reality, but bad policy for the victims. Republicans understood the policy issue but were too cowardly to confront their political adversaries over it. One of the sources of the cowardice was their lack of clarity on the issue of homosexuality itself. If Republicans were clear that their task as a political party is not to manage private morality, they could have responded to the crisis of a vulnerable community whose leaders had betrayed it. Compassion for the victims of the epidemic, whose government failed to protect them, should have inspired Republicans to support the public health measures that were discarded. But so far it hasn't.

Republicans and Democrats alike should consider the implications of what has happened. The very activists who assaulted and undermined the public health system are currently mounting new attacks on traditional institutions that are vital to the welfare of America's communities. Holding them to account for the damage they have already done would be a first step in stopping them from doing more.

PART IV

Feminist Assaults

I

The Unforgiving

For nearly two decades after the Sixties, the military remained the one institution able to withstand the baleful influences of the progressive attack on American culture. Now that the cold war is over, this immunity appears to have ended. A series of minor incidents at the Navy's "Tailhook Convention" have fueled a national hysteria about "sexual harassment" and triggered a political witch-hunt which threatens to deconstruct that institution in the same way others have been deconstructed.

Guilty associations with the incidents—a drunken party at which crotches were grabbed in a gantlet ritual, and a skit with sexual innuendos mocking an anti-military female member of Congress—have already ended the careers of the Secretary of the Navy, four admirals, a military aide to the president, and three "top gun" flight commanders. In addition, a question mark has been placed over the careers of thousands of officers, while star-chamber interrogations have been authorized to ferret out even more culprits. And it doesn't end even there. Every male serviceman in the Navy, judged guilty *before* the fact under the new Puritanism, has been condemned to 8 hours of re-education in "sensitivity training classes," provided to purge their corrupt souls.

September 1992, *Heterodoxy* magazine, http://www.discoverthenetworks.org/Articles/1992%20September%20Vol%201,%20No4.pdf

The fires of this investigative fury have been fanned by a group of feminist legislators led by Democrat Pat Schroeder, ranking member of the Armed Services Committee, author of a bill to allow women in combat and the congresswoman pilloried in the skit. In a July 9 letter to Defense Secretary Dick Cheney, she put the Pentagon on notice that "Tailhook '91 is a symptom of a larger problem;" that the resignation of the Navy Secretary does not begin to address the problem; and that further investigations and prosecutions are in order. The skit that pilloried Schroeder was part of "Tom Cat Follies," a private show in the officers' club at the Miramar Naval Station. The show included lampoons of George Bush and Dan Quayle, but it was the two skits about Pat Schroeder that provoked the lightning. So horrible were the thought-crimes committed on stage that no major medium has seen fit to report them, perhaps because the offense is laughable. I have no such compunctions.

The first Schroeder skit was an altered nursery rhyme: "Hickory dickory dock, Pat Schroeder sucked my cock." The second was an episode in which Schroeder goes to Europe for a sex-change operation. A photo of the new Pat Schroeder is then produced, and lo! It is Dick Cheney. Not far off the mark, considering that Schroeder has been mentioned as a possible Secretary of Defense in a Clinton Administration. Fearful of retribution from a Congressional antagonist, the Navy terminated the commands and careers of five "top gun" officers who were merely present at the Tom Cat Follies. Although two were later reinstated, the Navy made it clear that they were still associated with an unspeakable outrage and that their tarnished reputations would not be fully restored.

What is going on in America when seasoned fliers can have their careers blighted because of a possible offense to a politician? What is the problem with feminists who can't handle this kind of trivia, and yet claim the right to enter a war zone as combatants? Schroeder's combat bill would also make women eligible for a military draft, though no one in the media is mentioning this. It is seen by advocates as a wedge measure that would mean the end of what Schroeder calls "institutional bias against women" in the military. A presidential commission has been appointed to review the issue and is scheduled to make a recommendation in November.

The feminist argument is familiar: by excluding women from combat, the patriarchy undermines women's self-esteem, causes them to be perceived as inferior and thus "structures" their oppression. Anyone who fails to be impressed by this formula is self-convicted as a sexist bigot. In fact, studies conducted at West Point have identified 120 physical differences between men and women that may bear on military requirements.[1] Notwithstanding these real-life barriers to equality in military service, in the wake of "Tailhook" the U.S. Naval Academy has been excoriated for not moving fast enough to increase its female enrollment. Senator Barbara Mikulski has demanded "an attitude change" at the academy, and an official "Committee on Women's Issues" headed by Rear Admiral Virgil Hill has called for the "immediate dismissal of senior officers who question the role of women in the military." To question—to *question*—the role of women in the military is now regarded as unacceptable sexism and grounds for dismissal by the military itself.

Under the guidance of its feminist commissars, our newly sensitized military has moved into the realm of the utterly surreal. Thus the Air Force has established a SERE program (Survival, Evasion, Resistance and Escape), including its own "prisoner of war" camp in the state of Washington, to de-sensitize its male recruits so that they won't react protectively, i.e., like men, when female prisoners are tortured. In other words, Schroeder and her allies have harassed the military into creating a program that brainwashes men so that they won't care what happens to women, as they normally do. That's consciousness-raising, feminist style.

---

[1] Military Academy—United States General Accounting Office—Report to Congressional Requesters, *Gender and Racial Disparities*, March 1994, http://www.gao.gov/assets/160/154159.pdf

Another form consciousness-raising takes is the suppression of inconvenient facts. At the commission hearings on Schroeder's bill, testimony was given about the suppression of a report on the performance of female troops in Desert Storm. In particular, women were unavailable for duty at a rate three to four times that of the men recruits.[2] Non-deployability, the technical term for this critical form of absenteeism, has serious implications for unit cohesion and combat effectiveness in war situations. But no matter, we can't embarrass the women.

Another immediate consequence of ignoring differences in the name of political correctness is "gender norming," the practice of creating double standards so that women are measured in performance against other women rather than men. Gender norming is now the rule at all military service academies, and so is the cover-up of the practice. At West Point, the official position is that there have been no negative effects of admitting women to the academy. The facts, as a recent Heritage Foundation study by Robert Knight points out, are different. Women cadets take what is euphemistically called "comparable" training when they cannot meet the physical standards for male cadets. In load-bearing tasks, for example, 50 percent of the women score below the bottom 5 percent of the men.[3] Women's scores in exercises are routinely "weighted" to compensate for their deficiencies, while peer ratings have been eliminated altogether because women were scoring too low.

The men's training program has been downgraded as well. Cadets no longer train in combat boots because women were experiencing higher rates of injury. Running with heavy weapons has been eliminated because it is "unrealistic and therefore inappropriate" to

---

[2]Air Command and Staff College Air University, *The Impact Of Pregnancy On U.S. Army Readiness*, Merideth A. Bucher, Major, U.S. Army. April 1999, p. 4, http://www.au.af.mil/au/awc/awcgate/acsc/99-016.pdf
[3]The Center for Military Readiness, *Army Gender Integrated Basic Training (GIBT) 1993–2002*, May 2003, Appendix C, pp. C-1, C-2, http://www.cmrlink.org/data/sites/85/CMRDocuments/Army-GIBT_Finding052003.pdf

expect women to do it. The famed "recondo" endurance week, during which cadets used to march with full backpacks and undergo other strenuous activities, has been eliminated, as have upper-body strength events in the obstacle course.

It is one thing to have second-rate professors in the humanities because of affirmative-action quotas that lower standards. But a second-rate officer corps? Not surprisingly, resentment on the part of male cadets is high.[4] One indication is that more than 50 percent of the women cadets at West Point reported that they had been sexually harassed last year. It is a perfectly sinister concoction. Rub men's noses in arbitrariness and unfairness, and then charge them with sexual harassment when they react. It is also a perfect prescription for accumulating power and controlling resources. Which is what this witch-hunt, no different from any other, is ultimately about. For every male who falls from grace because he is suspected of sexual harassment, or of defending standards that may be unfavorable to women, or of not reacting strongly enough to sexual harassment, there is a politically correct career officer or politician ready to achieve grace by advancing the progressive cause. Representative Beverly Byron, a Schroeder ally, has been mentioned as a possible Secretary of the Navy; Pat Schroeder has her sights set on Defense.

What qualifies a Pat Schroeder to shape the American military through the next generation? During the Cold War, Schroeder and her supporters in the congressional left worked overtime to hobble the efforts of the United States in confronting the Soviet threat. In 1982, with the Red Army occupying Afghanistan, with 50,000 Cuban troops waging civil war in Ethiopia and Angola, with a Communist base established on the American mainland in Nicaragua, with a Communist insurgency raging in El Salvador, with thousands of nuclear warheads in Central Europe aimed West and Warsaw Pact forces outnumbering NATO troops by a two-to-

---

[4]United States Military Academy, *The Annual Report of the Superintendent*, West Point, NY, 1986–1987, p. 47

one margin, Congresswoman Schroeder authored an amendment to reduce the number of U.S. military personnel stationed overseas *by half*. In recent editions of the *Congressional Quarterly*, she has been noted for her efforts against nuclear testing, while the Soviets were still our adversaries, against further development of the MX missile, against proposed funding for the strategic defense initiative and the B-2 bomber, and against authorizing the president to use force to stop Saddam Hussein.

The one American institution that survived the radical decades intact is under attack from progressives like Schroeder. Let's not add the destruction of America's military power to the depressing list of its utopias that failed.

2

Tailhook Witch-Hunt
(co-authored with Michael Kitchen)

According to Navy Lieutenant Paula Coughlin, a helicopter pilot and aide to Rear Admiral John W. Snyder, she had no idea that she would be walking into sexual hell around midnight on September 6, 1991, when she went up to the third floor of the Las Vegas Hilton to visit the hospitality suites at the Tailhook Association's annual convention. But as she entered the hallway of the hotel, she immediately found herself in a sea of leery male faces swollen with sexual energy. A taunting chant arose: "Admiral's aide! Admiral's aide!" A man bumped her from behind, grabbing both of her buttocks and lifting her up off the ground. Then, as she spun to confront this attacker, someone else grabbed her from behind. She felt hands going down the front of her blouse.

The scandal broke when Coughlin told her story. It would eventually shake the American military, and the culture that supports it, more than any event since the trial of Lieutenant Calley for the My Lai massacre two decades ago. Just as Calley's trial became a symbolic event for a military haunted by losing the war in Vietnam, so the Tailhook scandal was a symbolic moment for a profession still trying to accommodate the requirements of a gender-integrated force. These requirements had already produced dramatic changes inside the military; yet feminist critics claimed

October 1993, *Heterodoxy* magazine, http://www.discoverthenetworks. org/Articles/1993%20October%20Vol%202,%20No.pdf (Michael Kitchen, a former Navy officer, attended the court proceedings, and both authors interviewed defense attorneys involved in the Tailhook prosecutions.)

that women still were assigned second-class status, since they were restricted from combat and thus from careers that conferred the highest rank and esteem. When the annual bash of the Navy's and Marine Corps' elite top guns seemed to have turned into an orgy of wholesale sexual harassment and assault, it also appeared to prove everything the critics had charged, presenting a picture of the male military culture not only resistant to change but morally degenerate and out of control. When Navy brass sought to cover up the scandal, it was taken as proof that an Old Boy Network would stop at nothing to protect its own. Critics of the military like Representative Patricia Schroeder said that heads would roll, and roll they did.

Two years and many military careers later, these images of sexual barbarism and cover-up are still firmly fixed in the public mind. Perhaps they always will be. But as the Tailhook investigations have been completed and the trials and court-martials of alleged criminals have begun, a very different picture of what took place that fall weekend emerges. That the late evening hours of Friday and Saturday nights on the third floor of the Las Vegas Hilton constituted a mob scene, which to some extent was out of control, is beyond dispute. That some $23,000 worth of damage was done (albeit mostly the result of stains on carpets) cannot be doubted. That there was in fact public lewdness and sexuality, some drunken brawling, and a general groping of females by intoxicated military personnel has been proven. Some civilian women who strayed into the third-floor party unsuspectingly were indeed verbally and physically abused, and there were perhaps one or two cases of real sexual assault.[1]

But all this notwithstanding, the Pentagon investigation conducted by civilian federal agents and involving several thousand interviews with witnesses—along with detailed reports on the

---

[1] "Report of Investigation: Tailhook 91, Events of the 35th Annual Tailhook Symposium—Part 2," Inspector General—Department of Defense April 12, 1993, 229 pages, http://www.dtic.mil/cgi-bin/GetTRDoc?AD= ada269008

night's activities in every one of the 26 hospitality suites—shows something else as well: that many victims who were identified as victims in the press, and who are identified as victims even in the Pentagon report, do not consider themselves victims; that many who do consider themselves victims, including the chief accuser, Paula Coughlin,[2] were willing collaborators in the sexual frivolities that spilled over into the abuse of innocents; that when the party was over, and Coughlin and her cohorts appeared to advance a cause, it was not the cause of "duty, honor, country" but a gender cause that regards the military as an enemy to be defeated by a war of social attrition.[3]

From the beginning, the Tailhook scandal had the air of a public burning rather than a dispassionate inquiry into the facts of the case. Before a single participant in Tailhook was given his day in court, the Secretary of the Navy and six admirals, including the commander in charge of the Navy's own investigation, had been sacked and their careers terminated; 4,000 Navy and Marine Corps promotions were held up; and the entire male enlisted corps was required to attend sessions that added up to a million hours of sensitivity training.[4]

The tangled chronology of investigation began with Paula Coughlin. She did not report her assault to the Hilton security staff or to the police the night it allegedly occurred, but the next morning she did file a complaint with her boss, Rear Admiral Jack Snyder. After reading it, Snyder did not regard the complaint as warranting any action (a judgment that would cost him his career). After several weeks without a response to her complaint, Coughlin wrote to Vice Admiral Richard M. Dunleavy and Dunleavy notified his superior, Admiral Jerome Johnson, the vice chief of Naval Operations. On October 11, 1991, the head of the Tailhook

---

[3]"A Tale of Two 'Paulas'," *MilitaryCorruption.com*, 2003, http://www.militarycorruption.com/paulas.htm
[4]"Where Are They Now?," *MilitaryCorruption.com*, 2011,http://www.militarycorruption.com/paulas2.htm

Association sent a letter to squadron officers who had attended the bacchanal, rebuking them for the excesses at the Hilton. "Let me relate just a few specifics to show how far across the line of responsible behavior we went," his letter said "We narrowly avoided a disaster when a 'pressed ham' [naked buttocks] pushed out an eighth floor window.... Finally, and definitely the most serious, was 'the Gauntlet' on the third floor. I have five separate reports of young ladies, several of whom had nothing to do with Tailhook, who were verbally abused, had drinks thrown on them, were physically abused and were sexually molested." This letter was leaked to the *San Diego Union* on October 29, triggering a full-scale inquiry by the Naval Investigative Service (NIS) and producing the national scandal that has determined the dynamics and shaped the meaning of the case ever since.

Two thousand one hundred witnesses were summoned for questioning about Tailhook by agents of the NIS—100 more than the number of those actually registered for the convention. Many were subjected to mandatory lie detector tests and other Star Chamber methods of interrogation that would not have been allowed under a civil investigation. When this exhaustive dragnet identified only 26 assault victims, the small number was taken as a sign of the Navy's willingness to "whitewash" the problem. A clamor went up from gender radicals, demanding a larger body count. If 4,000 men attended Tailhook, the reasoning went, there had to be more culprits. Summoning the Joint Chiefs before the House Armed Services Committee, longtime foe of the military Patricia Schroeder interrogated them in a voice dripping with sarcasm: "Is the bottom line that most of you think you can operate without women?"[5]

As a result of this political pressure, the head of the Naval Investigative Service, Rear Admiral Duval Williams, was removed

---

[5]"The Tailhook Scandals," Elaine Donnelly, *Center for Military Readiness*, January 14, 2002, http://cmrlink.org/content/article/34430/THE%20TAILHOOK%20SCANDALS

from his command. According to the subsequent Pentagon report, one of the admiral's sins was to comment, according to his female special assistant Marybel Batjer, "that, in his opinion, men simply do not want women in the military." His other two sins, according to the report, were his reluctance to interview admirals who had attended Tailhook, and "his repeatedly expressed desire to terminate the investigation." A key testimony to this allegation was a female agent's claim that "Admiral Williams said that NIS did not have 'a fart's chance in a whirlwind' of solving this investigation." Two days after the submission of the initial Navy Investigative Services report, the Secretary of the Navy—whom the Navy report had failed to place at Tailhook, even though he had been present on the third floor—was summarily cashiered.

Embarrassed by the Tailhook publicity and feeling itself vulnerable to increased budget cuts and the downsizing policy of the Bush administration, the Pentagon brass capitulated to the pressure of powerful legislators, like Schroeder, who controlled its purse strings. On June 24, 1992, a second investigation was ordered, this time by the Pentagon. Federal agents normally accustomed to tracking white-collar crimes were dispatched by the Inspector General's office of the Defense Department to investigate not only the Tailhook convention but the naval investigation itself. Their bottom-line assignment was clear: to produce a more satisfactory result.[6]

In this second effort, 22,000 man-hours were allotted to the investigation of the first investigation alone. Instead of being criticized, the Star Chamber methods of the failed Navy investigation were intensified. Eight hundred more witnesses were interrogated. Immunity was given freely in exchange for incriminating testimony. At least one senior Marine officer was put on notice by investigators that, if he did not cooperate, he would be audited by

---

[6] "Top Brass Oppose Women In Combat," *Chicago Tribune*, July 31, 1992, http://articles.chicagotribune.com/1992-07-31/news/9203080972_1_combat-exclusion-combat-positions-tailhook-scandal

the IRS (and subsequently was). Other officers were told that, if they did not comply, their names would be given to the media. These techniques of intimidation paid off. This time 90 assault victims were identified, including 83 women and 7 men. (The male assaults were the result of brawls.) Penalties assessed for these and other charges ranged from fines to dismissal from the service to possible prison terms.

These ongoing inquiries have adversely affected more careers than any similar investigations since the 1950s. Like the McCarthy hearings of that era, they have created their own drama with their own heroes and villains. And, as was the case then, the morality play also has a political text. The heroine the media came to fix on was Lieutenant Paula Coughlin. Her complaint, that she had been sexually assaulted during the Saturday night revelries at the Las Vegas Hilton, was the smoking gun that led to the investigations and the incident that dramatized the public scandal surrounding them. On the same day the Pentagon began its investigation, Coughlin surfaced on a television show, revealing herself eager to step into the role of a military Anita Hill, and to play her part in the unfolding "rights" drama. The Hill-Thomas hearings had begun the very month of the Tailhook party and Anita Hill was—by Coughlin's own account—her role model and inspiration. The press was more than willing to facilitate her new career as an icon of feminist courage and progress. Coughlin's name was soon enshrined in Women of the Year stories in the national media and canonized in feminist political circles. Commander Rosemary Mariner, a prominent feminist naval officer (and herself a lifetime member of the Tailhook Association) compared Coughlin to Rosa Parks, the pioneer of the black civil rights movement: "When one individual has the courage not to accept something that's wrong, it inspires other people to have the courage to stand up."[7]

---

[7]http://en.wikipedia.org/wiki/Tailhook_scandal

But, like Anita Hill's story, Coughlin's has proven problematic, to say the least. It is a story whose hasty stitching begins to unravel under close scrutiny. In the same way that Hill's presentation of herself at the time of the hearings as a Bork conservative with no hidden political agendas has been effectively refuted by David Brock in *The Real Anita Hill,* Coughlin's presentation of herself as a morally outraged whistle-blower with no ulterior motives has been undermined by the testimony (including her own) given to government interviewers. Far from being an unsuspecting bystander who stumbled into the raunchy, raucous, intoxicated, and sometimes sexually explicit atmosphere on the Hilton's the third floor the night of September 6, Coughlin was returning to a scene with which she was already familiar. She knew that the wild party was part of a tradition that went back more than a decade; she had been to Tailhook six years earlier, in 1985. The sexual aggression she encountered this time was neither new nor unexpected. According to the Pentagon report, "Throughout the investigation, officers told us that Tailhook '91 was not significantly different from earlier conventions with respect to outrageous behavior." The report lists the Tailhook traditions that "deviated from the standards of behavior the nation expects of its military officers," including the "gantlet," ball walking (exposing the testicles), "sharking" (biting the buttocks), leg-shaving, mooning, streaking and lewd sexual conduct.

Lieutenant Paula Coughlin was an active participant in at least two of these traditions—the gantlet and leg-shaving. Leg-shaving is described in the Pentagon report in these terms: "Most of the *leg* shaving activity at Tailhook 91 occurred in the VAW-110 suite. A banner measuring approximately 10 feet long and 2 feet wide reading, FREE LEG SHAVES! was posted on the sliding doors of the VAW-110 suite in plain sight of large portions of the pool patio. According to the witnesses and the officers involved, the leg shaving was a rather elaborate ritual that included the use of hot towels and baby oil, as well as the massaging of the women's legs and feet. The entire process took between 30 and 45 minutes per shave.

Other activities often accompanied leg shaving. For example, officers in the VR-57 suite reportedly licked the females' legs with their tongues to ensure 'quality control.' Several witnesses observed nudity in conjunction with leg shaving. Three instances were reported where women exposed their breasts while being shaved in the VAW-110 suite. Witnesses related that some women wore only underwear or bikinis during leg shaving, or pulled up their shorts or underwear to expose the areas they wanted shaved." Some of the women volunteers were strippers who bared their breasts and then demanded money to remove their underpants. "One uncorroborated witness reported seeing a female naval officer having her legs shaved while wearing her whites." That woman, according to one of the Tailhook defendants, was Lieutenant Paula Coughlin.

Lieutenant Rolando Diaz, an E-2C Hawkeye pilot, made this accusation to the Pentagon team, which suppressed it. A sixteen-year veteran, Diaz had been recently selected for promotion to Lieutenant Commander. Diaz had previously attended Tailhook 90, where he performed leg-shaving without incident. For his 1991 leg-shaving, a court-martial has charged Diaz with disobeying the order of a superior commissioned officer not to shave above the mid-thigh. He has also been charged with conduct unbecoming an officer. Diaz told the Pentagon investigators and the press that he shaved Coughlin's legs twice during Tailhook 91 in the VAW-110 suite. On Friday, September 6, Diaz claims, he shaved Coughlin while she was in uniform, and the next day—the day of her alleged harassment—while she was in civilian clothes. Diaz did not ask any money for his service but requested that customers sign his banner. Diaz says that Coughlin signed the banner thus: "You make me see God. The Paulster."

The banner is now official evidence held by the Inspector General's office. Diaz's attorney, Colonel Robert Rae, has said that, if needed, he will call in handwriting experts to identify Coughlin's script. Diaz reported this incident during his official interview with Pentagon investigator Special Agent Patricia Call. But this part of his testimony was not included in Call's report. Similar omissions from the investigators' reports, damning to the male participants and protective of female participants, were widespread, according to officers who were interviewed.

Paula Coughlin also participated in the "gantlet," the most notorious Tailhook ritual. The earliest reported existence of the gantlet was contained in a Navy commander's testimony that he heard the term in the early 1980s when it referred to the hallway outside the hospitality suites as it filled with drunken officers who had overflowed the rooms. Another officer thought "the practice started in 1983 but was not termed a gantlet until 1986." At this time, Tailhook conventions were mainly stag affairs and, as women walked through the hallway, officers would call out ratings of the women who passed through. A large proportion of the women who attended the earlier Tailhook conventions were groupies and prostitutes. Wives generally did not attend, and the Las Vegas setting was treated as a port of call away from home. The Pentagon report notes that this was the first Tailhook after the Gulf War and was treated as a kind of victory celebration by the aviators. One rationale for the Tailhook behavior, according to the report, "that of returning heroes, emphasizes that naval aviation is among the most dangerous and stressful occupations in the world. During Desert Storm, for example, the U.S. Navy suffered six fatalities, all of whom were aviation officers.... Over 30 officers died in the one-year period following Tailhook '91 as a result of military aviation related accidents. Others were found to have died in nonmilitary plane accidents, in vehicle crashes and, in at least one incident, by suicide."

According to the Pentagon report, "inappropriate" touching was for the most part consensual and the women involved were "aware of and tolerant of the consequences of walking through a hallway lined with drunken male aviators." The aviators would loudly call out either "clear deck," "wave off," "foul deck" or "bolter," indicating the approach respectively of attractive females, unattractive ones, senior naval officers or security personnel. Any approaching females not turned away by these loud and raucous ratings would be warned of what lay ahead by another of the rituals associated with the antics of the gantlet—men pounding on the walls and chanting on their approach. Moreover, the dangers of a walk on this wild side were well known.

According to the official report, "indecent assaults" dated back to at least the '88 Tailhook convention. These assaults included breast, crotch and buttocks feels and efforts to put squadron stickers on the "tail" areas of the women. By 1991, these activities had clearly gotten out of hand. One female Navy lieutenant told the investigators that her squadron mates had warned her, "Don't be on the third floor after 11:00 PM." Apparently she disregarded their advice, because she told the investigators that between 10 and 10:30 PM on Saturday night the hallway was transformed from "a quiet place with 20 people" to "an absolute mob scene." The Pentagon report on this mob scene states: "Our investigation revealed that many women freely and knowingly participated in gantlet activities. A significant number of witnesses reported that women went through the gantlet and seemed to enjoy the attention and interaction with the aviators. Those witnesses, both men and women, generally stated they could tell the women were enjoying themselves because, despite being grabbed and pushed along through the crowd, they were smiling and giggling. Some of the women were observed going repeatedly through the gantlet. Many women who went through the gantlet told us they did so willingly and were not offended by the men touching them."

As an attendee at Tailhook previously, Paula Coughlin knew beforehand what the ritual entailed. Moreover, the evidence shows that she purposefully showed up on the third floor of the Hilton when the dangerous hours had begun. That Saturday morning, Coughlin had attended a Tailhook symposium at the Hilton, as Admiral Snyder's aide. When evening came, she went to the group's banquet wearing what she described to investigators as "a snazzy red silk dress" she had bought from Nieman Marcus. After dinner, according to her own testimony, she left the Hilton, went back to her own hotel (the Paddle Wheel), changed into a tube top, short denim skirt and "little black cowboy boots," and went back to the PM when she claims to have been assaulted, the gantlet was reaching its frenzied pitch. It is hard to believe that Paula Coughlin strayed into the hallway carnival unsuspectingly, or that she did not have a hidden agenda in putting herself into a situation where she knew she was going to be "harassed."

According to Coughlin, as she entered the hallway, the men started chanting, "Admiral's aide! Admiral's aide!" Marine Corps Captain Gregory J. Bonam bumped into her from behind. "He grabbed both my buttocks and lifted me off the ground almost," she testified. She spun around and their faces were within six inches of each other. "What the fuck are you doing?" she asked him. She immediately noticed his eyes and his burnt orange shirt with the monogram "Boner" across the chest, as she later testified. Then somebody else grabbed her from behind; Bonam forced his hands down the front of her blouse and squeezed her breasts. When Bonam let go, she turned and faced him. "He had his hands across his chest," she testified, "with his chest out proud and he smiled." At the trial, Bonam denied assaulting Coughlin and testified that he had spent most of the evening out of the hallway in a suite nicknamed the "Rhino Room" in honor of his squadron's mascot. His attorney produced a photograph taken that night, showing Bonam dressed in a green "Raging Rhino" shirt—not the orange shirt that Coughlin alleged.

Paula Coughlin was not the only "victim" with problems sustaining her testimony in the legal proceedings. Ensign Elizabeth Warnick had accused Navy Lieutenant Cole Cowden of holding her "down on a bed, pulling off her underwear, kissing her thighs and touching her pubic area," and attempting with two other officers to gang-rape her. Providing more detail, Warnick told the Pentagon investigators that she had a dinner date with Lieutenant Cowden and arrived at his room at 7:00 PM. The door was ajar, so she knocked and entered. As she stepped into the dimly lit room, three men grabbed and blindfolded her, threw her on the bed and

274 VOLUME V: CULTURE WARS

began to take her clothes off. But she was able to kick one of them off and fight her way free from the other two and flee the room. She did not report the incident or talk about it to anyone until the scandal broke.

The reason she kept silent was that her story was made up, or embellished so as to transform its meaning. Under repeated interrogations, Warnick changed her story considerably. In the new version, she sat down on the bed with Cowden, who began to kiss her. She responded and they moved to more heated necking and she helped him take off her stockings. While they were on the bed, she felt the presence of a second man and they began a 2 v. 1 (fighter lingo for a threesome). For a while, according to Warnick, it "felt good." Then she became uncomfortable, kicked Cowden off the bed and fled the room.

But even this version of the story was false. Warnick's motive in lying, as she admitted under oath, was to deceive her fiancé and prevent him from learning that she had cheated on him at Tailhook. Warnick had told investigators that she was disgusted with Tailhook after her experience at the previous convention. But, under oath, she admitted she had engaged in leg-shaving, had allowed Cowden and others to drink "belly shots" of liquor out of her navel, and had had sex three times with a lieutenant commander (whom she falsely accused of sexually harassing her). Excerpts from the transcript are unambiguous:

> **Defense Atty:** Now, you indicated already that you lied on your initial account of having been assaulted?
> **Warnick:** Yes, sir.
> **Defense Atty:** You also indicated you lied about having sex with Lieutenant Commander X?
> **Warnick:** Yes, sir.
> **Defense Atty:** Initially you denied having consensual sex with Lt. Cowden at Tailhook '90?
> **Warnick:** Yes, sir.
> **Defense Atty:** Is that a fair summary of your testimony?
> **Warnick:** Yes, sir.

As a result of the exposure of Warnick's perjury, all charges against Cowden were dropped.

Far from being unique, the complicities of Warnick and Coughlin were the rule at Tailhook, revealing the scandal as a witch-hunt driven by political agendas. The true scandal is that the vague accusations of "sexual harassment" became imprinted as facts of "sexual assault" on the public mind. As the investigations have moved into various military courts, the flimsy evidentiary base has crumbled, producing a dissonance not unlike when Senator Joseph McCarthy would emerge from a Senate cloakroom claiming that there were 247 or 81 or 23 Communist agents in the State Department, depending on who was asking and with how much specific knowledge. Thus, press accounts of Tailhook will mention 175 or 140 or 83 officers as having been involved in "assaults" or "sexual misconduct" or "conduct unbecoming" during the Las Vegas party, while the bottom line is this: after nearly two years and $4 million of investigations, the Pentagon has felt on solid enough ground to bring only 3 such charges of sexual assault.[8]

As the Pentagon's official report makes clear, this result is not really surprising. There were 100 Hilton security guards on duty during the Tailhook convention, 12 of whom were present and patrolling on the third floor during the gantlet revelries where the scandal-making incidents occurred. The exhaustive summary of the Pentagon investigation describes each intervention by the Hilton staff. The security officers "stopped three aviators from carrying off a wall lamp they had torn from a wall; [they] broke up a large crowd of aviators who were chanting at a woman in an attempt to encourage the woman to expose her breasts; [they] stopped an intoxicated naked male who had walked out of room onto the pool patio and returned him to his room; [they responded

---

[8]Neil Lewis, "Tailhook Affair Brings Censure of 3 Admirals," *The New York Times,* October 16, 1993; http://www.nytimes.com/1993/10/16/us/tailhook-affair-brings-censure-of-3-admirals.html

to] incidents involving public urination, physical altercations and aviators expectorating ignited alcohol." In another incident, a security officer was walking with a woman on the pool patio when she was "grabbed on the buttocks." The report then states: "The woman verbally confronted her attacker but the security officer, at the woman's request, took no action."

The Pentagon summary then describes "the most significant incident reported by a security guard." Hearing a commotion, security guards approached a crowd of men in the hallway and "witnessed a pair of pants being thrown up in the air." On closer examination, they saw an intoxicated woman, naked from the waist down, lying on the floor of the hallway. The security officers assisted her and reported the incident to the executive director of the Tailhook Association, "warning him that improper conduct by attendees had to cease or the hotel would be forced to close down all activities in the hallway." In addition, there was an assault reported by two women who also reported the matter to the Las Vegas police. The police referred them back to hotel security because the women refused to return to the third floor and attempt to identify their attackers. This was the only report of an assault made that night by any alleged victim, either to hotel security or to the Las Vegas police: "The security officers told us that, excluding the aforementioned incidents, no women reported being assaulted nor did any of the security officers witness any assaults."[9]

After the fact, during the Navy and Pentagon investigations, when pressed by military investigators, many Tailhook participants claimed to have witnessed "indecent assaults" which were not reported at the time. In a section of the Pentagon report titled "Victims," the claim is made that, in the four days of Tailhook,

---

[9]"Report of Investigation: Tailhook 91, Events of the 35th Annual Tailhook Symposium—Part 2, Section IX," Inspector General—Department of Defense April 12, 1993, http://www.dtic.mil/cgi-bin/GetTRDoc? AD=ada269008

"at least 90 people were victims of some form of indecent assault," including 83 women and 7 men.[10] According to the report, 68 of the assaults took place on Saturday evening and, except for one, all of those took place on the third floor. The report adds the astonishing fact that 10 of the women had been assaulted at previous Tailhook conventions. It also reports that 8 were assaulted more than once, 4 on more than one occasion that evening, while 9 "did not consider themselves to be a 'victim,' even though they had been subjected to indecent assault." But if they did not consider themselves to be victims, how could the incidents be described as assaults? In an intriguing footnote, the report explains: "We have used the term 'victim' to describe any individual who was subjected to a nonconsensual indecent assault," i.e., even when the victim does not consider herself victimized.

Lacking a real criminal dimension, the only way Tailhook could be made to appear an epoch- making scandal was to use the strictly military charge of "conduct unbecoming an officer" to inflate the number of total offenses into "140 acts of assault and indecent conduct." But when it eventually came time to prosecute, this method of raising the body count did not hold up in court. Thus Lieutenant Cowden, alleged attacker of Ensign Warnick, was charged with "conduct unbecoming" on the basis of a picture the Inspector General's office found of him with his face pressed against a woman's breast. His tongue was sticking out and her hand was behind his neck, apparently pushing his head down. IG agent Peter Black tracked the woman down and interviewed her in Las Vegas.[11] During the interview, the woman told Black

---

[10]"Report of Investigation: Tailhook 91, Events of the 35th Annual Tailhook Symposium—Part 2, Section VI," Inspector General—Department of Defense April 12, 1993, http://www.dtic.mil/cgi-bin/GetTRDoc? AD=ada269008

[11]"Tailhook Investigator Eavesdropped On Phone Call," William H. McMichael, *Daily Press*, September 8, 1993; http://articles.dailypress. com/1993-09-08/news/9309080015_1_navy-s-tailhook-investigation-thomas-r-miller-tailhook-scandal

that she did not consider herself to be a victim or to have been assaulted. She added that she did not want Cowden to get in trouble for the picture. Ignoring the woman's expressed views, Agent Black had her sign a statement that he wrote to include all the elements of a sexual assault case.

The cross-examination at Cowden's court-martial proceedings revealed the lengths to which the government agents were prepared to go in order to produce culprits:

Defense Atty: That first statement by Ms. M., who wrote that?
Agent Black: I did, sir.
Defense Atty: Did she tell you that she didn't consider that an assault?
Agent Black: Yes, sir.
Defense Atty: Did she tell you that she didn't appreciate the government telling her whether or not she's been assaulted?
Agent Black: That I don't remember, sir.
Defense Atty: You explained it to her that it was an assault whether or not she considered it to be an assault Correct?
Agent Black: That's correct sir.

The defense attorney, Lieutenant Commander Jeffrey Good, then turned to the woman's own statement, producing an even more chilling look at the mentality of the government's agents:

Defense Atty: Have you read her subsequent statement that she provided?
Agent Black: Yes, sir.
Defense Atty: It's a lot different than her first statement.
Agent Black: Yes, sir.
Defense Atty: So, the statement that you wrote out [made it seem that Cowden's behavior] constituted an assault even though the woman clearly told you that she had not been assaulted?
Agent Black: Yes, sir.
Defense Atty: Now, looking at the second statement, it's pretty clear that she hasn't been assaulted. Correct?
Agent Black: In her view, yes, sir.

Defense Atty: Whose view is important here, the view of the victim or the view of you?
Agent Black: Well, I would answer that question, sir, by saying that . . .
Defense Atty: No, the question was whose view is important. If you're talking about an assault, a woman has been assaulted, whose view is important?
Agent Black: In this instance, the government.

Thus, in the Tailhook investigation, it appears, the United States government has taken the position immortalized by Lavrenti Beria, the head of Stalin's secret police, who said, "You bring me the man, I'll find the crime." This of course is merely a particularly brutal way of expressing what has become the cardinal principle of the new feminist jurisprudence, which maintains that, where gender is concerned, the crime is in the eye of the accuser and, when the accuser won't accuse because of false consciousness or some other defect, it is in the eye of the government.

Almost as illuminating as the government's prosecution of Lieutenant Cowden was its failure to charge Lieutenant Diaz with "conduct unbecoming" for shaving the legs of Lieutenant Coughlin, an infraction he freely admits. Diaz is indeed facing a court-martial for leg-shaving but on a different legal ground. As the *San Diego Union* reported the story, "Rather than charge Diaz with conduct unbecoming an officer—a charge that might also have been made against Coughlin and the two other female officers identified by the Pentagon inspector general as having had their legs shaved—the Navy took a different tack. Diaz was charged with disobeying an order from a Navy commander instructing him not to shave a woman's legs above the knees." What the *Union* failed to add was that if such an order had indeed been given (as Diaz denies that it was), it would itself have been an illegal order, since it had no bearing on military duties, and military orders must relate to military purposes. A naval officer can't be ordered to mow a superior's lawn, let alone shave a leg below the thigh.

The charges based on "conduct unbecoming" expose the political nature of the entire Tailhook prosecution. No similar charges have been leveled at any females, even though culpable activities like leg-shaving and "belly shots" could not have taken place without the willing participation of female officers. Lieutenant Elizabeth Warnick has not been charged with perjury, nor faced with any disciplinary measures for lying under oath, let alone with any conduct-unbecoming charges for her participation in belly shots and the "lewd behavior" which made her male partners culpable. Nor has Lieutenant Coughlin. Nor has any other female been faced with disciplinary action for leveling false charges or (as in the case of one female Navy lawyer) parading around the entire evening topless. "The agenda of the Pentagon Inspector General did not include looking at the misconduct of women," a senior naval officer told *San Diego Union* reporter Greg Vistica, the journalist who broke the Tailhook story.[12] "It was a conscious decision," the officer added, "to punish male aviators for misconduct. That was the direction, and investigators were not going to get sidetracked by the misconduct of women." Sidetracked indeed. Sidetracked from justice, or from advancing a feminist agenda?

The Navy brass had set out to appease the feminists in Congress, and to forestall military spending cuts by showing that it would prosecute men. As acting Navy Secretary Sean O'Keefe said in unveiling the Pentagon report at a press conference on September 24: "I need to emphasize a very, very important message. We get it. We know that the larger issue is a cultural problem, which has allowed demeaning behavior and attitudes toward women to exist within the Navy Department. Over the past two and a half

---

[12]"Hooked! ('The San Diego Union-Tribune' military affairs reporter Greg Vistica)," Bill Wright, *The Quill*, September 1, 1992, http://www.access-mylibrary.com/article-1G1-13836784/hooked-san-diego-union.html
[13]Melissa Healy, "Pentagon Blasts Tailhook Probe, Two Admirals Resign," *Los Angeles Times*, September 25, 1992; http://tech.mit.edu/V112/N44/ tailhook.44w.html

months, the Navy Department has pursued an aggressive campaign to address this issue."[13]

To prosecute the women involved in the Tailhook party would have punctured a fatal hole in the feminist myth that all women on the third floor were victims. Before the appearance of the final report, Elaine Donnelly, a former Pentagon official and head of the Center for Military Readiness, complained to Navy Secretary John H. Dalton about the selective prosecution of male officers, to no avail. She later commented, "The apparent double standard at work here is both demoralizing to Navy men and demeaning to military women. I am disappointed ... that you apparently have no intention of issuing a general statement of principle that prosecutions must be conducted fairly, without regard to rank or sex of the person who allegedly engaged in improper conduct at the Tailhook convention."[14]

The Pentagon's disregard for the principle of fairness began with the second investigation by the Inspector General, which was specifically tasked with finding out why the first Navy investigation didn't come up with the requisite number of criminals. Barbara Pope, an Assistant Secretary of the Navy, threatened to resign in the middle of the 1992 presidential election campaign unless all of the commanding and executive officers of squadrons who attended Tailhook were fired.[15] Rather than stand up to this latter-day McCarthyism in which the officers would be assumed guilty before trial, Secretary of Defense Cheney acquiesced in the witch-hunt, which had the immediate effect of increasing the body count of the Navy probe.

"I have been a Navy prosecutor, and I worked in the state's attorney office. I've been on both sides, but I have never seen the likes of this ever, anywhere," commented defense counsel Robert

---

[14]Letter supplied by Elaine Donnelly to the authors.
[15]"Tailhook Scandal," *Wikipedia,* http://en.wikipedia.org/wiki/Tailhook_scandal

Rae of the suppression of evidence and extralegal methods used by the government investigators in their attempts to come up with a sufficient number of victims that would satisfy Barbara Pope and Pat Schroeder. "People are charged with felony offense-level charges with no evidence or evidence patently insufficient and totally without any credible testimony."[16]

Commander Jeffrey Good, the lawyer for Lt. Cowden, was of a similar mind. "The reports of interview are shoddy and can't be relied on," he told *The Washington Times*. "I think Tailhook is a mountain out of a molehill from what I have seen. There certainly was some misconduct there, but I think it's been blown out of proportion and I think the Navy is overreacting with these prosecutions."[17]

What Tailhook really represents is another skirmish—along with the clash over gays in the military—on the most important battlefield of the new diversity. Until recently, the military was the sole institution to remain relatively protected from the malign influences of the social engineers. But that is no longer the case. The Pentagon report is fully aware of the culture war that enveloped its investigation. The report notes that the 1991 Tailhook convention was affected by the victory in the Gulf War, the downsizing of the military which would most affect the junior officers involved in the Tailhook excesses, and the growing debate initiated by ranking Armed Services Committee member Pat Schroeder about women in combat. A GAO report, not mentioned in the Tailhook summary, estimated that 90 percent of the "sexual harassment" charges in the military as a whole stemmed from resentment over double standards and the role of women in previously male preserves.

The double standards present in the Tailhook investigations are merely extensions of the double standards that have come to pervade the military in the last decade, as a result of pressure from feminists like Schroeder. These range from double standards in performance tests at all the military academies (except the

---

[16]Authors' interview with Robert Rae
[17]William H. McMichael, "The Mother of All Hooks: The Story of the U.S. Navy's Tailhook Scandal," Transaction, 1997

Marines') to double standards in facing death. Women failed to be ready for battle at a rate three to four times that of men during Desert Storm, mainly as a result of pregnancy; in one notorious instance, 10 percent of the female sailors aboard the Navy ship *Arcadia* became pregnant after leaving port in California for the Gulf, thus avoiding the risks of actual combat.[18] Not one of the women was court-martialed. Instead the military financed the births and the maternity leaves for the women involved.

This debate was in the air when the Tailhook convention took place in Las Vegas in September 1991. Five weeks before Tailhook, Paula Coughlin was lobbying on Capitol Hill for a repeal of the restriction on women in combat. According to the testimony of one Navy commander present at Tailhook, Lieutenant Paula Coughlin became embroiled in an argument with him on Friday night, before the Saturday night gantlet and other capers, over just this subject. Coughlin, it was well known, was chafing under the restrictions that prevented her from piloting a combat helicopter. During the argument about women in combat, Coughlin angrily told the commander that "a woman getting pregnant was no different than a man breaking a leg." If Coughlin felt she didn't get the best of the argument on that Friday evening in Las Vegas, the subsequent scandal she triggered changed its dynamics dramatically. In her new persona as a national heroine, she told the Los Angeles *Times:* "I look at many of these guys—who still don't get it—and I think to myself: 'It *was* their Navy. It's soon going to be *my* generation's Navy.'" Whether this would make it a more efficient killing machine and defender of the nation, neither Coughlin nor Schroeder had anything to say.

Nor was the issue of women in combat only on the mind of Paula Coughlin at Tailhook, although she may have been the only one who acted on her convictions. The conflict over the policy, recently proposed by Schroeder, to allow women to fly combat aircraft was "the single, most talked about topic" at the convention, according to

---

[18]"36 Women Pregnant Aboard a Navy Ship That Served in Gulf," *New York Times, AP,* April 30, 1991; http://www.nytimes.com/1991/04/30/us/36-women-pregnant-aboard-a-navy-ship-that-served-in-gulf.html

the Pentagon investigation. At the "Red Flag Panel" where the issue of women flying combat aircraft was discussed, the issue "elicited strong reactions from attendees." These included both cheers and applause when one male officer forcibly stated his personal objections to women in combat, and complaints from the women when a male Vice Admiral failed to provide "sufficient support" for their position. One female aviator complained to Pentagon investigators that, immediately following the Flag Panel, she was "verbally harassed by male aviators who expressed to her their belief that women should not be employed in naval aviation. They also accused her of having sexual relations with senior officers while deployed on carrier assignment."

Instead of allowing the dispute to work itself out within the military community—perhaps with the restoration of single standards for both genders, which would eliminate much of the male resentment— the Tailhook scandal tipped the scales in favor of the feminists. In the wake of Tailhook and Clinton's election, an executive order by the new Secretary of Defense allowed to women fly combat planes for the first time—a victory achieved by scandal rather than by demonstrated competence.

Meanwhile, the trials continue. Symbolic of the tragedies that resulted from the witch-hunt is the case of Commander Robert Stumpf. An 18-year veteran in the military's most dangerous and demanding profession, he was commander of the Blue Angels, the Navy's elite flight demonstration team. An F-18 pilot and Gulf war hero, Stumpf received the Distinguished Flying Cross for his heroism in Desert Storm. He came to Tailhook to receive the Estocin Award for the best F/A-18 squadron in the Navy. But he found himself removed from his command without a single charge being filed against him. His crime was to have visited in a private room (not on the third floor) where a stripper performed fellatio on an aviator, after Stumpf had left.[19]

---

[19]Interview with Commander Robert Stumpf, *PBS Frontline,* 1993; http://www.pbs.org/wgbh/pages/frontline/shows/navy/oldnew/stumpf2 .html

Commander Stumpf is like the thousands of victims of the witch-hunt that scarred our country several decades past. But there is one big difference. The vast majority of those who lost their jobs because of McCarthyism were supporters of a police state which was their country's enemy. The crime of Commander Stumpf was to serve his country and risk his life, as a male, to defend it.

3

The Feminist Assault
on the Military

For nearly two decades after the Sixties, the U.S. military remained the one institution that had withstood the baleful influences of the radical left. Now that the Cold War is over, this immunity appears to have ended. A series of relatively trivial incidents—a joke about women's sexual excuses, a skit with sexual innuendos mocking a female member of Congress and a drunken party at which crotches were grabbed in a gantlet ritual—have triggered a national hysteria and political witch-hunt that is threatening the very foundations of the military establishment.

The dimensions of what is happening are only dimly appreciated by the American public. The case of three-star Admiral John H. Fetterman, Jr., a naval aviator with thirty-seven years of service, provides some clues. A family man with conservative moral values and a reputation for honesty and integrity, Fetterman had earned respect as the "people's admiral," for his concern for the "little guy" and his advocacy of a wider role for women in the Navy. Capping his long and distinguished career, he had headed the Navy's air forces in the Pacific before being appointed chief of

The Presidential Commission on the Assignment of Women in the Armed Forces, 1992, http://www.cmrlink.org/content/women-in-combat/34414/women_in_land_combat?year=2004; Presidential Commission on the Assignment of Women in the Armed Forces—Alternative Views; Executive Summary, 1992, http://www.cmrlink.org/data/sites/85/CMR-Documents/PCAWAF-AV.pdf; *The Feminist Assault on the Military*, David Horowitz, Center for the Study of Popular Culture, 1992

naval education and training, the Navy's number-one shore command. A month after the Tailhook revelations, Fetterman was busted in rank. Days later, he took an early retirement.

Fetterman's crime? He had been accused anonymously over a harassment "hotline" of shielding an aide from naval investigators. The aide, a chief petty officer, had made a pass, while drunk, at another enlisted man. In less fevered circumstances this incident might have slipped by without notice. But in the wake of Tailhook, the furies of sexual purity demanded blood. One female officer, among the hundreds who rallied to Fetterman's support, told the *San Diego Union* in horror, "They're going after the wrong admiral. This shows you the whole world is upside down."

In justifying an otherwise incomprehensible act against one of its most respected commanders, the Navy hierarchy reached for the blunt instrument of innuendo. In an official statement, the Navy said that the relationship of Fetterman and his wife with the chief petty officer "appears to have been unduly familiar." In a poignant defense to his commanding officer, Fetterman replied:

That conclusion is based upon observations that my wife extended the courtesies of our home to the chief in question. In response, I must note my wife is a caring and gracious person. She has always made all members of the Navy family feel like they are part of our family. That particular attribute is one of her greatest strengths and one for which I will not apologize.

Then he warned that the measures being taken to root out sexual harassers might end up doing "irreparable damage to the military."

For the past few months, we have seen the reputations of honorable men and women tarnished by innuendo, falsehood and rumor. Enough! Our Navy is populated by decent, honest and dedicated people. They need to be recognized as such.

But it will be a long time before the Navy's honor is restored and the concept of innocent until proven guilty is respected again in military quarters. The feminist movement leading the current witch-hunt is far from spent. It began in earnest a decade ago, when the army attempted to introduce a sex-neutral system to test the physical strength of recruits. Designed to match individual abilities to military requirements, the Military Enlistment Physical Strength Capacity Test (MEPSCAT) provoked objections at the time from feminists inside and outside the military, who feared that sex-neutral standards might cause women to be barred from certain roles, particularly combat roles, which were the keys to military status and advancement.

Although the Air Force held out and maintained the objectivity of the test, the Army and Navy caved in to feminist critics. As the feminists' objections were met, the MEPSCAT test was reduced to a "guidance tool." The double standard had taken its first step in becoming a way of life in the military, as it has in other institutions of American life. The only area where a true standard remained in force was combat itself. Now, ten years later, combat has become the issue and, with incidents like Tailhook ripe for exploitation, the pressure to surrender to the feminist levelers appears all but insurmountable.

That pressure is embodied in the "Schroeder Amendment," which would open the door to women to fly combat missions. The Amendment is named after its sponsor, liberal Democrat Pat Schroeder, who appears to be the aspiring Senator McCarthy of the current investigative frenzy. (*I have in my hand a list of harassers* . . .) In a July 9 letter to Defense Secretary Dick Cheney, Schroeder put the Pentagon on notice that "Tailhook '91 is a symptom of a larger problem" and that the resignation of Navy Secretary Garrett does not begin "to address the problem." To do *that*, the congresswoman wants investigations and prosecutions that will enable the navy to purge itself of sexual miscreants: "The Navy's inability to complete an accurate investigation and the failure to identity *and prosecute* the attackers . . . sends a clear message." [emphasis added] In addition, Schroeder demands (and has succeeded in getting) re-education classes—"sexual harassment training [for] all personnel"—to cleanse the Navy of bad attitudes.

Schroeder's bill to allow women in combat, which would also make women eligible for a future military draft, is the other face of the feminist juggernaut. Its supporters see it as a "wedge" measure that would lead to expanded combat roles and true institutional equality for women. A presidential commission has been appointed to review the issue and is scheduled to make a recommendation in November.

While the primary concern in making such a decision ought to be its possible impact on military capabilities, many of the advocates of change, and many of those who will actually decide the issue, have shown little interest in the maintenance of an effective defense. Schroeder, for example, was an antiwar activist before entering the House where, as a ranking member of the Armed Services Committee, she has been a longtime proponent of reductions in America's defense budget. Serving alongside her on the committee are feminist allies Beverly Byron, who has demanded that every officer merely present at Tailhook be thrown out of the service, and California antiwar Senator Barbara Boxer. Another ranking committee member and ardent Schroeder supporter is radical congressman Ron Dellums. Among other things, Dellums is a camp follower of Fidel Castro and other U.S. adversaries; an opponent of U.S. military interventions over the last three decades who denounced the Carter White House as "evil" for opposing Soviet aggression in Afghanistan; and a legislator who every year has sponsored an alternative defense authorization bill mandating crippling cuts in America's military forces.

When New Left radicals like myself launched the movement against the war in Vietnam, we did not say we wanted the Communists to win—which we did. Instead we said we wanted to give peace a chance; we wanted to bring the troops home. By persuading well-meaning Americans to take up our cause and by forcing Washington to bring the troops home, we accomplished our objective: the Communists won, with disastrous consequences for Vietnam and the world.

Examples of this kind of double agenda abound in the current feminist campaign; they can be found in testimony before the Presidential Commission on the Assignment of Women in the Armed

Forces. Dr. Maria Lepowsky, a graduate of Berkeley and an associate professor of anthropology and Women's Studies at the University of Wisconsin, provided testimony in support of a combat role for women. Professor Lepowsky asked: "What would be some possible consequences ... if women were put in combat—on American cultural values and American society...?" Then she answered her own question: "I think there might be increased concern about committing troops to combat, also perhaps a good thing...."[1] In other words, Lepowsky was advocating that women be put in combat roles because to do so would make it more *difficult* to commit troops to combat. This kind of candor is unusual for the left.

The feminist movement, which supplies the ideological framework for witnesses like Professor Lepowsky and advocates like Pat Schroeder, is typical of those in which radicals have played significant roles. It is a coalition of different voices in which radicals set the political agendas, but not all the agendas are on the surface. Moderate feminists generally are seeking modest reforms in American society. Technological developments in the 20th century have dramatically changed women's social roles. Women no longer risk death in the normal course of childbirth, and can choose whether to become pregnant or not. Together with labor-saving devices in the home, which have reduced the demands of maintaining a household, these technological advances have freed women to consider careers in the world at large, including in the military, where they have historically made significant contributions.

Naturally these changing opportunities for women have required some adjustments in the culture, particularly since many of the developments occurred in a relatively short time-span.

---

[1] The Presidential Commission on the Assignment of Women in the Armed Forces, 1992, http://www.cmrlink.org/content/women-in-combat/34414/women_in_land_combat?year=2004; Presidential Commission on the Assignment of Women in the Armed Forces—Alternative Views; Executive Summary, 1992, http://www.cmrlink.org/data/sites/85/CMRDocuments/PCAWAF-AV.pdf

When women entered the work force in unprecedented numbers, attitudes had to be adjusted and laws had to be changed; some traditions had to be modified and others abandoned. America is a remarkably open society, with remarkably responsive institutions, and these changes have taken place with consequent alacrity. And they are still taking place. The best and most constructive way for them to take place is deliberately, with careful consideration of possible consequences, and special respect for consequences that may be unforeseen. As the inhabitants of the former Soviet empire discovered at great human cost, revolutionary cures can often be worse than the diseases they were prescribed for.

This is a lesson lost on feminism's radical wing, whose ideology has been described by philosopher Christina Sommers as "gender feminism." Sommers contrasts this with "equity feminism," a moderate position that really means getting a fair shake. When advocates of reform speak of "gender integration" of the military, they are often invoking the ideas of the radical feminists without acknowledging what they are. Gender feminism is a bastard child of Marxism. It is the dominant ideology of women's studies departments in American universities and of feminist groups like the National Organization for Women. Gender feminism holds that women are not women by nature, but that patriarchal society has "constructed" or created them female so that men could oppress them. The system that creates females is called a patriarchy. As the source of their oppression, patriarchy must be destroyed.

Radical feminists are social engineers in the same way that communists are social engineers. They deny there is a human nature, and they deny there is a female nature, that human biology in any way fundamentally influences who or what we are. The solution to all social problems, conflicts and disappointments in life is to manipulate laws and institutions so as to create liberated human beings—beings who will not hate, or have prejudices, or exhibit bad sexual manners, or get into conflicts that lead to war. By changing institutions, especially powerful institutions like the military, and using their administrative power to brainwash people into adopting attitudes that are politically correct, these radicals believe that the problems that have plagued mankind since the dawn of creation will be miraculously cured.

Social engineers like the gender feminists have little interest in questions of America's national security—not because they are in the pay of foreign powers, but because they believe that America is a patriarchal, sexist, racist oppressor and that its institutions must be destroyed or transformed beyond recognition, if women and other oppressed groups are to achieve their liberation. Of course, the gender feminists are not so naive as to admit their radical agendas outside the ideological sanctuaries of women's studies departments. In testifying before presidential commissions, they sound like equity feminists. They will say that placing women in combat positions is merely an extension of women working outside the home, and of expanding equal opportunity

But placing women in harm's way and training them to kill one-on-one is not a mere extension of working outside the home. Furthermore, there are definite limits to equal rights and equal opportunity when biology is involved. Do I, for example, as an American male, have a right to bear a child? Do I have an equal opportunity with women to do so? Do they have an equal aptitude for combat? Ninety percent of the people arrested for violent crimes in the United States are, and always have been, male. From this statistic alone, it would be possible to conclude that males have a distinct advantage over females when it comes to mobilizing an instinct for aggression for the purposes of organized combat.

One of the leading military advocates of equal roles for women and men is Commander Rosemary Mariner, a nineteen-year career naval officer. In June, Commander Mariner testified before the presidential commission that women should not be excluded from

---

[2]The Presidential Commission on the Assignment of Women in the Armed Forces, 1992, http://www.cmrlink.org/content/women-in-combat/34414/women_in_land_combat?year=2004; Presidential Commission on the Assignment of Women in the Armed Forces—Alternative

combat because "separate is inherently unequal."[2] Perhaps, but so what? The founding documents of this country recognize the rights to life, liberty and the pursuit of happiness. They do not recognize the rights of short people to be tall, of less intelligent people to have higher intelligence, of physically weaker people to be stronger, of less aggressive people to be more aggressive, or of women to be deployed in military combat.

Men and women are different *and unequal* in various abilities. To all but gender feminists, that is an obvious, indisputable fact. The question is, what are the consequences of that fact? The difficulty in answering the question is the emotional element that is introduced into the discussion by the moral and political claims of the feminist left. Mariner's testimony before the commission, a testimony infused with radical nostrums and logically incoherent, is instructive: "As with racial integration the biggest problem confronting gender integration is not men or women, but bigotry. It is bigotry that is the root cause of racial and sexual harassment. From common verbal abuse to the criminal acts of a Tailhook debacle, sexual harassment will continue to be a major problem in the armed forces because the combat exclusion law and policies make women institutionally inferior."[3]

The basic elements of the radical view are all here. Sexual relations between men and women are to be understood in terms of racial relations between blacks and whites. The problems between men and women are analogous to racism and unrelated to biology or the different sexual drives of men and women. The root of the problem is not individuals but institutions. "Tailhook '91," wrote Schroeder in her letter to the Secretary of Defense, "is the symptom of a larger problem: institutional bias against women." In feminist terms, the social construction of women that renders them different from men is made possible by the patriarchal system

---

Views; Executive Summary, 1992, http://www.cmrlink.org/data/sites/85/CMRDocuments/PCAWAF-AV.pdf

[3] Ibid.

that causes them to be perceived as inferior. In the eyes of the gender feminists, the exclusion of women from combat is a keystone of this system. If women were to be included in combat, if gender roles were to be abolished, then sexual harassment would cease to be a significant problem.

Consider the proposition: For five thousand years men have been more aggressive sexually than women. Recognizing this, societies have universally established different sexual rules for men and women. And, for all that time, some men have failed to heed those rules and have overstepped the boundaries of decent behavior. But according to the gender feminists, that is merely the past. Now the U.S. military has a chance to solve this problem once and for all—by passing the Schroeder amendment and removing the barriers to women in combat. As soon as the exclusion law is changed, women's self-esteem will rise, men's respect for women will increase, and—*mirabile dictu*—sexual harassment will cease.

It is difficult to believe that rational people could propose such nonsense; but this is the fundamental idea that feminists promote from their pulpits *ad nauseam.* And to which our military brass and political leadership are kowtowing at an alarming pace. It is an instructive example of how radical ideology can glue up the brain. If people were seriously looking at the question of military effectiveness, they would see that the greatest threat to military morale today is being created by the onslaught of half-baked feminist ideas that are making every male in the military—from the highest brass to the lowliest grunt—guilty before the fact, guilty just because he is a male.

- Item: This summer, Jerry Tuttle, a three-star admiral who had been nominated by the president for one of the 12 top posts in the navy, was subjected to public humiliation when the president was forced to withdraw his nomination. Why? Because a newsletter for which he was responsible printed the following joke: *Beer is better than women because beer never has a headache.*

- Item: Three top gun fliers were relieved of their commands because of their participation in, or witnessing of, a privately shown skit in the annual Tom Cat Follies at the Miramar Naval Station. The skit lampooned Congresswoman Schroeder.

What is going on in America that a three-star admiral can be denied a promotion over a lame male joke that he didn't even make? Or that seasoned fliers can have their careers terminated because of possible offense to a politician? How could a Republican president and Navy Department cave in to pressures like this, and why isn't there national outrage over the injustice and stupidity of it? And, finally, what is the problem with feminists who can't handle this kind of trivia and yet want to enter a war zone and engage in combat!

There *is* a big problem out there and it is this: We are fast becoming a nation of hypocrites and liars in our unseemly haste to humor ideological bluenoses like Mariner and Schroeder, and to submit the lives of honorable, dedicated men like Admiral Tuttle and the Miramar commanders to the tender mercies of the feminist thought-police. Thanks to Representative Schroeder, her supporting wolf-pack and the weak-kneed defense brass who won't stand up to them, the men in our armed services are now guilty for being men: for having encountered women who have used headaches as an excuse for not wanting sex; for suffering the abuse of a vindictive congresswoman in silence; and for making lame jokes to ventilate their frustrations.

According to feminists like Commander Mariner, people who even suggest that it might not be a good idea to include women in combat are hereby put on notice that they are encouraging bigotry and most likely are bigots themselves. Studies conducted at West Point have identified 120 physical differences between men and women that may bear on military requirements. Yet the U.S.

Naval Academy has been criticized for not moving fast enough to increase its female enrollment on the grounds that this is mere prejudice. Meanwhile, an official Committee on Women's Issues headed by Rear Admiral Virgil Hill has called for the "immediate dismissal of senior officers who question the role of women in the military." To question—*to question*—the role of women in the military is now regarded as bigotry by the military itself.

The word "bigot" has resonance. It is meant to invoke the specter of racism and, simultaneously, to appropriate the moral mantle of the civil rights movement for the feminist cause. This feminist attempt to hijack the civil rights movement has always struck me as spurious and offensive. Women, as a gender, were never oppressed as American blacks and their ancestors were oppressed. It is the big lie of feminism to speak of "patriarchy" as a system of oppression—to see women's restricted social roles as unrelated to restrictions imposed by their biology and the state of technological development.

Black people were enslaved for centuries. Their slavery was justified by whites who judged them to be less than human. That was racism. *Sexism*, by contrast, is a mind-numbing term invented by Marxist radicals to stigmatize their opponents, while appropriating the moral legacy of the struggle against racism to make their attacks seem righteous. No western civilization, let alone western democracy, ever regarded women as inferior in the sense that blacks were. None has ever failed to value and cherish them. Despite the fog of feminist propaganda, we don't need elaborate studies to prove this. Men's feelings for women have been richly recorded in Western culture. Homer's *Iliad*, which gives expression to the informing myths of Hellenic society, and is a founding document of Western civilization is about a war over a woman. Even the most dimwitted ideologue should be able to see that there is power in womanhood there.

As for more recent attitudes, anyone who thinks that, before *The Femine Mystique*, women in America were denigrated as mere bodies without character or brains should catch the next showing of any Katherine Hepburn film on *American Movie Classics*. In *Adam's Rib*, a film made in the 1940s, Hepburn and Spencer Tracy play husband and wife lawyers who wind up on opposite sides of a major case. The wife, who is clearly the smarter and more mature individual, wins. And this is only one of scores of such popular expressions of women's prowess. Only in Betty Friedan's febrile imagination was the American family a "comfortable concentration camp" before the advent of NOW.

Yet the argument is still made that the decision to put women in combat is somehow crucial to women's self-esteem and to men's respect. It is a constant theme of the presidential commission hearings. In discussing the inclusion of women in combat, for example, Professor Lepowsky had this to say: "There might be a significant impact ... on female self-esteem, especially for young girls and young women, the idea that male fraternity and male respect of women was possible."[4]

On what planet is Professor Lepowsky living? Including women in combat would give women the idea that male friendship for and respect of women was *possible?* If men don't respect women, why do women fall in love with men and marry them? Is there something wrong with women? Are they so brain-deficient or brainwashed as a gender to be involved intimately with a species that doesn't respect them? Only a feminist ideologue could explain that. It only serves to confirm the suspicion that, behind every radical feminist's concern for what women might be, there lies a profound contempt for who they are. Yet this is the kind of thinking that is being factored into the future of our armed forces.

What is truly worrying about all this is that there is now an atmosphere of intimidation in the public sphere that prevents any

---

[4]The Presidential Commission on the Assignment of Women in the Armed Forces, 1992, http://www.cmrlink.org/content/women-in-combat/34414/women_in_land_combat?year=2004; Presidential Commission on the Assignment of Women in the Armed Forces—Alternative Views; Executive Summary, 1992, http://www.cmrlink.org/data/sites/85/CMRDocuments/PCAWAF-AV.pdf

candor on these issues. Jobs can be and are being lost, careers are being ruined, reputations are being tarnished because of politically incorrect views on these issues. These are disgraceful times, and they are fraught with danger where national security matters are concerned.

In its Washington session in June, the presidential commission also heard testimony from William S. Lind, former defense advisor to Gary Hart. In his testimony, Lind referred to the suppression of information vital to the decisions the commission was going to make. According to Lind, the Army Personnel Office has detailed information on problems encountered with women troops in Desert Storm, which had not been released to the public. They include the fact that the non-deployability rate for women in the Gulf was many times higher than that for men. Specifically, when the troops were called to battle, between three and four times as many women per enlisted personnel were unavailable for duty. The inability to deploy women troops apparently caused immediate turmoil with negative effects on unit cohesion, which is a primary component of combat effectiveness. Another piece of important information that was not made public is the fact that, despite rigid measures taken in the field, there was no drop in the pregnancy rate through the period of deployment. Pregnancy during Desert Shield was the primary reason for non-deployability.

Why is this information on the back burner? Where are the famous investigative reporters from "60 Minutes" and *The Washington Post,* ever vigilant against the evils of military censorship? Perhaps our politically correct media lack interest in information that could sow doubts about the case for gender integration—even if the suppression of that information might jeopardize our men on some future field of battle. Suppression of information about women's actual performance in some traditionally male jobs is not unique to the military. As a journalist I have interviewed policemen who will talk—off the record—of the dangers they face because of women partners who are not as physically intimidating as men. I have talked to construction workers who will talk—off the record—of having to carry women the law has forced onto their crews, even though they are not physically strong enough to do a full share of the work.

The suppression of information has provided one answer to these problems. Gender norming provides another. This is the practice of institutionalizing the double standard so that women are measured in performance against other women, rather than against men who can outperform them. Gender norming is now the rule at all military service academies, as is the cover-up of the adverse consequences of the new policies of admitting women. The official position at West Point, for example, is that there have been *no* negative effects stemming from the admission of women to the Academy. The facts, as revealed in a recent Heritage study by Robert Knight, are quite different. Knight's information is drawn from the sworn testimony of a West Point official taken in a Virginia court:

- When men and women are required to perform the same exercises, women's scores are weighted to compensate for their deficiencies.
- Women cadets take comparable training when they cannot meet the physical standards for male cadets.
- In load-bearing tasks, 50 percent of the women score below the bottom 5 percent of the men.
- Peer ratings have been eliminated because women were scoring too low.

To appease the heightened sensitivities of women in the present political atmosphere, even the *men's* training program has been downgraded:

- Cadets no longer train in combat boots because women were experiencing higher rates of injury.
- Running with heavy weapons has been eliminated because it is "unrealistic and therefore inappropriate" to expect women to do it.

- The famed "recondo" endurance week, during which cadets used to march with full backpacks and undergo other strenuous activities, has been eliminated, as have upper-body strength events in the obstacle course.

It is one thing to have second-rate professors in the humanities because of affirmative-action quotas that lower standards. But a second-rate officer corps?

Not surprisingly, resentment on the part of male cadets is high. One indication is that more than 50 per cent of the women cadets at West Point reported that they had been sexually harassed last year. It is a perfectly sinister formula. Rub men's noses in arbitrariness and unfairness, and then charge them with sexual harassment when they react. It is also a perfect prescription for accumulating power. Rosemary Mariner is a candidate for admiral; Beverly Byron has been mentioned as a possible Secretary of the Navy; Pat Schroeder has her sights on a cabinet post, perhaps Secretary of Defense. Who is going to pay the price for these ambitions on the field of battle?

This brings us to another problem raised by William Lind— unit cohesion and combat effectiveness. In combat, men will act to protect the women and this will undermine the effectiveness of the unit. The male soldier's protective instinct is heightened by his knowledge of what the male enemy will do to females taken prisoner of war. This is not mere theory. The Israelis, who pioneered the introduction of women in combat during their war of liberation, now bar them. What they found is that "if you put women in combat with men, the men immediately forget about their tactical objective and they move instead to protect the women." The Israelis abandoned the practice of putting women into combat positions because it weakened their forces and exposed their fighting men to even greater risks.[5] Is there is a rea-

---

[5]Scott Tips, "The Real Reasons Why Women Should Not Be Allowed In Combat," NewsWithViews.com, April 24, 2012, http://www.newswith-views.com/Tips/scott113.htm

son for Americans to repeat the Israelis' mistakes just to humor the feminist left?

No amount of sensitivity training, no amount of brainwashing can alter human nature. The communists proved that at unbelievable cost. They could not make a new socialist man (or woman) who would be cooperative and not competitive under a social plan; who would respond as effectively and efficiently to administrative commands as they had to market incentives; who would be communist and not individualist. The communists killed tens of millions of people and impoverished whole nations trying to change human nature, all the time calling it liberation, just as radical feminists do. It didn't work. Social experiments that disregard fundamental human realities in the name of abstract pieties will always fail. But they will cause incalculable social damage and irreparable human suffering before they collapse. Yet, under the guidance of feminist social engineers, our newly sensitized military leadership marches on. The Air Force has established a SERE program (Survival, Evasion, Resistance and Escape), including its own "prisoner of war" camp in the state of Washington to de-sensitize its male recruits so that they won't react like men when female prisoners are tortured. In short, in their infinite wisdom, Ms. Schroeder and her feminist allies have enlisted the military in a program to brainwash men so that they won't care what happens to women. That's progress and social enlightenment, feminist style.

It is not necessary to gain access to the information that the military has suppressed, or to be familiar with military terms like "unit cohesion," to see that America's war-making ability has already been weakened by the decision to deploy large numbers of women on battlefields overseas, even when they do not have combat roles. Who does not remember the poignant stories, which the networks elaborated in lavish detail, about the children left behind by their mothers on duty in the Persian Gulf? In fact, there were 16,337 single military parents and 1,231 military couples who left anxious children behind during the Gulf War. In the irresponsibly gifted hands of network reporters, even the family pets orphaned by their owners became objects of national concern, and for some occasions to oppose the war.

The net result is that an American president now is under pressure to win a war in four days or risk losing the war at home. How many dictators are going to test the will of America s liberated military and compassionate citizenry in future conflicts? These changes have implications for diplomacy and long-term national security that are literally incalculable. Yet Schroeder and company want them decided on the basis of cheap slogans like "separate is inherently unequal."

The military establishment has rolled over before an all-out assault on America's armed services by Congresswomen Schroeder, Byron, Boxer, Mikulski et al. In the reigning atmosphere of political intimidation, even an offending skit can send career servicemen to the stake. Among the public figures lampooned in the Tom Cat Follies were President Bush and Vice President Quayle. But it was a rhyme about Representative Pat Schroeder that sent the Navy brass into paroxysms of fear and scrambling for a sword to fall on. When it was over, three dedicated careers were down the drain because of this nonsense. Three careers destroyed as a result of Navy hypocrisy and fear of the wrath of one bigoted U.S. congresswoman. When the history of this sorry episode is written, maybe someone will call it the Feline Follies.

One might well ask what qualifies someone like Pat Schroeder to intimidate the American military establishment and to shape its destiny through the next generation. During the Cold War, Pat Schroeder and her supporters in the congressional left worked overtime to hobble America in the face of the Soviet threat. In 1981, when Soviet armies were spreading death and destruction across Afghanistan and the United States had boycotted the Olympics in order to isolate the Soviet aggressor, Pat Schroeder and a group of left-wing House members hosted a delegation from the World Peace Council, a proven Soviet propaganda front, providing a KGB operation with a forum in the halls of Congress.

In 1982, with Soviet armies occupying Afghanistan, with 50,000 Cuban troops waging war in Ethiopia and Angola, with a Communist base established on the American mainland, with a Communist insurgency raging in El Salvador, with thousands of nuclear warheads in Central Europe and Warsaw Pact forces outnumbering NATO troops by a two to one margin, Congresswoman Schroeder proposed an amendment to reduce the number of U.S. military personnel stationed overseas *by half*.[6] If ever a member of the U.S. government proposed a prescription for national suicide, this was it. Fortunately, Democrats joined Republicans in defeating Schroeder's amendment on the House floor. In the *Congressional Quarterly*, Pat Schroeder is noted for her efforts against nuclear testing while the Soviets were still our adversaries; against further development of the MX missile; against proposed funding levels for the Strategic Defense Initiative and the B-2 bomber— and against authorizing the president to use force to stop Saddam Hussein. Maybe Ms. Schroeder's Denver constituents approve of the attitudes these positions reflect. For most Americans, however, Pat Schroeder's credentials on issues of national defense will be cause for alarm.

The military is the one American institution that survived the 60s intact. Now it threatens to become a casualty of current radical fashions. Of far more concern than any possible injustice that might be associated with the exclusion of women from combat is the assault on the military that is now being conducted in the name of gender integration, the elimination of sexual harassment and the purging of male bigots. The worst crimes of our century have been committed by idealists attempting to eradicate just such "injustices," to stamp out politically incorrect attitudes and reconstruct human nature. Let's not add the weakening of America's military to the depressing list of disasters of these utopias that failed.

---

[6]*Congressional Record*, July 22, 1982, pp. H4515–H4522

4

Gender Travesties

Almost everyone knows about the latest sexual harassment scandal in the Army involving seven officers at the
Aberdeen Proving Grounds. The officers are accused of
sexual abuses against females under their command, including
charges of rape, sodomy and assault. But until the NAACP stepped
into the case a week ago, few people were aware that all seven officers are black while most of their alleged female victims are white.
It also appears that the facts of the case are not so simple as first
presented. Five women "victims" now say that military investigators, eager to show that the Army knows how to deal with sexual
harassers, intimidated them into transforming consensual sex to
the serious criminal charges that have been filed against the black
officers.

Both the sex scandal and the racial cover-up are products of political correctness, the progressive party line that continues to threaten
the efficacy of the one institution which previously appeared imper-
vious to such assaults. The Aberdeen case is reminiscent of the infamous 1991 Tailhook affair involving the U.S. Navy. Although
thousands of servicemen were punished by the military, when the
Tailhook targets were tried in court the government prosecutors
were unable to get a single conviction. This was because, when
cross-examined, the women 'victims' admitted to having consensual
sex. They, too, told stories of military investigators threatening

Monday, March 17, 1997, http://archive.frontpagemag.com/Printable.
aspx?ArtId=24411; http://www.salon.com/1997/03/17/horowitz970317/

them and putting words in their mouths. Yet, despite these acquittals, none of the ruined careers of the defendants were restored. Unlike the cases at Aberdeen, none of these facts are well known because the white males caught up in the Tailhook witch-hunt did not have an NAACP to intervene in their behalf. Without the race card to trump the gender card, they were hung out to dry.

The national hysteria over Tailhook that has been whipped up by the feminist left ended the careers of hundreds of seasoned officers, admirals of flag rank, war heroes, and thousands more who, though they were not even at the Tailhook convention or did not participate in its celebrated events, were punished as well. The pressure to destroy the "male culture" of the military led to more lost careers than were ever destroyed by Senator McCarthy, whose targets were members of an organization dedicated to advancing the interests of a foreign power. The crisis in military morale resulting from the feminist assault has decimated the ranks of American patriots who served their country and served it well.

These assaults have been mounted under the banner of "desexegrating" the military, an offensive term coined by the leader of the crusade, former Representative Pat Schroeder. The goal is to put women in combat and combat-support roles once reserved for men; the term "desexegrating" is designed to dismiss the problems associated with such a profound change, while insinuating that existing military arrangements are no different than Jim Crow—the racist rationale of white supremacists to enforce segregation in the South. As a result of this false melodrama, at least one female navy pilot, Kara Hultgreen, is dead.

Kara Hultgreen was a Navy pilot who would have been grounded before her death had she been a man and held to normal Navy standards of performance. But feminist politicians in Washington, led by Schroeder who was, at the time, the ranking member of the Armed Services Committee, were so determined that the Navy qualify females to fly advanced combat planes that normal standards were thrown overboard. Despite her documented inadequacies, Hultgreen's trainers pushed her beyond her ability and continued to do so until, in 1994, she crashed her $40 million F-14 into the sea while trying to land on the aircraft carrier Abraham Lincoln. Nobody, either in the Congress or the media, has looked into the possibility that Schroeder's "desexegration" agenda may have been to blame.

Schroeder is a left-wing Democrat whose entire career could be viewed as an assault on America's defense establishment. Entering Congress in 1974, she pledged to cut off all military aid to Cambodia and South Vietnam. The aid was cut, the anti-Communist regimes fell, and two million Indochinese were slaughtered in the bloodbath that followed. Untroubled, Schroeder went on to oppose every subsequent use of American military power over the next 20 years, right up to the Gulf War. Fortunately, Republican presidents, with the assist of a battalion of "boll-weevil" Democrats, were able to maintain America's military posture adequately and to sustain the standards that have kept America's fighting force the best in the world.

During the Bush administration, a Presidential Commission on the Assignment of Women in the Armed Forces specifically recommended that women *not* be assigned to combat for reasons that lie at the heart of the above-mentioned incidents. Four years ago, however, the American people elected Bill Clinton as their commander-in-chief. Encouraged, the Schroederites resumed their agenda, disregarding the recommendations of the presidential commission. The death of Kara Hultgreen is one result; the sexual fiasco at Aberdeen is another.

Undaunted by these travesties, a Schroeder-sponsored group called WANDAS (Women Active in our Nation's Defense and their Advocates and Supporters) is busy keeping the faith alive. Following the Hultgreen tragedy, the *San Diego Union* and *The Washington Times* published charges made by Elaine Donnelly of the Center for Military Readiness that the military was preparing to qualify a second inadequate female flyer (known as "Pilot B"). WANDAS sued Donnelly and both newspapers on behalf of "Pilot B" on the grounds that they had defamed her flying skills. Whatever the legal case, the upshot is this: Pilot B is no longer flying any planes. After the military invested a million dollars in her training, she became pregnant and is now the mother of a baby daughter.

5

Military Justice

On Wednesday, the Army filed charges against its top enlisted man, Army Sgt. Maj. Gene McKinney, for allegedly committing adultery, demanding sex during a business trip and obstructing justice. McKinney is black. The previous day, Staff Sgt. Delmar Simpson, one of 12 accused black Army trainers at the Aberdeen Proving Ground in Maryland, was convicted of rape and other sexual offenses against enlisted women. Simpson was sentenced to 25 years in prison, about the same as for an average civilian homicide. But, for some, even this punishment wasn't enough. "This doesn't seem to be terribly severe," said Georgia Sadler, founder of Women in the Military Information Network. Karen Johnson, a former Air Force colonel and a vice president of the National Organization for Women, agreed. The sentence, she said "sends a message to women in the military that the talk of zero tolerance is just talk."[1]

What did Simpson, convicted on 18 counts of rape, do? He didn't actually rape the women trainees, at least not in the civilian sense of the term. He may have used his rank as a coercive tool, but his acts did not involve violence. Even feminist lawyers have admitted that, if committed in the non-military world, Simpson's crimes would amount at best to sexual harassment—and no one

---

May 8, 1997, http://www.salon.com/1997/05/08/news_364/

[1] "Army Sergeant Gets 25-Year Term for Rapes," Paul Richter, *Los Angeles Times*, May 7, 1997, http://articles.latimes.com/1997-05-07/news/mn-56313_1_25-year-term

has yet suggested 25-year terms for sexual harassment. But, under the military code, rape occurs if the woman feels she had no choice, even if no physical force was present. Classmates of two of the white recruits, who told the military court that Simpson had raped them, testified that the alleged victims had previously said they wanted to have sex with him. One was in the habit of walking past the drill sergeant's office wearing "little short shorts" and skimpy tops. One of Simpson's victims said she had been raped by Simpson on eight different occasions, yet had taken a shower at his quarters afterwards while he went to sleep. Under the influence of its feminist advisors, the Army calls such situations "constructive rape."

In fact, consensual sex among the ranks was so common at the Aberdeen Proving Ground that the base seemed to be closer in spirit to "Animal House" than to a U.S. Army installation. Yet none of the women reported "rape" until after the military investigators moved in. Attempting to explain this under oath, the women testified that they were too proud, too embarrassed or too frightened to make an accusation. If they had complained, they said, no one would believe them. Is this a plausible excuse in the post-Anita Hill, post-Paula Coughlin world? Would it not be more likely for them to think that making the accusations would land them a photo-op at *Newsweek* or a docudrama by Disney (as it did Coughlin)?

On the other hand, if they had indeed been having consensual sex with the officers, the prospects they were facing were not attractive. Consensual sex between officers and enlisted personnel is forbidden by the military. An investigator happening upon such facts can confront a female recruit with the choice of becoming a "victim" by claiming rape, or going to prison and getting a dishonorable discharge. Five of the women who originally reported being raped at Aberdeen have already publicly recanted their stories, claiming that investigators threatened them in precisely this manner and pressured them into testifying against the officers.

In fact, the Army itself admits that as many as 40 percent of the female "victims" at Aberdeen had consensual sex or were having personal relationships (also a violation of regulations) with the accused sergeants. Significantly, the Army has not punished any of the women for these violations, lending fuel to the suspicion that this is just another anti-male witch-hunt similar to the Navy precedent at Tailhook, where none of the consenting female officers were prosecuted either.

The Secretary of the Army now has a feminist advisor on contract from Duke Law School to tell him that the military culture has to be changed. In place of the "masculinist" influences that are "rape-conducive," the Army must create an "ungendered vision," and teach male and female dogfaces to live as a "band of brothers and sisters." Thus the political visions of the 60s have finally invaded the military and apparently conquered its leaders. The head of the Army is on record proclaiming it his mission to "desexualize" the military. The result of such attitudes is the travesty at Aberdeen.

When rape is "constructed" first by feminist theorists and then by military bureaucrats, the results are bound to be Orwellian. This is a tragedy for Sgt. Simpson and the other black soldiers who have found themselves in a judicial environment eerily similar to the Southern courts before which black males were hauled a generation ago, where the rules seemed calculated to convict them. The NAACP and other civil rights organizations which have protested the Aberdeen charges believe that there is a racial witch-hunt in the making. And like every witch-hunt, the appetite for transgressors grows, as Army Sgt. Maj. Gene McKinney—whose alleged crime appears to have been making a clumsy pass at a female officer during a business trip to Hawaii—is about to find out.

This is an ominous development for the nation, and not just in terms of racial relations. As Sgt. Simpson's attorney, Frank Spinner, put it: "What this really comes down to is that any woman can come in and say she had sex with a drill sergeant and was raped. Discipline in the Army is going to break down—if it hasn't already broken down—because who has the power now? The drill sergeant or the trainee?"

Somewhere out there, Saddam Hussein and other potential adversaries are surely taking note.

6

Godmother of Feminism

What is it with progressives that they feel the need to lie so relentlessly about who they are? Recently Rigoberta Menchú's autobiography was exposed as a hoax.[1] Now it's Betty Friedan's turn to have her fibs unraveled. In a new book, *Betty Friedan and the Making of the Feminine Mystique*, Smith College professor Daniel Horowitz (no relation) establishes beyond doubt that the woman who has always presented herself as a typical suburban housewife before she began researching her path-breaking manifesto was in fact nothing of the kind. Under her maiden name, Betty Goldstein, she was a political activist and professional propagandist for the Communist left for a quarter of a century before the publication of *The Feminist Mystique* launched the modern feminist movement.

Professor Horowitz documents that Friedan was a Stalinist from her college days until her mid-30s, the political intimate of the Communist leaders of America's fifth column, and for a time the lover of a young Communist physicist working on atomic-bomb projects in Berkeley's radiation lab with J. Robert Oppenheimer. Her notorious description of America's suburban family as "a comfortable concentration camp" in *The Feminine Mystique* had more to do with her Marxist hatred for America than with her

---

January 19, 1999, http://archive.frontpagemag.com/Printable.aspx?ArtId=24283
[1]"Rigoberta Menchú: Tarnished Laureate," Larry Rohter, *FrontPageMagazine.com*, December 15, 1998, http://archive.frontpagemag.com/readArticle.aspx?ARTID=24215

actual experience as a housewife or mother. Far from being house-bound and confined to "female roles," she was, like her husband, Carl, "in the world during the whole marriage," and "seldom was a wife and a mother." Friedan had a maid, lived in a Hudson River mansion, and was supported full-time in her writing and research by her husband Carl, facts that were inconvenient both to the persona and theory she was determined to promote, which is why she suppressed them.

It is fascinating that, in writing her book, Friedan not only lied about her actual views and life experiences but that she still feels the need to lie about them now. Although the academic author of the new biography is a sympathizing leftist, Friedan refused to cooperate with him once she realized he was going to tell the truth about her life as Betty Goldstein. After he had published an initial article about Friedan's youthful work as a "labor journalist," Friedan maligned him, saying to an American University audience, "Some historian recently wrote some attack on me in which he claimed that I was only pretending to be a suburban housewife, that I was supposed to be an agent."[2] This was particularly unkind, because Friedan's professor-biographer is such a fellow-traveler that he bends over backwards throughout the book to sanitize the true dimensions of Friedan's Communist past. Thus he describes Steve Nelson, a colleague of Friedan's, as "the legendary radical, veteran of the Spanish Civil War and Bay Area party official." In fact, Nelson was a Soviet agent notorious for his espionage activities in the Berkeley radiation lab where Friedan's boyfriend worked. Nelson had been in Spain as a Communist Party commissar to make sure the party line was obeyed.

Professor Horowitz also bends over backwards, and at length, to defend Friedan's lying as a response to "McCarthyism." When she makes the ridiculous accusation against the professor that he is

---

[2]Daniel Horowitz, *Betty Friedan and the Making of the Feminine Mystique: The American Left, the Cold War, and Modern Feminism*, University of Massachusetts Press, 1998, p. 15

planning to use "innuendoes" to describe her past as a justification for refusing to grant him permission to quote from her unpublished papers, he is all-too-understanding. The word "innuendoes," he explains, was often used by people "scarred by McCarthyism."

Reading this reminded me of a C-Span BookNotes program on which Brian Lamb asked the president of the American Historical Association, Eric Foner, about his father, Jack. Foner claimed that Jack Foner was a man "with a social conscience" who made his living through public lectures and who, along with his brothers Phil and Moe, was persecuted during the McCarthy era. When Lamb asked Foner why they were persecuted, Foner responded that his father had supported the loyalist side in the Spanish Civil War. But no one was persecuted for simply siding with the Spanish Republic in the Spanish Civil War. The Foner brothers were fairly famous Communists, one a Communist Party labor historian and another a Communist Party union organizer and leader. It is an indisputable fact that Communist-controlled unions in the CIO, on orders from Moscow, opposed the Marshall Plan's effort to rebuild Western Europe. The Marshall Plan was in part designed to prevent Stalin's empire from absorbing Western Europe as it had its satellites in the east. That is why socialists like Walter Reuther purged the Communists from the CIO, and also why Communists like Foner's uncle came under FBI scrutiny and were "persecuted" in the McCarthy era—because they were working for America's enemy.

That Communists like the Foners lied at the time was understandable. They had something to hide. But why are their children lying to this day? And why are people like Friedan lying long after they have anything to fear from McCarthy-like committees? Surely no one seriously believes that people who reveal their Communist pasts these days have anything to fear from the American government. Angela Davis, for example, was once the Communist Party's candidate for vice president and served the Soviet empire until its very last gasp. Her punishment for this was to have been appointed one of only seven "President's Professors" at the state-run University of California, and to be officially invited at exorbitant fees by college administrations across the country to give ceremonial speeches on public occasions.

Folk singer Pete Seeger, who has been a party puppet his entire life, is a celebrated entertainer and was honored recently at the Kennedy Center with a Freedom Medal by President Clinton. In the midst of the Vietnam War, Jane Fonda went on Radio Hanoi to incite American fliers to defect. She then returned to the United States to win an Academy Award and eventually become the wife of one of America's most powerful media moguls, where she oversaw a 24-episode CNN special purporting to be a history of the Cold War. Bernardine Dohrn, leader of America's first political terrorist cult, who once officially declared war on "Amerika," and who has never conceded even minimal regret for her crimes nor hinted at the slightest revision of her views, has just been appointed to a Justice Department commission on children. The idea that America punishes those who betray her is laughable, as is the idea that leftists have anything to fear from their government if they tell the truth.

So why the continuing lies? The reason is this: The truth is too embarrassing. Imagine what it would be like for Betty Friedan (the name actually is Friedman) to admit that, as a Jew, she opposed America's entry into the war against Hitler because Stalin told her that it was just an "inter-imperialist" fracas? Imagine what it would be like for America's premier feminist to acknowledge that, well into her 30s, she thought Stalin was the Father of the Peoples, that the United States was an evil empire, and that her interest in women's liberation was just a subtext of her real desire to create a Soviet America. No, those kinds of revelations don't help a person who is concerned about her public image and wants to influence masses.

This is why it seemed better just to lie about her real agendas all these years. Politically speaking, it certainly has worked, and Betty Friedman-Friedan has become the godmother of modern feminism. At a personal level, however, the problem is that lying can't be contained. One lie begets others until lying becomes a way of life, as President Clinton could tell you. On the other hand, political lies can equip their purveyors with new weapons that serve their ends. Denial of one's Communist past, or of the real-world consequences of that past, generates an exaggerated view of "McCarthyism" and its alleged injustices. Fear of McCarthyism then becomes an excuse for cover-ups of activities that would otherwise be seen as treasonous. Instead they become resistance to American oppression. Watergate reporter Carl Bernstein once referred to McCarthyism as a "reign of terror" in justifying his father's lies about his own Communist beliefs. But no lives were lost as a result of McCarthy's 18-month reign; while the number of people who lost their freedom was minimal, a score of Communist leaders whose convictions were soon reversed.

Yet Friedan's left-wing biographer claims that McCarthyism even stunted women's development before the appearance of her feminist tract. "Even though increasing numbers of [women] entered the work force, the Cold War linked anti-Communism and the dampening of women's ambitions. With *The Feminine Mystique*, Friedan began a long tradition among American feminists of seeing compulsory domesticity as the main consequence of 1950s McCarthyism." Brain-dwarfing characterizations like this are the currency of American progressives and are being sold to the next unsuspecting generation by their left-wing professors; and such perverse views are sure to have unforeseen consequences for the American future.

7

V-Day: Feminist War Against Love

When Jane Fonda was thirteen years old, her mother went into the family bathroom, closed the door, and slit her throat from ear to ear. Just outside the door, she left a note for the maid that there was a mess inside and to please clean it up. That evening, Jane's father, Henry Fonda, went on stage, as usual, to perform the role of Mr. Roberts in the Broadway play in which he was starring. He never told his daughter her mother had committed suicide. She was to learn about it three years later at summer camp, in the pages of a movie fan magazine.

These biographical details are brought to mind by the "V-Day Demonstrations," scheduled for 50 cities, over 200 college campuses and Madison Square Garden, which Jane Fonda has bankrolled to the tune of $1 million. These are an effort by feminists across the country to transform Valentine's Day, a millennia-old celebration of romance and friendship, into a "Violence Against Women Day," an orgy of self-pity and hatred against men. A novelist could not have formed the metaphor of Jane's childhood trauma more acutely: Valentine is Violence.

But, even though Jane Fonda has provided the organizing funds, the event itself is not merely an expression of personal distress. It is a social movement, a statement by the political left. The manifesto of the organizers proclaims "Valentine's Day as V-Day until

February 9, 2001, http://archive.frontpagemag.com/Printable.aspx?ArtId= 19926

the violence stops. When all women live in safety, then it will be known as Victory Over Violence Day."

Of course, the idea that someday all women will "live in safety" is a utopian fantasy - the impossible dream of a kingdom of heaven on earth, where the sick will be healed and the wounded made whole. How is this world - the real world of flesh-and-blood human beings—ever going to be made safe for children like Jane? Or for any human being—female or male—given what human beings are and what they have shown themselves to be capable of since the beginning of time?

The messianic illusion that will energize the thousands of women who flock to Jane's cause reflects the fact that the cause itself is not so much a political movement as a crypto-religion; a yearning for redemption without God but through their own political action. It is a substitute for a God who could accomplish the miracle they yearn for, but who—for whatever reason—is absent in their hearts. The actress Glenn Close, who is adorning the event, put it succinctly when she described the woman who actually came up with the idea for V-Day this way: "She is giving us our souls back."

Like all political religions, it is also a religion of hate. In authentic religions, God judges, God redeems and God forgives. In authentic religions, we understand ourselves as sinners. No one mistakes himself or herself as a redeemer. In political religions, on the contrary, human beings act as God, judging and condemning; and there will be no redemption. This is the bloody history of the left—the saga of the guillotine and the gulag, which continues now into the new millennium.

This is why the left wants to take the one holiday a year that is dedicated to the love human beings do manage to show for each other, and turn it into a day when women can vent their rage against men. According to the organizers of V-Day, "22 to 35 percent of women who visit emergency rooms are there for injuries related to ongoing abuse." This would make the United States one of the most repressive and barbarous places on earth for women. But, as Christina Hoff Sommers notes, the actual figure of abuse according to Bureau of Justice statistics is one-half of one percent.[1] Why the exaggeration? To foment hate against the devil. As Sommers puts it: "The true numbers are apparently not high enough for V-Day proponents. They are determined to implicate the average American man in an ongoing social atrocity and to place the United States on a moral par with countries that practice genital mutilation and bride burnings."

Jane Fonda's adult life has been consumed with hatreds like this in the name of love. She committed treason in Vietnam, indicting American soldiers over Radio Hanoi as "war criminals," and abetting their torturers on a visit to the infamous "Hanoi Hilton," which housed our prisoners of war. She once said at a college rally in Michigan: "I would think that if you understood what communism was, you would hope, you would pray on your knees that we would someday become communist."

Jane's hatred for America and her love for communism have been central tenets of the leftist religion for nearly a century now. There are not many leftists any longer who would defend the Soviet gulag as they once did. Even Marxism has undergone revisions. In the old days, the crypto-religion demonized the "ruling class." Now a trinity of hate—race/gender/class—has been overlaid on the old formula of belief. It was prominent in the chants at the inauguration of a Republican president just this January: "George Bush go away—racist, sexist, anti-gay." The same exaggeration, the same will to believe in themselves as the saviors of us all.

The founder of V-Day is Eve Ensler, author of *The Vagina Monologues*, a cornucopia of hatred against men. Celebrities like

---

[1] "V-Day Twists Holiday into Male-bashing Event," Christina Hoff Sommers, February 8, 2001, http://www.usatoday.com/news/comment/2001-02-08-ncguest2.htm

Fonda and Close refer to themselves as soldiers in "Eve's Army." How fitting. Eve, the mother of us all, who was tempted by the Serpent to "become as God" but instead led our Fall into the vale of suffering and tears from which the left now promises to redeem us.

PART V

The Government's Left-Wing Network

The Politics of Public Broadcasting

The public television system is one of the last El Dorados of the Great Society. It was created by the Public Broadcasting Act of 1967 with the express caveat that it *not* become a "system" competing with other networks. But from relatively modest beginnings it has grown into a $1.2-billion leviathan which is virtually free of accountability to taxpayers, who still shell out an annual $250 million to subsidize the system while also enabling it to get funding from private individuals, foundations and corporations. Of these private benefactors, the most important historically was the Ford Foundation under the leadership of McGeorge Bundy in the late 60s and early 70s. Having helped orchestrate the Vietnam War as national security adviser to John F. Kennedy and Lyndon B. Johnson, Bundy became one of a large crowd of liberals to leave the sinking ship when their policies

This article was originally published as "The Politics of Public Television" in *Commentary*, December 1991; http://frontpagemag.com/2010/ 10/28/the-politics-of-public-television/print/ [A note on sources] John P. Witherspoon and Roselle Kovitz, "A Tribal Memory of Public Broadcasting Missions, Mandates, Assumptions, Structure," 1986, privately circulated typescript; Robert K. Avery and Robert Pepper, *The Politics of Interconnection: A History of Public Television at the National Level*, National Association of Educational Broadcasters, 1989; *A Public Trust, The Report of the Carnegie Commission on the Future of Public Broadcasting*, 1979; AIM Reports, 1975–1991; John W. Macy, Jr., *To Irrigate a Wasteland*, 1974; author interviews with Michael Hobbs, Bob Kotlowitz, Richard Brookhiser, James Day, and James Loper. See also David Horowitz and Laurence Jarvik, eds., *Public Broadcasting and the Public Trust*, Center for the Study of Popular Culture, 1995

failed. In 1966 he found refuge in the presidency of the Ford Foundation, where he told intimates he intended to make public television one of the special objects of his attention.

Before Bundy's arrival, Ford had already funded many of the hundred or more educational stations around the country, investing $150 million, a prodigious sum for the time, establishing the rudiments of a fourth national network. Before this intervention, educational stations had been homegrown, do-it-yourself, garden-variety enterprises. Operating on average only eight hours a day and mainly associated with universities and schools, they devoted themselves to no-frills instructional fare tailored to their respective locales. "Shakespeare in the Classroom," "Today's Farm," "Parents and Dr. Spock" or "Industry on Parade" were typical titles of the programs that were often bicycled in tape form from one station to the next, because there was no interconnection link at the time. The unifying element in all these educational productions, distinguishing them most clearly from commercial TV, was their low budget.

So great was the change when Ford entered the picture with its massive investments that there is no organic relation between the high-tech professionalism of public television as we now know it and the modest efforts of the pioneers in the field. An hour of the MacNeil/Lehrer NewsHour (perhaps the best product of the post-Bundy system) costs $96,000, while a similar segment of a series like Cosmos or Masterpiece Theater might cost three or four times that much. These figures are certainly much lower than those for comparable commercial shows (partly subsidized by special discount arrangements with unions and talent), but they are still out of reach for any university or community group. Despite this qualitative change, executives of the Public Broadcasting Service (PBS) still portray their network as if it were a decentralized service to diverse publics, the very incarnation of America's democratic spirit. Thus, a typical official statement reads: "PBS is owned and directed by its member public television stations, which in turn are accountable to their local communities. This grassroots network is comprised of stations operated by colleges, universities, state and municipal authorities, school boards, and community organizations across the nation."

Notwithstanding organizational complexities of Rube Goldberg dimensions and the lack of a single programming authority, PBS is ruled by a centralized power that creates its characteristic voice. Of the 44 million taxpayer dollars annually available for programs to the 341 separately-owned PBS stations across the nation, $22 million or half the total goes to just two: WGBH in Boston and WNET in New York. Another $10 million goes to a group of producers affiliated with WNET, to three other stations and to PBS itself, which brings the centralized figure to 77 percent of the total funds. This money is then leveraged against grants from private foundations and other sources by a factor as great as two, three or even five times the original amount. The result is that most major public-television series—MacNeil/Lehrer, American Playhouse, Frontline, NOVA, Sesame Street, Great Performances, Masterpiece Theater, and Bill Moyers's ubiquitous offerings—are produced or "presented" by the two powers in the system, WNET and WGBH. Others are produced by a group of stations known as the "G-7," often with WNET and WGBH as the dominant partners.[1]

When creating the new system in the late Sixties, its architects attempted to square the circle of a government-funded institution independent of political influence. The result was a solution in the form of a problem: a private body—the Corporation for Public Broadcasting (CPB)—that would distribute the government funds. Compromise was the order of the day. The Carnegie Commission, whose report had led to the 1967 Public Broadcasting Act, wanted the governing board of CPB to be composed of eminent cultural figures; Lyndon Johnson wanted (and got) political appointees. Carnegie wanted a permanent funding base in the form of an

---

[1]The other G-7 stations are WETA (Washington, D.C.), WTTW (Chicago), WQED (Pittsburgh), KCET (Los Angeles), and KQED (San Francisco).

excise tax on television sets; Congress said no. But as a sop to the broadcasters, emphasis was placed on the private nature of CPB as a "heat shield" to insulate the system from governmental influence. Congress also limited CPB's mandate, insisting that it be established on the "bedrock of localism." The idea of an elite network financed by the taxpayer (which is what the system turned out to be) would have been political anathema. To prevent CPB from creating a centralized fourth network, Congress barred it from producing programs, operating stations, or managing the interconnection between them. In addition to insisting on the safeguards of a decentralized system, Congress inserted a clause into the Public Broadcasting Act requiring "fairness, objectivity, and balance" in all programming of a controversial nature.

Such was the plan; the product proved otherwise. Once Congress had agreed to provide a fund to finance the stations, Ford's McGeorge Bundy recruited David Davis of WGBH to connect them into a national voice. Together with Ward Chamberlin of CPB, Davis engineered the new interconnection, which began operations in 1970 as the Public Broadcasting Service. To meet congressional concerns about preserving localism, the new service was to be controlled by a board of directors elected by the "grass-roots" subscribing stations. But Ford ensured that they, in turn, would be dominated by the powerful inner circle of metropolitan stations it favored. The new PBS president was Hartford Gunn, the manager of WGBH.

While this process was unfolding, political events were moving in ways that would fatefully shape the future of public broadcasting. Until 1968, the disaffected liberals who had a share in creating public television had been engaged in a family quarrel with their fellow Democrats. The Vietnam War had cast them unexpectedly in an adversarial posture toward the anti-Communist liberals who remained committed to the Vietnam policy they themselves had once supported. But, in 1968, the presidency fell into unfriendly Republican hands and, worse still, into the hands of the man who, since the trial of Alger Hiss, had been their most hated political antagonist. With Richard Nixon in the White House, the Vietnam nightmare was no longer a liberal war. It was in this period that LBJ's press secretary, Bill Moyers, joined WNET. It was at this time, too, that the Ford Foundation announced the creation of a news center in Washington that would be staffed by prominent luminaries from the media fraternity, several of whom the Nixon White House regarded as political enemies. Among them were Elizabeth Drew, Robert MacNeil and Sander Vanocur.

The loading of these cannons was duly noted by the White House; in June 1972, Nixon retaliated by vetoing the CPB funding bill. CPB's president and several Johnson-appointed board members resigned and were immediately replaced with Nixon nominees. For all the good it did him, Nixon might have saved himself the trouble. Two weeks earlier, five men had been arrested while breaking into the Watergate apartment complex in Washington. By the end of the year, the most watched show on public-television stations was the congressional hearing to decide whether to impeach him. True to its promise to offer fare that the commercial channels would not or could not provide, PBS featured the hearings on prime time when the networks had turned to other entertainments. The result was a groundswell of support from new members and contributors. Even the more conservative stations, which had been at loggerheads with PBS, joined hands to fight the common foe.

Once the Democratic Congress had finished humbling the president, it rushed to aid the network that had been its ally in the Watergate battles. One of its first measures was to authorize a significant increase in funds for public television and, more importantly, to commit three years of funding in advance. Congress also acted to tie CPB's unreliable hands. Fifty percent of its non-discretionary program grants were now earmarked for the stations as "general support"—a percentage that would rise even higher in the following decade. The stations, in turn, kicked back a portion of their grants into a newly created program fund, further depriving CPB of influence over the system product. When the dust had

settled, CPB was discredited and crippled, while the Ford Foundation's protégé, the anti-Nixon, antiwar PBS, emerged as the newly
dominant power at the center of the system. Public television's
birth by fire in the crucible of Vietnam and Watergate created its
political culture, which today often seems frozen in 60s amber.
The one area of its current-affairs programming which managed to
escape this fate, ironically, is the one where the battle with the
Nixon White House was most directly joined.

Robert MacNeil was among the liberal journalists singled out
by the Nixon administration as political antagonists. But the program he launched on WNET in 1975, in collaboration with Jim
Lehrer, turned out to be reasonably fair and balanced. Originally
devoted to a single subject per evening, The MacNeil/Lehrer
Report provided in-depth analysis that network sound-bites could
not duplicate, and it went on to prosper more than any other public-television show besides Sesame Street. But MacNeil/Lehrer,
along with a few other talking-head shows, most notably Tony
Brown's Journal and William F. Buckley's Firing Line, proved to be
the exceptions. In other crucial areas of current affairs programming, a different standard was set. Especially in film documentaries, where subjects were treated in a magazine-like setting that
made it possible to tell a story whole but with an editorial thrust,
the political personality of the system soon showed another, more
radical face.

In fact, the protest culture, which everywhere else had withered
at the end of the 60s when its fantasies of revolution collapsed, discovered a new base of operations in public television. A cottage
industry of activist documentarians had sprung up during that
decade to make promotional films for the Black Panther Party, the
terrorist Weather Underground, and other domestic radical groups;
as well as for Communist causes like Cuba and Vietnam. This
group now began its long march through the institutions by taking
its political enthusiasms, its filmmaking skills, and its network of
sympathetic left-wing foundations into the PBS orbit. The integration of these radicals into the PBS community was made easier by

the convergence of political agendas at the end of the Vietnam War, when supporters of the Communist conquerors were able to celebrate their victory over a common domestic foe in the Nixon administration alongside Democrats who had only desired an American withdrawal. Another convergence occurred around the post-60s romance between New Left survivors and the "Old Left" Communists, whom cold warriors like Nixon had made their targets. Most liberals shared the radicals' antipathy for the anti-Communist Right, along with their sense that any political target of the anti-Communists was by definition a victim of persecution.

A prime expression of this liberal-left convergence was the airing in 1974 of "The Unquiet Death of Julius and Ethel Rosenberg," a two-hour special which attempted to exonerate the most famous spies of the anti-Communist Fifties, and which PBS described as "the kind of programming that we enjoy presenting [and] hope to continue to present."[2] What was striking about the film was not just that it cast doubt on the verdict of the Rosenbergs' trial; or that it did so even as massive FBI files released under the new Freedom of Information Act were confirming their guilt; or even that it went beyond the airing of questions about the case to imply that there had been a government frame-up and that the verdict was an indictment of American justice. What was most disturbing, and prophetic in terms of future PBS productions, was that the film also amounted to a political brief for the Communist left to which the Rosenbergs had belonged. Thus, the narration introduced the Rosenbergs in these words: "With millions of others they question an economic and political system that lays waste to human lives. Capitalism has failed. A new system might be better. Socialism is its name. For many the vehicle for change is the Communist Party."[3] The film then cut to an authority explaining that Communists were people

---

[2]Reed Irvine, "A Watergate Cover-up By the Media," *Accuracy in Media*, December 12, 1975, http://www.aim.org/publications/aim_report/1975/75_12_12.html
[3]Ibid.

who "believed that you couldn't have political democracy without economic democracy.... Being a Communist meant simply to fight for the rights of the people. ..." The authority was the long-time Stalinist Carl Marzani.[4]

Four years later, to mark the 25th anniversary of the execution of the Rosenbergs, PBS ran the documentary again, adding a half-hour update. The update confirmed just how determinedly ideological some regions of PBS had become. The original two-hour program had been based on the standard argument for the Rosenbergs' innocence developed in a well-known book by Walter and Miriam Schneir. In the interim, a definitive study of the case, *The Rosenberg File* by Ronald Radosh and Joyce Milton, had appeared, based on the new FBI materials and on original interviews with principals. Because *The Rosenberg File* had been so widely praised as a "definitive" account, PBS executives asked the producer of the documentary, Alvin Goldstein, to interview Radosh as part of the "update." After he had seen the program that PBS aired, Radosh commented: "I couldn't believe the final product when I saw it. He cut out everything I said that contradicted his film, and left only the parts that supported his claims: the failure of the government to make its case against Ethel, the injustice of the sentence. Whereas our book totally demolished the argument of his film, viewers watching it would think I endorsed his claims. Moscow television couldn't have done better. It was outrageous."[5]

Far from being an isolated example, the PBS film on the Rosenbergs proved typical. Individual Communists who were later admiringly profiled on PBS specials included Paul Robeson, Angela Davis, Dashiell Hammett, Bertolt Brecht, and Anna Louise Strong.

---

[4]When the Soviet archives were opened after the fall of the Communist system, they revealed that Marzani was also a Soviet agent. This didn't prevent his propaganda for Stalin from becoming a source for Oliver Stone's pro-Communist 10-part series for Showtime, *The Untold History of America*. See "Oliver Stone's Communist History," in *Progressives*, Volume 2 in this series.

[5]Interview with the author.

These were amplified by the collective portrait "Seeing Red" (1986), a 90-minute celebration of American Communists as progressive idealists, and "The Good Fight" (1988), a nostalgic tribute to the Communists who volunteered to fight for Stalin in the Spanish Civil War. In a clear violation of PBS's enabling legislation, this opening to the discredited pro-Soviet left was never balanced by any reasonably truthful portrait of American Communism; nor was it matched by any provision of equal time to anti-Communists, whether of the left or right. Thus, although there were specials on the personal trials of American radicals who had devoted their lives to a political illusion and an enemy power, there was nothing on the tribulations of those former radicals who had changed their minds in order to defend their country and its freedom, such as Max Eastman, Jay Lovestone, James Burnham, Elizabeth Bentley, Bella Dodd, Whittaker Chambers, Bayard Rustin and Sidney Hook. Instead, while PBS searched for silver linings in the dark clouds of the Communist left, it found mainly negative forces at work in those American institutions charged with fighting the Communist threat, in particular the Central Intelligence Agency, which became a PBS symbol of American evil. In 1980, PBS aired a three-hour series called "On Company Business," which its producers described as "the story of 30 years of CIA subversion, murder, bribery, and torture as told by an insider and documented with newsreel film of actual events."[6]

The CIA insider on whom the PBS film relied for editorial guidance was Philip Agee, a CIA defector to the Soviets who in a 1975 *Esquire* article had written after his defection: "I aspire to be a Communist and a revolutionary."[7] The same year, a Swiss magazine asked Agee's opinion of U.S. and Soviet intelligence agencies. He

---

[6]Reed Irvine, "Soulmates: PBS and the Christics," *Accuracy in Media*, February 1989, http://www.aim.org/publications/aim_report/1989/02b.html

[7]Reed Irvine, "The Public Broadcasting Disinformation Service," *Accuracy in Media*, June 1980, http://www.aim.org/publications/aim_report/1980/06b.html

replied: "The CIA is plainly on the wrong side, that is, the capital-istic side. I approve KGB activities, Communist activities in gen-eral, when they are to the advantage of the oppressed. In fact, the KGB is not doing enough in this regard because the USSR depends upon the people to free themselves. Between the overdone activi-ties that the CIA initiates and the more modest activities of the KGB there is absolutely no comparison."[8] Agee had been expelled from the Netherlands, France, and England because of his contacts with Soviet and Cuban intelligence agents, but the PBS special identified him only by the caption "CIA: 1959-1969." When Reed Irvine of Accuracy in Media and other critics objected to the pro-gram's "disinformation," they were dismissed out of hand by Barry Chase, the PBS vice president for News and Public Affairs. Chase then sent a memo to all PBS stations describing "On Com-pany Business" as "a highly responsible overview of the CIA's his-tory and a major contribution to the ongoing debate on the CIA's past, present, and future."[9]

PBS's next summary view of American intelligence was a Bill Moyers special called "The Secret Government" (1987), which insinuated what no congressional investigation had ever estab-lished—that the CIA was a rogue institution subverting American policy. The wilder shores of this kind of conspiracy thesis were subsequently explored in two Frontline programs, "Murder on the Rio San Juan" (1988) and "Guns, Drugs, and the CIA" (1988), which leaned heavily on the fantasies of the radical Christic Insti-tute. "The Secret Government" was followed by a four-part series called "Secret Intelligence" (1988), which, like all three of its pred-ecessors, rehearsed the standard litany of left-wing complaints, including the Fifties *coups* in Iran and Guatemala, the Bay of Pigs, and the ouster of Allende's Castroist regime in Chile, culminating in a one-sided view of the Iran-contra affair as an anti-constitu-tional plot. All these programs characterized the CIA as more of

---

[8]Ibid.
[9]Ibid.

a threat to American institutions than a guardian of American security.

While PBS officials continued to pay lip service to the idea of "balance," no sympathetic portrait of the CIA's cold war activities was ever aired, no equally partisan account of its role in supporting the anti-Communist rebels in Afghanistan or Angola. In the absence of countervailing portrayals, the indictments presented in PBS documentaries amounted to an editorial statement. As far as PBS was concerned, the United States was an imperialist, counter-revolutionary power whose national security apparatus was directed not at containing an expansionist empire but (in the words of the producers of "On Company Business") at suppressing "people who have dared to struggle for a better life."[10] "The American Century" was yet another propaganda event in this series—a five-part, five-hour program that was written and hosted by the editor of *Harper's* magazine, Lewis Lapham, purporting to chart the course of American foreign policy from 1900 to 1975. The final segment traced American Cold War policy from 1945 to 1975. It did not pay tribute to the heroic efforts of containment, which prevented a tyranny as great as the world has ever known from conquering more countries than it already had. It rehearsed, instead, the familiar left-wing litany—Guatemala, Iran, the Bay of Pigs—to claim that, in the name of anti-Communism, Third World progress had become the victim of greedy U.S. corporations and their secret allies in the U.S. government, which Lapham described as "the agent of the reactionary past."[11] The summary segment of the series, called "Imperial Masquerade," appeared in December 1989, even as the inhabitants of the Soviet gulag were tearing down the Berlin Wall.

---

[10]Ibid.
[11]Reed Irvine, "The Ugly American Century," *Accuracy In Media,* December 1989, http://www.aim.org/publications/aim_report/1989/12b.html

This view of America as an evil empire was powerfully rein-
forced by PBS's treatment of post-Vietnam Communism in other
documentary programs on the taxpayer-funded network. In 1975,
PBS aired "China Memoir," a show purportedly about Mao's para-
dise narrated by actress Shirley MacLaine. So wide-eyed was its
view of Mao's gulag that PBS's own chairman was forced under
pressure to concede that it was "pure propaganda." "China Memoir" was followed by "The Children of China" (1977), which was
praised by Communist officials as helping Americans to "understand the new China." The "new" North Korea and the "new"
Cuba were also the focus of promotional features in the PBS shows
"North Korea" (1978), "Cuba, Sport and Revolution" (1979),
"Cuba: The New Man" (1986), and "Cuba in the Shadow of
Doubt" (1986), about which even the *New York Times* reviewer
commented: "At its best, the documentary has a romantic infatu-
ation with Cuba; at its worst, it is calculated propaganda."[12]

As the locus of the Cold War shifted to Central America in the
1980s, documentary after documentary appeared on PBS celebrating the Sandinista dictatorship in Nicaragua and the FMLN terrorists in El Salvador. These efforts included "From the Ashes ...
Nicaragua Today" (1982), "Target Nicaragua" (1983), and "El Salvador, Another Vietnam?" (1981). The producers of these programs, all of which were presented by WNET, were the radical
activist filmmakers who had come in from the Seventies cold,
among them World Focus Films of Berkeley, the Women's Film
Project, and the Institute for Policy Studies. As with its celebra-
tions of American Communism and one-sided views of the Cold
War with the Soviet Union, PBS showed no readiness to balance
this advocacy with other views. In 1983, the American Catholic
Committee offered WNET a program critical of the Marxist
regime: "Nicaragua: A Model for Latin America?" The Catholic

---

[12]John Corry, "Cuba: In the Shadow of Doubt," *New York Times*, October
2, 1986, http://www.nytimes.com/1986/10/02/movies/tv-reviews-cuba-
in-the-shadow-of-doubt-on-13.html

film was based on documentary footage and dealt with government repression of the press, the Roman Catholic Church, and independent labor unions. WNET rejected the film, on the grounds that it had "a better way to handle this information."[13]

To be fair, in 1985, a Frontline program called "Central America in Crisis" did take a critical look at the various sides of the conflict; while, in 1986, "Nicaragua Was Our Home," a film focusing on the plight of the Miskito Indians, was aired in response to the protests over WNET's previous offerings. But, for the most part, the "better way" to handle information about Nicaragua turned out to be pretty much the way it had been handled before. In 1984, the Frontline series featured "Nicaragua: Report From the Front," whose message, in the words of *New York Times* reviewer John Corry, was: "Sandinistas are good: their opponents are bad. There is no middle ground." The same wisdom was the message of two subsequent Frontline reports: "Who's Running This War?" (1986), which portrayed the contras as *somozistas* bent on violating human rights, and "The War on Nicaragua," which was named one of "The Worst Shows of the Year" in 1987 by the liberal critic of the *San Francisco Chronicle*, John Carman, who called it "shoddy, unfair, and manipulative journalism." The PBS attitudes displayed towards the Marxist dictatorship in Nicaragua were mirrored in the programs it aired about the conflicts in other Central American countries. Thus "Guatemala: When the Mountains Tremble" (1985) was panned by *The New York Times* as a "vanity film" because of its agitprop character. *The Washington Post*'s TV critic, Tom Shales, summed it up in the following terms: "The film is bluntly didactic and one-sided in portraying Guatemalan rebels as noble freedom fighters and Guatemalan peasants opposed to the present regime as the victims of repression, torture, and squalor."

---

[13]Richard Bernstein, "Group Accuses Channel 13 of Pro-Sandinist Bias," *The New York Times*, June 21, 1983; http://www.nytimes.com/1983/06/21/movies/group-accuses-channel-13-of-pro-sandinist-bias.html

At least four of the programs on Central America that PBS chose to air during the crucial decade before Communism's collapse were the work of a single director and radical ideologue, Deborah Shaffer, whose "solidarity" with the Communist dictators of Nicaragua, and their guerrilla allies in El Salvador and Guatemala, was a proudly displayed item in her *curriculum vitae*. Her most celebrated documentary, "Fire From the Mountain" (1988), an aggressive promotion of Sandinista myths, was based on the autobiography of the Sandinista secret police chief, Omar Cabezas, while her other films, "El Salvador: Another Vietnam?" (1981), "Witness to War: Dr. Charlie Clements" (1986), and "Nicaragua: Report From the Front" (1984) all reflected her commitment to the politics of Central America's communist guerrillas.

In 1988, the Congressional Oversight Committees for Public Television, led by their Democratic chairmen, Representative Edward Markey and Senator Daniel Inouye, institutionalized this revolutionary front inside PBS by authorizing the transfer of $24 million of CPB monies to set up the Independent Television Service (ITVS) as a separate fund for "independent" filmmakers. Representing the independents in testimony before the committees were Deborah Shaffer's producer, Pam Yates of Skylight Productions, and Larry Daressa, co-chairman of the National Coalition of Independent Public Broadcasting Producers. Daressa, who later turned up on the ITVS board, was also the president of California Newsreel, flagship of the radical film collectives and producer of such 60s classics as "Black Panther" and "The People's War," a triumphalist view of the Communist conquest of Vietnam.

Daressa returned the favor by biting the hand that had fed him so generously, for not being radical or generous enough: "Independent producers have found themselves progressively marginalized in this brave new world of semi-commercial, public pay television. Our diverse voices reflecting the breadth of America's communities and opinions have no place in public television's plans to turn itself into an upscale version of the networks. We have found that insofar as we speak with an independent voice we have no place in public television."[14] But, as one veteran member of the public-television community scoffed on hearing this testimony: "These people are not diverse, they're politically correct. Nor are they independent. These are the commissars of the political Left. These are the people who basically owned the Vietnamese and Cuban and Nicaraguan franchises, who got so close to Communist officials and guerrilla capos that if you wanted to get access for interviews or permission even to bring camera equipment into the liberated zone in certain cases, you had to go through them."

All during its tenure, the Reagan administration battled Soviet-backed Marxists in Central America and the Sandinista dictatorship in Nicaragua. Yet there was no direct White House response to the PBS attacks on its Central American policies, or even to PBS's propaganda war in behalf of the Communist enemy. Far from attempting to control public television through CPB, as the Nixon administration had (unsuccessfully) done, the Reagan White House even reappointed Sharon Rockefeller, a Carter nominee and liberal Democrat, as CPB chairman. Penn James, who handled White House appointments, recalls: "Our intention had been to remove her as chairman, just as we tried to do with every other agency. But when we announced our intention, her father, Senator Charles Percy, was outraged. He went storming over to the White House and told the President: 'If you want my cooperation on the Foreign Relations committee, you'd better reappoint my daughter.' So we did."[15]

With Reagan's reelection and her father's defeat, Rockefeller was replaced as chairman by Sonia Landau. The following spring, a Reagan appointee, Richard Brookhiser, offered a modest proposal to the CPB board. Brookhiser suggested that CPB undertake a scientific

---

[14]"The Political Film and Its Audience in the Digital Age," remarks delivered by Larry Daressa, co-director of California Newsreel since 1974, at Northwestern University's "Symposium on Social Issue Media," May 10, 2008, http://newsreel.org/articles/newsreel40.htm

[15]Penn James, "The Politics of Public Television," *Commentary*, December 1991, p. 30

"content analysis" of the current-affairs programs it had funded to see if they were indeed tipped to one side of the political scale. The board would be "derelict," he said, if it did not try to assure the "objectivity and balance" of its programming as the 1967 Act had mandated. It seemed a straightforward request, but the reaction was almost entirely negative. Charges of "neo-McCarthyism" were hurled in Brookhiser's direction, and PBS vice president Barry Chase scolded: "It is inappropriate for a presidentially appointed group to be conducting a content analysis of programming. It indicates that some people on the CPB board don't fully understand the appropriate constraints on them."[16] In an interview with the *Los Angeles Times*, Bruce Christensen, president of PBS, was less restrained: "In 1973, President Nixon in fact tried to kill federal funding for public television through his political appointees to the board, and the kind of chicanery that went on at the time. They didn't do a 'content analysis.' Content analysis seems to me a little more sophisticated way of achieving those ends."

Such accusations were sufficiently intimidating to stall the proposal. Brookhiser could not secure enough support even from the Reagan-appointed majority to get approval. Meeting in June, the CPB board decided to postpone its decision on the study until September. But, before it could do so, a new controversy erupted which demonstrated just how weak the conservatives' influence on public television was, and how powerful their liberal adversaries had become. The *casus belli* was "The Africans," a nine-part series on Africa presented by WETA. "The Africans" had been underwritten by more than $1 million in grants from PBS, CPB, and the National Endowment for the Humanities (NEH). When Lynne Cheney, the chairman of NEH, received an additional request from WETA for $50,000 to promote the series, she decided to screen it. Her response was outrage: "I have just finished viewing

---

[16]David Crook, "Proposed Analysis Of Public TV Sparks Debate," *Los Angeles Times*, July 8, 1986, http://articles.latimes.com/1986-07-08/entertainment/ca-22747_1_public-broadcasting

all nine hours of 'The Africans.' Worse than unbalanced, this film frequently degenerates into anti-Western diatribe.... [One entire segment, "Tools of Exploitation"] strives to blame every technological, moral, and economic failure of Africa on the West.... The film moves from distressing moment to distressing moment, climaxing in Part IX where [Moammar] Qaddafi's virtues are set forth."[17] Shortly after that scene, pictures of mushroom clouds filled the screen and it is suggested that Africans are about to come into their own because, after the "final racial conflict" in South Africa, black Africans will have nuclear weapons. Cheney told WETA that not only would she not finance the promotion of the series, but she wanted the NEH credits removed from the print. "Our logo is regarded as a mark of approbation, and NEH most decidedly does not approve of this film."

PBS defended its series by disclaiming all responsibility for the product that bore its imprint. Said Christensen: "We don't make the programs at PBS, and we have no editorial control ultimately over what is put in the program.... Until a series is delivered to PBS for distribution, we have no editorial input or oversight over the producer or anyone connected to the project." It was an evasion that the bureaucratic complexities of the system made possible. True, PBS did not actually "produce" programs and, in that most technical sense, could not be held responsible for what was in them. But this was to beg the question. As "gatekeeper" for the national distribution of programs, PBS daily rejected projects on grounds that they "did not meet PBS standards." A thick volume of "Standards and Practices" is, in fact, distributed to independent producers, warning them that public television has to "maintain the confidence of its viewers," and that, consequently, producers have to adhere strictly to the official PBS quality guidelines.[18]

---

[17]Judith Michaelson, "'The Africans': An Insider's Non-western View," *Los Angeles Times*, October 6, 1986, http://articles.latimes.com/1986-10-06/entertainment/ca-4362_1-i-m-african

[18]"Perceptions of Integrity," *COMINT* Magazine, Vol. 1, Issue 2, Spring 1991, p. 1, http://www.discoverthenetworks.org/Articles/JCMI-1.pdf

Moreover, once a series like "The Africans" is aired, it bears the PBS logo and is promoted and distributed by PBS on cassette and in companion book form, with educational aids, to schools and libraries. Such activities constitute an active endorsement and, like the decision to air the programs in the first place, is not merely an imposition, as Christensen implied.

In seeking support from the press and Congress, PBS executives deployed an argument other than their alleged impotence. For NEH or PBS to exert any judgment on the quality of "The Africans," they claimed, however implausibly, would be to engage in a form of censorship. NEH, Christensen told the *Los Angeles Times*, is "not the Ministry of Truth," and warned that, if Cheney were to insist on entering the editing room, "there will be no NEH funding in public television."[19] This line of reasoning was more effective but no less disingenuous. It simply ignored the right (let alone the obligation) of a funder to impose guidelines and conditions on the recipients of its gifts. It also ignored the fact that CPB's own standard contract with producers stipulated that it would be allowed to see rough cuts and make changes it regarded as necessary. Christensen's argument also ignored PBS's own responsibility, emphasized by PBS officials on other occasions, regarding the character of programs they distributed and promoted.

With PBS again polarized as the public's David against the government Goliath, Brookhiser's proposal was doomed. A move by 57 House members to stimulate an inquiry into the matters that Brookhiser had raised was easily rebuffed by committee head, Democrat John Dingell. To consolidate these victories, PBS appointed a committee to review its own procedures. Stacked with an in-house majority, the committee avoided any systematic review of programming and concluded with a pat on its own back:

---

[19]Judith Michaelson, "PBS Chief Raps Endowment Over Its 'Africans' Actions," *Los Angeles Times*, October 31, 1986; http://articles. latimes.com/1986-10-31/entertainment/ca-8301_1_public-television-programming

"PBS's procedures ... have encouraged programs of high quality that reflect a wide range of information, opinion, and artistic expression and that satisfy accepted journalistic standards." The fact that business would proceed as usual became quickly apparent. In the fall of 1989, WNET presented a 90-minute documentary about the Palestinian intifada titled "Days of Rage," a catalogue of horror stories about the Israeli "occupation" featuring interviews with Palestinian moderates and Israeli extremists, and omitting any mention of Palestinian terrorism. During the battle over "Days of Rage," WNET was besieged by public protests and membership cancellations but held fast to its decision. Reflecting later on his role in airing the program, WNET vice president Robert Kotlowitz displayed an attitude that was both perverse and at the same time characteristic of other public television officials: "I thought the *intifada* program was a horror. It was a horror. And I wasn't happy with having it on the air. But I'm still happy that we made the decision to go with it."

In arriving at such attitudes, PBS executives frequently invoke their loyalty to the network mission, which they see as a mandate to give the public what commercial television won't, because, in the word of Bruce Christensen, it is "constrained by the commercial necessity of delivering mass audiences to advertisers." The mission is what makes public television "public." It is its life principle and *raison d'être*. It is what justifies the hundreds of millions of government and privately contributed dollars necessary to keep the system going. But the mission is also what provides a rationale under which extreme left viewpoints have a presumptive claim on public airtime. This is the rationale that justifies the indefensible propaganda of programs like "Days of Rage" and the propaganda films for Communist guerrillas in Central America, unbalanced by opposing views. It is the rationale under which a partisan journalist like Nina Totenberg, who was involved in the leak that nearly destroyed the nomination of future Supreme Court Justice Clarence Thomas, could be assigned by PBS as its principal reporter and commentator on the hearings triggered by the leak.

Just how much a part of the ethos of public television this attitude has become can be seen in a recent controversy involving Bill
Moyers, who has been praised as a "national treasure" by the present PBS programming chief, Jennifer Lawson. Moyers had come
under fire as the author of PBS's only two full-length documentaries on the Iran-contra affair, "The Secret Government" (1987)
and "High Crimes and Misdemeanors" (1990), which not so subtly
suggested that President Reagan was guilty of impeachable
offenses. Critics, of whom I was one, questioned whether these
programs met the standards of fairness and balance that public television was legally supposed to honor. Moyers's response was a
tortured invocation of public television's mission: "What deeper
understanding of our role in the world could we have come to by
praising Oliver North yet again, when we had already gotten five
full days before Congress, with wall-to-wall coverage on network,
cable, and public air-waves, to tell his side of the story? In fact, it
hardly seems consistent with 'objectivity, balance, and fairness'
that the other side of his story got only two 90-minute documentaries on public television."

For anyone not steeped in Moyers's own political bias, this was
an eccentric view of what had taken place. North had not produced his own network documentary. He had been hauled before a
congressional committee dominated by political enemies who
were bent on exposing him as a malefactor, and on discrediting the
administration in which he had served. Yet, because he had turned
the tables on his inquisitors and emerged from his ordeal with a
positive approval rating from the general public, Moyers proposed
that the networks had been telling only North's side of the story.
In short, in Moyers' view, the mission of public television was not
to present a balance of views, as its enabling legislation required,
but to attack North more successfully than the Democratic
stagers of the hearings had managed to do.

Quite apart from its absurdity, Moyers's statement reveals how
the concept that originally inspired public television has grown
out of date. All three networks aired the Iran-contra hearings,

which were a Democratic attempt to impugn the integrity and even the legitimacy of the Reagan presidency. In other words, public television can no longer position itself as the only channel on which such hearings critical of a sitting president can be broadcast. Responding to this turn of events, public television has sought a new space in the media spectrum by positioning itself even more firmly to the left.

Another factor in public television's identity crisis is the advent of cable and the fact that commercial stations have begun to compete directly with its offerings. The Arts & Entertainment network was started by the head of PBS's cultural programming, and its schedule of European films, serious drama, and biographies of historical figures is comparable to anything PBS has to offer. Another cable channel, Bravo, features drama from Aeschylus to O'Neill, film from Olivier to Buñuel, and music from Monteverdi to Messiaen. The Discovery Channel now repeats the nature shows that enhanced PBS's early career, while C-Span provides round-the-clock political interviews and discussions at the most serious level, including live sessions of Congress, and political conventions and meetings. The one PBS feature that these channels do not offer is the monotonous diet of left-wing propaganda.

But if a fare of left-wing politics is PBS's ill-conceived solution to its identity crisis, it is also the key to its financial unease. As the country has become more conservative, PBS's radical posture has alienated a major part of its audience as well as its Republican constituency in Congress. Indeed, it is only because Congress has remained stubbornly Democratic that public television is not in even deeper financial trouble. But the current situation is inherently unstable, and will remain so for as long as public television fails to live up to its statutory mandate by presenting a fair balance of views reflecting the broad interests of the population that is being taxed to help support it.

2

PBS Promotes the Black Panthers

The Black Panthers were an emblematic group for the 60s. They were regarded as heroes by the New Left, SDS leaders designated them the "vanguard of the revolution," and Tom Hayden called them "America's Viet Cong." At the same time, they were feared and reviled by the "silent majority" who saw them as street hoodlums made doubly dangerous by their adoption of a revolutionary rhetoric that brought battalions of white radicals and left-wing lawyers to their defense. These progressives viewed the Panthers as both passive victims of a racist power structure and the active agents of revolutionary revenge. History has not proved kind to the leftist embrace of this violent gang. An investigative *New Yorker* article by Edward Jay Epstein exploded the myth of police conspiracy and Panther victimhood, while a *New Times* report by left-wing journalist Kate Coleman documented the brutal felonies, including murder, arson, and rape, that the Panthers themselves committed against other ghetto blacks. But if investigative research has exposed the heroic myth of the Panthers, public television has done its best to restore the aura. In the PBS series "Eyes on the Prize II," in "Making Sense of the 60s," and especially in "Black Power, Black Panthers," a one-hour KQED-produced documentary, the Panthers are back in all their presumed innocence and revolutionary glory.

This article originally appeared in *COMINT* magazine, Spring 1991. *COMINT* was a publication of the Center for the Study of Popular Culture.

At a time when even the Kremlin fabulators are making efforts to restore respect for historical truth, is it too much to ask PBS to take steps to rectify its own abuse of the historical record? On August 20, 1990, the magazine I edit about public broadcasting, *COMINT*, appealed to the management of KQED in San Francisco to look into the matter of "Black Power, Black Panthers." While purporting to be a documentary history of the Black Panther Party, the program suppressed widely known facts about the Panthers' criminality, including the murders of at least a dozen Bay Area residents, while presenting them as victims of a governmental conspiracy to eliminate black civil-rights activists. In making their "documentary," the producers ignored half a dozen Bay Area reporters who had covered the story, in some cases risking their lives to do so. Pearl Stewart, a black reporter for the *Oakland Tribune*, for example, had her car firebombed after breaking the first local story about the Panthers' criminal operations.

Made by political activists, the KQED "documentary" is little more than a promotional film for a group of Panther veterans led by ex-felon David Hilliard, who were attempting to revive the party's apparatus and newspaper. The first issue of the revived paper, *Black Panthers*, appeared in early 1991 with an editorial proposing that, in the 60s, it had been "an uncompromising voice for exposing attacks on the 'Afrikan Amerikkkan' community and for advocating an implacable stand to redress them.... History once again demands that we take action."[1]

The letter *COMINT* sent to KQED president Anthony S. Tiano called the film "a disgrace to KQED and a public outrage." It noted that the distortions of the film served to feed the racial paranoia that has done so much to poison the public atmosphere. The clear message of the tendentious history in "Black Power, Black Panthers" is that white America, and white American law enforcement

---

[1] Black Panther Newspaper Committee, December 1990, http://freedom archives.org/Documents/Finder/DOC510_scans/New_Afrikan_Prisoners/510.correspondence.from.black.panther.newsletter.Dec. 1990.pdf

agencies in particular, conducted an "assassination" campaign against the leaders of the Black Panther Party, although the evidence shows that the reverse is closer to the truth. The letter concluded by demanding that KQED remove its name from the film, conduct an inquiry into how such a travesty could have occurred, and provide funding for a film that would be a corrective to the distorted version of events it had sponsored.

KQED's response to this appeal was written by station manager David H. Hosely, who glossed over its charges and defended both the filmmaker and his subjects. "We believe that, by adding to the body of information on this historic political movement, we encourage multi-dimensional analysis, and ultimately, understanding," he wrote. "We are proud of this contribution and our association with it." Having been rebuffed by KQED staff, *COMINT* turned to the KQED board, requesting an opportunity to present its concerns. An invitation was duly extended, and on December 6, 1990, with PBS programming chief Jennifer Lawson in attendance, I spoke to the KQED Board. This is what I said:

"I am here to discuss the KQED-produced film 'Black Power, Black Panthers.' This film portrays the Black Panther Party as an idealistic organization of ghetto youth, driven to violent but essentially innocent posturing and rhetoric by brutal police forces in the 60s. According to the film, as the party's influence grew among the oppressed, its leaders were targeted by the FBI and other law-enforcement agencies for assassination and were murdered, jailed, and, in the case of their founder Huey P. Newton, driven to desperate, drug-influenced courses of action that ended in sordid and violent death. Thus, even Newton, whom the film criticizes for creating a 'cult of the individual,' is presented as a victim of assassination (albeit psychological) by the powers that be.

"I understand the seductive appeal of this image of the Panthers (which is, after all, their self-image) as victims of a white racist society bent on destroying any black person who dared to challenge its oppressive order. It was this image that brought me into close association with Huey Newton and the Black Panther

Party in the early Seventies. I did not especially like their violent rhetoric. I was suspicious of their gang-like behavior. But I basically believed the radical and liberal apologists for the Panthers who, like the KQED filmmakers, assured us all that they were really the well-intentioned victims of racist authorities, vicious police agencies, and a hostile media.

"Influenced by these deceptive images, I agreed to work with the Panthers. I raised over $100,000 and created the Oakland Community Learning Center, which is improbably featured in the KQED film as 'an internationally recognized school' that provided free meals for children and which was, in fact, the party's showpiece and base of operations throughout the Seventies. It was for embezzling money from this school that Newton was finally convicted and was about to be sent to jail when he was killed. The school was real, but it was also a front for a criminal gang attempting to control the illegal traffic of the East Oakland ghetto. My association with the Panthers terminated in 1974 when they kidnapped and murdered the woman I had engaged to do bookkeeping for the school, Betty Van Patter, a well-known member of the radical community and the mother of three children. Huey Newton, the only Panther the KQED film finds fault with, was in Cuba when Betty was kidnapped and murdered. Ericka Huggins, who is featured in the film as an idealistic Panther leader, was the head of the Panther school at the time. Elaine Brown, who is celebrated in 'Eyes on the Prize II,' was the head of the Party. Betty's death is not mentioned in the KQED film.

"In the years after Betty's murder, partly because of the horror that many working Bay Area journalists felt over her death, reporting on the Panthers began to change. Despite considerable risks to their personal safety, a number of journalists—Lance Williams, Pearl Stewart, and Kate Coleman among them—gradually uncovered the true story of the Black Panther Party, its origins as a criminal gang, its assumption of a political personality, its continuing criminal activity, and the reign of terror it conducted mainly in the Bay Area's black community, during which more than a dozen people were killed. The positive effect of these stories was to warn others not to make the mistake that I and so many like me had made in responding to the Panthers' idealistic image a decade earlier. Under the impact of this adverse publicity, the Panther Party ceased to exist.

"Recently, however, some Panther veterans led by David Hilliard, a convicted felon and the principal on-camera 'authority' in KQED's film, have begun to organize a revival of the party in the Bay Area, appearing at demonstrations and promoting the same hate-filled rhetoric as in the past. KQED has produced the perfect vehicle to make this revival a success: A film posing as history that covers up as much of the truth that has been discovered about the Panthers as possible, while refurbishing their image as the idealistic victims of a white racist society that ruthlessly set out to destroy them.

"How could KQED finance and produce such an obscene rewrite of contemporary history? How could the KQED producers systematically ignore the well-known Bay Area reporters responsible for uncovering the truth about the Panthers in the past? Pearl Stewart, a black journalist who reported this story and whose life was threatened by the Panthers, has appeared on many programs on KQED. How could her testimony be ignored? How could this whole travesty have slipped by the KQED executives responsible for controlling the quality of the KQED product? What measures is KQED prepared to take to limit and/or repair the damage done by this film? What measures will it consider to prevent a repetition of this experience in the future?

"The present position of the KQED administration is that it is 'proud' of this film and stands by its producers. KQED management seems to have no interest in answering the troubling questions posed by the making of this film or in confronting the issues they raise. We are therefore placing our case before the KQED board. We would like to ask you first to set up a committee of inquiry to look into this matter and to provide us with a point of contact for our concerns, It has taken four months just to get to where this presentation could be made, a situation that is frustrating enough to actively discourage inquiries like ours. The reaction of KQED management to date says in effect that KQED has no interest in the fairness, objectivity, or integrity of its programming, something I am sure its board does not subscribe to.

"The committee of inquiry we are proposing should in our view be the prelude to the setting up of a permanent committee to handle questions of fairness, objectivity, and balance in KQED's programming. As you know, KQED is a taxpayer-funded institution with a responsibility to the public for fairness, balance, and objectivity that necessarily exceeds the responsibility of commercial stations that do not enjoy the benefits of governmental support. This is a trust that PBS and KQED officials have affirmed on numerous occasions and that is written into the law governing the Corporation for Public Broadcasting, which funds KQED. This law, Title 47, U.S. Code Section 396(g)(1)(A), specifies that the funds provided by the public will be used to: 'Facilitate the full development of telecommunications in which programs of high quality, diversity, creativity, excellence, and innovation, which are obtained from diverse sources, will be made available to public telecommunications entities *with strict adherence to objectivity and balance in all programs or series of programs of a controversial nature.'* [emphasis added]

"Presently, KQED has no institutional mechanism or corporate officer responsible for enforcing this policy. If there were such an office or officer, they would have been in touch with us four months ago. It is cause for concern that such a *lacuna* exists, but it does, and this is as good a time as any to begin to remedy the situation. The critical role of media— the problem of media responsibility in the functioning of a democracy—is universally acknowledged. Even a private media corporation like *The Washington Post* recognizes its public responsibility in establishing principles of fairness and balance in reporting. It has appointed an ombudsman to receive complaints and make periodical reports and recommendations to the staff of the paper in order to correct existing imbalances and redress grievances that its readers and the subjects of its coverage may raise. The existence of an ombudsman provides both a court of appeal for the complaints of the public and a disinterested perspective on the functioning of the organization, which can guide the staff towards better performance. We believe that in the case of publicly funded institutions like KQED, which enjoys the special privileges of a publicly supported medium and is therefore mandated by law to promote both fairness and balance, this ombudsman function should be the responsibility of a committee of the board, and not merely an individual.

"We would like to discuss these matters further, and hope to hear from your representatives soon. Thank you."

This appeal was made in December 1990. Four months later, there has not been a single word out of the KQED board, not a letter of inquiry, not an invitation to appear, not even a courtesy note. Meanwhile, "Eyes on the Prize II" is a constant re-run on PBS, especially during pledge-week; "Making Sense of the 60s" will be aired again this fall; and "Berkeley in the 60s," another tendentious self-celebration by the radical left complete with ritual glorification of the Black Panther Party, will be on PBS soon. Just in case we didn't get the point.

3

PBS Celebrates a Killer

"Well brother man you just keep passin' it on—passin' it on Lumumba, Dhoruba, Assata Shakur..."

In the 1960s, Martin Kenner was a New Left activist at Columbia University and supporter of the Black Panthers. In 1969, he organized the famous fundraiser for the Panthers at Leonard Bernstein's, which gave a new phrase to the language after it was satirized by Tom Wolfe in *Radical Chic*. Kenner is still a Panther stalwart and with his friend, writer Lewis Cole, helped Panther leader David Hilliard put together his memoir, *This Side of Glory*. In Hilliard's book, Kenner is quoted at length about a murder committed by a dissident Panther faction in New York: "Nothing ever shook me up in my political life as much as the murder of Sam Napier.... It was so unjust. Sam had never been involved in the military aspect of the Party He only worked on distribution [of the Panther newspaper]. He was defenseless and his murder was unspeakably brutal. He was caught unarmed and unprotected in the newspaper distribution office in Queens, tied to a bed, tortured, shot to death, then burned. The murder was fratricide. The assassins grabbed the two-year-old child Sam was taking care of in the office and literally threw him out the door, giving him lasting

---

This article was originally published as "Panther Outrage" in *COMINT* magazine, Fall 1994.

injuries, and two young neighborhood kids who happened to be in the office at the time were locked in a closet and left in the fire."

One of the dissident Panthers arrested for this crime was Richard Moore, a.k.a. Dhoruba Bin Wahad. Dhoruba Bin Wahad is familiar to PBS viewers as a panelist-expert on the two-hour show "A Question of Race," hosted by Phil Donahue, and as the subject of a celebratory one-hour PBS film "Passin' It On," produced by ITVS and shown on "POV," in which he is portrayed as a victim of police conspiracies, a champion of the oppressed, and a friend of Nelson Mandela. Dhoruba, whose criminal career by his own account began when he was eight, was tried with three other New York Panthers for the murder of Sam Napier. The trial ended in a hung jury, but the defendants then pled guilty in exchange for sentences of time served.

Dhoruba was the leader of an East Coast faction of the Panthers that broke from the party over Huey Newton's decision to "put down the gun" and turn away from "armed struggle." Newton was accused by Eldridge Cleaver, Dhoruba and others of betraying George Jackson, a San Quentin prisoner who had murdered a prison guard and whose brother Jonathan had been killed attempting to take hostages from a Marin County courtroom. Jonathan, a judge, and two other people were killed in the attempt. Dhoruba was also charged with killing two New York policemen in an ambush similar to the ambush of police that Eldridge Cleaver had arranged in San Francisco as part of the "armed struggle." After his conviction, Dhoruba served 19 years in prison before being released on a technicality. Dhoruba was linked to the ambush of the policemen because the machine gun used in the attack was found in his possession when he was arrested after holding up an after-hours club, where he had robbed the patrons of their drugs, jewelry and cash. In the PBS/POV/ITVS film, Dhoruba explains the robbery as a revolutionary attempt to "take drugs off the streets." In the context of the film, which is a political infomercial for Dhoruba and his agendas and which portrays local police forces as occupying armies in America's ghettos, even so transparent an alibi might seem to make sense to the uninformed viewer.

The title 'Passin' It On' is from a poem read at the beginning of the show that seeks to establish a link to the generational chain of Panther dissidents who lined up on the Cleaver-Dhoruba side of the Panther conflict. The Dhoruba faction formed the Black Liberation Army in the Seventies and defined its armed struggle as a quest to liberate "New Afrika," a territorial enclave in America with majority black populations. The Black Liberation Army, led by Lumumba and Assata Shakur (a.k.a. Joanne Chesimard), who are invoked in the poem as guiding spirits for Dhoruba and his followers, conducted an ambush of police officers in New Jersey similar to those led by Cleaver and Dhoruba. The Shakurs shot and killed two New Jersey state troopers. Assata Shakur fled to Cuba and is still wanted for the crime. The same military sect of black liberationists, led by Mutulu Shakur and aided by Weatherman Kathy Boudin and others calling themselves the "May 19 Communist Movement," attempted to rob a Brinks armored car in Nyack, New York, in 1982, killing three officers, including the only black policeman on the Nyack police force. The rantings of Mutulu Shakur and followers of George Jackson were recently featured on Pacifica public radio station KPFK in Los Angeles.

"Passin' It On" is only the latest in a series of PBS films promoting the political gang called the Black Panther Party, which committed hundreds of felonies in the 60s and 70s, murdered more than a dozen people, mainly black, and extorted the inner-city black populations of New York, Chicago and Oakland while committing rape, arson, armed robbery and other crimes. These crimes have been documented by black journalist Hugh Pearson, a reporter for Pacific News Service and well-known figure in the San Francisco Bay Area left. Pearson's new book, *The Shadow of the Panther*, was not reviewed on NPR's "Fresh Air." When contacted by Pearson's publisher, host Terry Gross said she would not review the book unless she could get a Panther to come on the program to defend the party. This is a curious attitude for a book reviewer. Similarly, NPR's "All Things Considered" and "Morning Edition," which mention new books and interview authors on a regular basis, rejected repeated requests that they bring Pearson's book to the attention of the public radio audience. The Panther story is so explosive, and so close to the interests of large sections of the public radio audience, that this can hardly be attributed to oversight.

Just as PBS has made no effort to balance its fawning service to the Panther cause with more responsible reporting, NPR has refused to conduct a journalistic investigation into the Panther story. This is in striking contrast to NPR's readiness to investigate claims of injustice when presented by leftist groups such as Joseph Lowery's Southern Christian Leadership Conference, which accused Mississippi prison officials of murdering black prisoners and making the racist murders look like suicides. NPR sent a team to Mississippi to investigate the charges, which it found to be baseless, when most of the reported suicides turned out to be white prisoners. While refusing to assign reporters to interview Pearson, "All Things Considered" editor Ellen Weiss offered a paid monthly commentary to Mumia Abu-Jamal, a Black Panther on death row for murdering a policeman. Only public outcries prompted wiser heads to reconsider the decision. Mumia was part of the same political network as Dhoruba and the Shakurs. His show can be heard regularly on the Pacifica network, which annually receives $1 million from the Corporation for Public Broadcasting.

The extreme left has established a pipeline into the PBS and NPR systems through friendly agencies like ITVS, POV and Pacifica. The editorial standards that should guard against this abuse are ignored, despite a congressional directive to put them in place. The unchallenged proliferation of propaganda over taxpayer-supported airwaves in behalf of violent radical groups like the Panthers is a disservice to the American public, which pays for public broadcasting, and a violation of the laws that make public radio and television possible.

4

NPR as a Political Weapon

In September 1992 the nation was treated to a spectacle that is regrettably becoming all too common a feature of our troubled democracy: trial by television. In this case, the trial was that of Clarence Thomas, the Supreme Court nominee accused of sexual harassment. His accuser was Anita Hill, a law professor who had worked for him when he was the nation's chief enforcer of civil rights. It is the nature of television trials that the accused has none of the protections of due process which our legal system provides. With his nomination in the balance, Thomas was forced to defend himself against charges about incidents that were alleged to have happened 10 years in the past, between two people, in private, where no witnesses were present. The charges, of course, had already been heard by the members of the Senate Judiciary Committee. These men, most of them lawyers, had decided that, as presented, the charges were not substantial enough to weigh in the balance against Thomas' nomination. The reason for their decision was so simple and so basic to American principles of equity and justice that it is hard to fathom that anyone should call their judgment into question, although that is precisely what happened. In the American justice system there is probably no principle so sanctified as a defendant's right not to be convicted on the basis of charges made by a faceless accuser. The right to cross-examine one's accuser and challenge his or her credibility is one of the

---

This article was originally published as "NPR and the Totenberg Affair" in COMINT magazine, Winter 1992.

cornerstones of a free society. The Senate Judiciary Committee members dismissed the claims of Anita Hill because she insisted on making her accusations anonymously; her affidavit was an attempt to destroy Clarence Thomas's career from the shadows. It was not because they were males that the committee members refused to admit Hill's unsubstantiated allegations as evidence, but because they were Americans, mindful of the rights that provide the foundations of the nation's democratic order.

It is there that these matters would have rested, except for the fact that someone with access to the committee's confidential files leaked Hill's accusatory affidavit to NPR reporter Nina Totenberg. This individual did so in violation of senatorial rules, common ethics, and possibly federal law. The leak provided reporter Totenberg with two stories. Both were sensational, and both had the potential to threaten the careers of national figures. But each had dramatically different political ramifications. The story she chose not to report was the leak itself. This breach of confidentiality was possibly not an isolated act but the culmination of a coordinated campaign to "Bork" the Thomas nomination—a verb coined to commemorate the character assassination that has become a feature of the nomination process in these divisive times. The leaker had violated a cardinal rule of the Senate, and possibly a federal law as well, in order to destroy a distinguished American's career. Was this a group effort? Were senators involved? Nina Totenberg now had the key, which if she had chosen to turn it would have broken a national scandal. Perhaps the repercussions of such a scandal would have led to the reform of the nominating process, which all parties seem to agree is needed. But, in exposing this scandal, she would also have ensured the confirmation of Clarence Thomas, which as a committed leftist she was not about to do.

Instead she chose the second reportorial path, which made her, willy-nilly, an accomplice to the unethical machinations of the anonymous party that sought to bring Clarence Thomas down. After receiving the confidential information contained in the affidavit, Totenberg made a hasty effort to substantiate the accusations.

She failed in this, just as the committee would fail in the hearings her revelations would make necessary. But she did succeed in acquiring the elements that would make it impossible for the committee to stick to its original position—a position that had protected both the accused and the accuser from the public circus that ensued. Totenberg managed to locate a "corroborating witness," Judge Susan Hoerchner, in whom Hill had confided about her alleged sexual abuse without being specific as to detail or to the name of the party she claimed had abused her.

How did Totenberg locate Judge Hoerchner? Perhaps through James Brudney, the Metzenbaum staffer who directed Anita Hill's performance and whose law-school roommate was Hoerchner's brother. In other words, perhaps by making herself even more complicit in the network that was conspiring to Bork the nomination. We don't know the answer, because Totenberg has chosen to maintain the confidentiality of *her* sources, while violating everyone else's. In any case, Hoerchner's testimony was inconclusive. In order to be able to go ahead with the second story, Totenberg had to flush Hill from her hiding place, where she had remained throughout the three months of the inquiry now concluded, and thus force her and Clarence Thomas to enter a debasing spectacle of accusation and counter-accusation about intimate matters without any possibility of resolution, all before a nationwide television audience.

Totenberg was able to accomplish this where the male members of the Judiciary Committee had failed, because she did not feel bound by those ethical scruples that had prevented them from compelling Anita Hill to go public against her wishes. It is one of the ironies of this whole affair that these much-abused males had more respect for the sensibilities and expressed concerns of Anita Hill than the female NPR reporter. Totenberg accomplished this end by threatening to divulge the contents of the confidential affidavit that Anita Hill had made and that some unscrupulous senator or Senate staffer had placed in unauthorized hands. Once Hill was confronted by Totenberg's threat, she consented to an interview.

This allowed Totenberg to go public with the interview rather than the leaked confidential affidavit, an act that might have exposed her to legal prosecution. With the interview in hand, Totenberg went on National Public Radio with her report: "[Hill] told the Senate Judiciary Committee and later the FBI that she'd been sexually harassed by Clarence Thomas when she worked as his personal assistant in the early 1980s.... According to Hill's sworn affidavit, a copy of which was obtained by NPR, Thomas spoke about acts that he'd seen in pornographic films involving group sex or rape scenes. He talked about pornographic materials depicting individuals with large penises and breasts.... She said she told only one person about what was happening to her, a friend from law school. The friend, now a state judge in the west, corroborated Hill's story, in part, both in an interview with the FBI and with NPR. She said that Hill had told her at the time of the alleged harassment in general, though not in detail."[1]

Totenberg's report was carried nationally. The revelation embarrassed the members of the Judiciary Committee, who were instantly accused of not taking Hill's accusations seriously because they were insensitive males. In fact, their only real crime was in being sensitive to the demands of a system which insists that anonymous accusers not be allowed to destroy an individual's reputation without subjecting themselves to cross-examination. By blackmailing Hill into coming forward, Totenberg had put the Judiciary Committee members in an impossible position. To get themselves off the hook, they decided to hold a supplemental hearing on the charges.

At this point, NPR faced its own test of principle as the following questions presented themselves: Was Nina Totenberg's action in leaking what amounted to a confidential personnel file ethical? Was Totenberg herself part of the network opposed to the Thomas nomination? Should an inquiry be held? Should she be censured?

---

[1]Nina Totenberg, "Thomas Accused of Sexual Harassment", Weekend Edition, NPR, Oct. 6, 1991; http://jwa.org/feminism/_html/_transcripts/transcript_JWA071a.htm

And, finally, should Totenberg be replaced as NPR's reporter for the hearings on Anita Hill's charges? This last question presented itself irrespective of the answers to the others. Totenberg had become an integral part of the Anita Hill story. It is a basic principle of journalism that, when a reporter becomes a part of the story, her objectivity has been compromised, and therefore she should be removed from the responsibility of reporting it. But NPR is apparently immune to considerations of its own partisanship, or to the professional standards that govern other members of the media, and chose to keep Nina Totenberg on the job, assigning her to anchor the Hill-Thomas hearing. These issues were raised with CPB, PBS, and NPR officials in a letter I wrote in behalf of our publication, *COMINT,* when the hearings were concluded: "We are concerned about the role NPR reporter Totenberg apparently played in this process and at the fact that her superiors have remained silent about her breach of professional ethics in publicizing [the] confidential material [contained in Anita Hill's affidavit] to the American public. We are appalled that even after the disclosure, NPR officials assigned Ms. Totenberg the responsibility of being the principal reporter and commentator for both NPR and the Public Broadcasting Service in respect to the Senate hearings made necessary by this leak."

On Saturday, September 12, 1992, Totenberg conducted a television and radio interview with Senator John Danforth, in which the Senator decried the unprecedented leaking of Anita Hill's accusations to the public as "despicable and disgraceful" and "probably illegal." As soon as the interview was over, with the senator was safely off camera and unable to reply, Totenberg told millions of public radio and television listeners across the country that "the history books are full of important things that have happened as the result of news leaks,"[2] thus justifying what she had

---

[2]L. Brent Bozell III, "'October Surprise' Unravels," *Media Research Center,* November 1991; http://archive.mrc.org/mediawatch/1991/watch 19911101.asp

done. She went on to cite her leaking of a file containing unsubstantiated allegations about the character of Clarence Thomas to
"the leaking of the Pentagon Papers" during the Vietnam War, as
an example of a public service. Thus was character assassination
by the press made into a virtue by the perpetrator.

Totenberg's abuse of the publicly funded broadcasting system
was not unprecedented. Totenberg had been instrumental in leaking rumors about the personal life of conservative Judge Douglas
Ginsburg that caused him to withdraw his name from nomination
to the United States Supreme Court. Totenberg, as was later
revealed, had purveyed the recriminations of an embittered ex-girl-
friend who told her that Ginsburg had smoked marijuana during
his college days, 15 years earlier.

In my letter to NPR I asked for an inquiry into the behavior of
Totenberg during the hearings process. NPR's response came from
its president, Douglas J. Bennet, which made clear that there was
not going to be an investigation of possible partisan politics in
NPR's reporting; nor was there going to be an apology for any
breach of journalistic ethics in having a story reported by a person
involved in the story in question. "November 4, 1991 NPR News
and PBS agreed to co-anchor the confirmation hearings jointly as a
public broadcasting experiment. PBS chose Paul Duke for its co-
anchor. NPR chose Nina Totenberg as its co-anchor, because she is
one of the most knowledgeable reporters in Washington in matters
involving the Supreme Court. When the Senate made the decision
to reopen the hearings, NPR and PBS agreed that this was a contin-
uation of the previous hearings, and therefore we decided to continue with the same anchors." This evasive explanation was
followed by the customary self-pat-on-the-back that has become
the signature of public-broadcasting officials: "NPR's editorial
process has been thorough, responsible, and in accordance with
the highest standards of journalism. Correspondent Nina Totenberg has provided excellent work as both a reporter and live-events
anchor on this story, as on many others. We are proud of her work

and the overall coverage of this matter by NPR news. Sincerely, Douglas J. Bennet."

In other words, NPR's president—a former bureaucrat in the Carter administration and now a potential appointee in the Clinton administration—regards his reporters as possibly above the law and certainly beyond the reach of the standards governing other professional journalists.

5

Hate Radio

For two days on the weekend of February 1, 1992, public radio station KPFK in Los Angeles turned over its transmitters from 9 AM to midnight to Louis Farrakhan, Leonard Jefries and a general parade of anti-Semitic racists, for what was billed as "Afrikan Mental Liberation Weekend." Farrakhan warned listeners that whites and Jews were "the pale horse with death as its rider and hell close behind" that for centuries had wreaked destruction on red, yellow, brown, and black peoples in Africa, Asia, and the Americas and on Palestinians in the Middle East.[1] Not to worry, Farrakhan continued, a "reckoning" was about to come. The organizer of the weekend event was Dr. Kwaku Person-Lynn, who had his own special message, which was as follows: Real Jews are black. White Jews are hypocrites for claiming to be Jews, and white Jews add injury to insult by forcing the real Jews, the Falashas of Ethiopia, to give up their original Judaism "in order to stay alive." As might be expected, this message elicited phone-ins by callers convinced that Jews were "devils."

"Afrikan Mental Liberation Weekend" is an annual production of KPFK. Its message is wholly in tune with the station's program-

---

Originally published as "Pacifica Radio Promotes Hate" in *COMINT*, Spring 1992.

[1]Phyllis Chesler, "Listener-Sponsored Hate Radio on the Left Coast," *FrontPageMagazine.com*, June 18, 2004, http://www.phyllis-chesler .com/136/listener-sponsored-hate-radio-on-the-left-coast

ming, which features fringe radicalism and general hatred of whites, America, and all things capitalist. Other KPFK programs have been devoted to hour-long diatribes by Farrakhan lieutenant Steve Cokeley, informing listeners that a recent measles epidemic was a "genocidal plot" by whites against the black community and that the problem with blacks was that they "didn't deliver retribution." During a recent fund drive, a KPFK station announcer decried the manipulative nature of commercial networks, which, by featuring stories on Olympic gold medal winner Kristi Yamaguchi, "tried to make us think America was a decent country." Another pledge-week announcer stressed that no other station had reported to its listeners the "fact" that orphans were being "disappeared" in Latin America by the U.S. government and "murdered for their body parts," which were then shipped to U.S. hospitals. Needless to say, there is not the slightest hint of the balance required by law in KPFK programming.

KPFK 90.7 FM Los Angeles is a Pacifica station and receives a Community Service Grant from the Corporation for Public Broadcasting of $134,126 a year. Why?

6

A Democratic Party Mouthpiece

Year after year, Republican legislators appropriate hundreds of millions of dollars to public radio and television broadcasters, who return the favor by promoting the agendas of their political opponents. During the 1992 presidential elections, public television ran two hour-long shows charging that then-President George H.W. Bush and former President Ronald Reagan "stole" the 1980 election by cutting a deal with the Ayatollah Khomeini to delay the release of American hostages in Iran. There was no opportunity given to Republicans to reply. Nor were any apologies or corrections offered by PBS when the "October Surprise" theory was dismissed as unproven even by a Democrat-controlled committee of congress. A year earlier, PBS had run a one-and-a-half-hour "documentary" on the Iran-*Contra* affair by Democrat Bill Moyers that accused President Reagan of "High Crimes and Misdemeanors." There was no opportunity for a Republican version of this history or a rebuttal of Moyers's partisan message.

During the 1992 election campaign, PBS ran six hours of programs by Moyers, a former LBJ speechwriter, and by another left-wing Democrat, William Greider, on how badly the country had fared under twelve years of Republican administrations. There was no opportunity given to Republicans for response. There were no shows about the unprecedented expansion of opportunities for

Originally published in *COMINT,* Fall 1994

Americans during the prosperity generated by the policies of the Reagan years. During the closing month of the 1992 election campaign, PBS also ran "LBJ," a four-hour celebration of Lyndon Johnson's Great Society programs. It also ran a four-hour tribute to the Kennedy family. What did public broadcasters do for Republicans in election year 1992? They ran a biography of Richard Nixon to remind the public that the only president ever forced to resign was a Republican. And this is just a sampling of the taxpayer-funded programs on public radio and television that helped to put the Democrats back in the White House.

Given this bias, it was hardly surprising that staffers at public station WGBH-TV, Boston, who were reporting the election results for the national PBS feed, cheered *on camera* when the announcement came that Clinton had gone over the top. It is indicative of the overall political culture of public television that PBS has never aired a program celebrating the victory in the Cold War that was won under the leadership of the Republicans and Ronald Reagan, even though this was the most important event of the last half-century. Perhaps that is because, during the last decade of the Cold War, PBS was running hour after hour of television programs praising the Marxist guerrillas in El Salvador and the Marxist dictatorships in Cuba and Nicaragua on the last Cold War frontier.

This political partisanship is a direct violation of the Public Broadcasting Act of 1967, which requires that taxpayer-funded public affairs shows be strictly balanced and fair. To rectify this, Congress took action in June 1992 to remind public broadcasters of their responsibilities under the law. Led by Senator Bob Dole, the Congress enacted amendments to the reauthorization bill that required the Corporation for Public Broadcasting to review its programming and take steps to balance its product. But, in the two years that have elapsed since this mandate, the CPB board has steadfastly refused to examine its programming and carry out this mandate. In that time, not a single program or programming schedule has been specifically reviewed for balance. Nor has a single program been funded for balance. CPB board chairman Sheila Tate has said categorically that the CPB board "does not intend to pass judgment on individual programs." In case after case, she has refused to look at the programming schedule of public radio and television stations for evidence of bias and has prevented CPB president Richard Carlson and his staff from doing so.

When media critics complained about the anti-Republican bias in public broadcasts during the 1992 campaign, PBS and NPR officials responded by saying that, as journalists, they were "adversarial to power" and would be just as critical of a Democratic administration as they had been of Republicans. This has proven to be an empty promise. We now have a Democratic administration. What has been public broadcasting's response? Now that a Democratic president has come under press scrutiny, public broadcasting has become the White House's most friendly network. There has not been a single documentary television program devoted to Whitewater or any other Democratic Party scandal, such as the Clinton Administration's attack on the Branch Davidian compound at Waco that left 50 children dead. While *The New York Times*, CNN, and the *Los Angeles Times* have vigorously pursued the Whitewater story, "All Things Considered" reporters Linda Wertheimer and Mara Liasson have applied their journalistic imaginations to suggesting excuses for the president and First Lady and commiserating with them over the prying sensationalism of the national press. Nina Totenberg, who bent journalistic ethics and skirted the borders of the law to break the story of Anita Hill's accusations against Clarence Thomas, dragged her feet in covering Paula Jones's complaint about Clinton's sexual harassment and played no role in getting her a public hearing. Nor has she expended any effort to get the many other women who have been identified by Arkansas troopers as victims of Clinton's advances to come forward.

While taxpayer-funded broadcasters circle the wagons around the Clinton White House, Republican legislators should be thinking about what this means for their own electoral chances this coming November. They should consider that public broadcasters estimate their audience at 100 million Americans a week; that National Public Radio reaches the most politically active and educated segment of the population; and that a poll of public broadcasters revealed that more than eighty percent of these on-air voices are liberal Democrats. Small wonder Senator Robert Dole has said that, every time he turns on NPR, he thinks he's listening to the Democratic National Committee. The public broadcasting network is, in fact, a Democratic lobby in every congressional district in the nation. This state of affairs violates the law and distorts the electoral process. Republican legislators—and all those interested in the health of the two-party system—should hold up reauthorization for the Corporation for Public Broadcasting until its board agrees to take steps to balance its programming and to abide by the spirit and letter of the public broadcasting law.

7

The Future of Public Broadcasting

At the heart of the present conflict over perceived bias in public broadcasting is a misconception by public broadcasters themselves about their mission. At the recent conference of the Central Educational Network, Michael Tracey, director of the Center for Mass Media Research at the University of Colorado, made the following observation:

> For me the most telling and disturbing discovery, as I have tried to understand the institution of public television, has been the deep ambivalence towards the public-as-audience. One gets a very real sense that the people in public television view American culture and society as something to be kept at arm's length, a dark and dangerous continent smothered by corrupted values and ethics, peopled by the fallen of mass culture, beyond redemption. Public television is to be a protected zone, safe and serious and pure, a kind of televisual green-lung amidst the devastation.

What Tracey characterizes as ambivalence on the part of public television towards its public is more accurately characterized as an *adversarial stance* towards its public—or, at least, the large element of its public that is not in a state of permanent war with American society and culture. It is this adversarial stance that produces the cultural isolation of public broadcasters and their present political problems with Senator Dole and other Republicans.

Originally published in *COMINT* magazine, Fall 1992

This is even more obvious in Tracey's account of public broadcasters' reactions to current critics:

> Those who broadly define themselves as the friends of public
> broadcasting appear to regard these ... attacks as badges of merit.
> They define the significance of the institution by the significance
> of those who assault it. If one is being attacked by the Republican
> leadership or by right-wing intellectuals ... one must be doing
> something right.

Whatever else may be said about this reaction, it is inappropriate and self-defeating for a public medium, publicly funded and
thus dependent on the support (or at least forbearance) of that
same Republican leadership and those same "right-wing intellectuals." It is not that public broadcasters cannot or should not have
political and cultural attitudes that are liberal and/or elitist. It is
that the *institution* cannot conceive its mission to mean advocacy
of a partisan vision, however "enlightened" or politically progressive its promoters deem it. If the public broadcasting community
understands its mission as partisan, it will inevitably find itself
locked into an adversarial stance towards the very audience and
community its looks to for support. Unfortunately, such partisanship is now an integral part of the self-understanding of many public broadcasters. It was on full display at the recent public
television conference in San Francisco,[1] where the implicit and
often explicit assumption of the thousand broadcasters present
was that the mission of public television was to function as an
agency of "social change."

Thus, in a crystallizing moment at the conference, moderator
Charlie Rose asked PBS president Bruce Christensen the following
question: "Let me raise this question David Horowitz and others
have raised. He says public broadcasting carries a strong liberal bias
that violates a provision for strict balance in the Public Broadcasting

---

[1] Steve Behrens, Public Television Annual Meeting, June 23, 1992,
Current, July 20, 1992, http://www.current.org/wp-content/themes/
current/archive-site/prog/prog213g.html

Act of 1967. I would like to turn to Bruce to respond to that, because that is part of the body of criticism that was aired on the floor of the Senate."

Christensen replied: "If you say our documentary programming has a liberal bias, and you define liberal as an argument for change or against the status quo, the answer is obviously, 'Yes, our [documentary] programs argue for change.'" The most important fact about this statement is that it was the first time any public-television official had conceded that documentary programming on the PBS schedule is in fact biased. For more than a decade, in celebrated controversies over "The Africans," "Days of Rage," and a series of documentaries celebrating Marxist revolutionaries in Central America, PBS officials generally (and Bruce Christensen in particular) had denied that there was *any* bias in PBS documentaries—even a bias in favor of change. But that was before Congress spoke. I welcome Bruce Christensen's belated admission that the objectivity and balance mandate has hitherto not been observed as a first step in correcting the problem.

But the second significant aspect of Christensen's statement is its conflation of the specific, and partisan, description "liberal" with the general, and neutral, category "change." The problematic programs argued in behalf of *Marxist* revolutions in Central America, PLO terrorists in the Middle East, and *socialist* solutions to Africa's problems. If public broadcast officials continue their one-sided support of Marxist revolutions and socialist "solutions" under the rubric of "social change," there will be no respite from their cultural isolation and political troubles.

The problems inherent in the prevailing conception of public broadcasting's mission surfaced in other ways at the PBS conference. Bob Larson, general manager of Detroit public television, talked for example about the importance of "serving the needs of gays and lesbians." This was a prominent theme of several other speakers as well, and was strongly affirmed by applause from those attending. These attitudes reflected a strong and articulated commitment of those assembled to the principles of diversity and tolerance and inclusion for all Americans. Well and good. This is an appropriate and important mission for public broadcasting. But would Bob Larson also have spoken of "serving the needs of Christian fundamentalists," a constituency practically invisible to public television audiences, yet representing a major component of the viewing and taxpaying public? And would the public broadcasters present have cheered him on? Certainly not. The same would apply to a proposal to serve the needs of any of America's religious communities, or any of its constituencies on the political and/or cultural right. The problem, thus, is a conception of its mission that puts public television on one side of the political and cultural barricades that now divide America's publics. As long as this conception prevails, public broadcasting will inevitably wind up somewhere in the firing line.

Is there a way out of this impasse? Is there an alternative conception of mission that will allow public broadcasters to honor the congressional mandate for balance and feel comfortable with themselves? Can they meet the congressional requirements and be satisfied that in their professional work they are acting to elevate the public consciousness and the culture in general? I think there is.

The mission of public broadcasting, as it relates to controversial public issues, should be to affirm and extend the foundations of America's pluralistic community. In the last three decades, America has become increasingly divided. Public broadcasting is uniquely positioned to help heal these wounds in the body politic and reunite America's warring communities in a forum characterized by democratic dialogue, tolerance, and mutual respect. Relatively free from commercial constraints, public broadcasting is able to devote itself to the "long form" and to seek the higher intellectual ground. It is a medium specially suited to provide the kind of forum that can strengthen the fabric of a national community, and can emphasize the *unum* in the *pluribus* of *e pluribus unum*.

This mission would cut right across the current debate. On this agenda (and perhaps this agenda alone), conservatives and liberals might agree. Liberals emphasize the *pluribus*, the importance of inclusion; conservatives emphasize the *unum*, the importance of the structure. Over differences in emphasis there can and will be disagreement; but disagreement is very different from ideological war. Take, as an example, one of the most volatile and difficult issues of conflict, that between religious orthodoxy and the gay community. The mission of public broadcasters should not be to resolve this conflict but to civilize it, by encouraging dialogue and respect and by emphasizing the tolerance that underpins America's pluralistic contract, the civic value that makes it possible for Americans to coexist with one another. Coexistence will not be furthered by excluding one party from the dialogue, as is presently occurring. Nor will it be encouraged by programs that assault a particular community, as was the case with the PBS program "Stop the Church." Other problems of the current schedule— those specifically affecting Republicans and Democrats—will be easier to resolve within this revised mission. It is exclusion that has created the ground of bitterness underlying the current conflict. The problems that now beset public broadcasting will remain insoluble if present conceptions persist. Thus, if conservatives are dismissed as selfish, complacent defenders of an unjust *status quo*, and if public broadcasters continue to understand their mission in terms of promoting "progressive" change, then public programming will maintain its present bias, and the conflict over its future will continue on its current course.

Index